Eyewitness Accounts of the American Revolution

The Graves Papers
and
Other Documents

Edited by
French Ensor Chadwick

The New York Times & Arno Press

THE GRAVES PAPERS

The R! Hon?.le THOMAS LORD GRAVES,

ADMIRAL OF THE WHITE.

From an original picture by Northcote

THE GRAVES PAPERS

AND OTHER DOCUMENTS

RELATING TO
THE NAVAL OPERATIONS OF THE
YORKTOWN CAMPAIGN

JULY TO OCTOBER, 1781

EDITED BY

FRENCH ENSOR CHADWICK

Rear-Admiral, United States Navy

NEW YORK
PRINTED FOR THE NAVAL HISTORY SOCIETY

M DCCCC XVI

CONTENTS

[xiii]

CONTENTS

[xiv]

CONTENTS

[xv]

ILLUSTRATIONS

INTRODUCTION

THIS book deals with a naval campaign, one of the most notable and momentous in history; for on its outcome, humanly speaking, depended whether, or no, the American colonies in revolt should remain a part of the British Empire.

Certain preliminaries are necessary to a clear understanding of events: as the character of the fleets employed; the tactics in vogue, and some account of the antecedent events leading up to the final British failure.

At the outbreak of the Revolution, the British fleet, which had been allowed to run down sadly after the Seven Years' War ending with the peace of 1763, was in a seriously unserviceable condition. The Admiralty administration was corrupt and inefficient beyond modern belief, the whole being under the influence of the party spirit which permeated every form of the public service and made both dockyard efficiency and sound discipline afloat impossible. And, too, besides the evils which come of party rancor in which admirals and generals took full part, it was a dishonest and corrupt period. There was peculation everywhere on the part of civilians connected with the public service, and often on a gigantic scale. Bribery, by the King, of members of parliament in order to retain a government majority, was the usual and recognized procedure. The paymaster-general of the forces built up a vast fortune, the

[xix]

dockyards, under civil control, were sinks of corruption. Honesty, in the modern sense, was almost unknown; the pursers afloat robbed the seamen with barefaced rapacity, and the higher officers were now and then not guiltless.[1] It was an age of what is now called "graft" with which the present cannot compare in theft efficiency.

At the outbreak of our Revolution only about 18,000 seamen were in the British service. These now and for long years after were largely the product of the "Press," an organized institution throughout England, by which in case of war every man who had remotest connection with the sea, and many who had none whatever, were ruthlessly seized and carried into service. Incoming merchantmen were boarded and the men, with their homes in sight, so to speak, taken aboard the men-of-war, leaving sometimes too few to work the ship safely into port, or manning them with men too old or weak to go to sea, who were known as "men in lieu [of]," and who were kept at hand for such purpose. Men-of-war cruised off the port in order to meet merchantmen and fill out their own crews, and if the unhappy sailormen escaped such big and little cruisers, there was an inner ring of small craft carrying press-gangs which completed the work. Rarely was any mercy shown poor Jack. "Thus the 'Monmouth's' men had in 1706 been in the ship 'almost six years, and had never had an opportunity of seeing their families but once.' In Boscawen's ship, the 'Dreadnought,' there were in 1744 two hundred and fifty men who 'had not set foot on shore near two years.' Admiral Penrose once paid off a seventy-

[1] Captain Young (Rodney's flag-captain) in the Barham Papers, [British] Navy Records Society, Vol. I, p. 75.

four at Plymouth, many of whose crew had 'never set foot on land for six or seven years'; and Brenton, in his Naval History, gives the case of a ship whose company, after having been eleven years in the East Indies, on returning to England were drafted straightway into another ship and sent back to that quarter of the globe without so much as an hour's leave ashore."[1]   It was a hard, rough age in which "man's inhumanity to man" still had fullest swing.   The press-gang was England's rough-handed, and in the main effective, *Inscription Maritime,* the best the Anglo-Saxon mind, never very ready in matters of organization, was able at that time to develop.[2]

The time of Hawke, Boscawen and Anson was just past, and Howe, Rodney, Hood, and not least from the point of promise, Kempenfelt, were coming forward as the prominent commanders.   The navy was, in a way, still so much a go-as-you-please institution, that uniform for officers had only a few years before been made a matter of regulation, the first order respecting this having been issued in 1754.   Until then dress had been much a question of individual taste.   The dress of the men continued for many years to be that common to all seafarers of the sailorman class.   Even so late as the thirties of the nineteenth century, one captain dressed his gig's crew in scarlet.

[1] J. R. Hutchinson, The Press-Gang, p. 441.
[2] Lieutenant Bartholomew James (later Rear-Admiral), belonging to the Charon (burned later at Yorktown), but serving temporarily in the Richmond frigate, describes a press in New York: "On the 27th [April, 1781], all the boats of the fleet having assembled by break of day on board the Rainbow, we landed at New York, and commenced a very hot press for six hours, having in the meantime taken four hundred seamen. The business of this morning furnished

Signals and tactics (of which more anon) were of the crudest, the latter being of a rigid order which required fleets to be practically equal in numbers and to be so handled that each ship should engage the ship holding the relative position in the opposite line, a rule which for nearly a hundred years stood for ineffectiveness and never brought a decisive action. These hard-and-fast rules, backed by the political rancor of the day, were to cause the putting to death of the unfortunate Byng. And these rules, which had had nearly a century of hold upon the service, combined with the inefficiency of the signal system which Kempenfelt tried so hard to reform and would have reformed much earlier than came to pass had he not been drowned in the tragic upsetting in Portsmouth harbor of the "Royal George," were to be a large element in the loss of America to England. For they were, through want of general knowledge of the new signals used by Graves (by order of the Admiralty), in part the cause of the loss by the British of the action between Graves and De Grasse off the Capes of the Chesapeake. Thus moved by comparatively simple things are even the greatest affairs of men. An indigestion, a delay of a few hours, a mistaken signal loses an empire.

The ships of the day were, as a rule, uncoppered and thus suffered from rapid fouling and the marine borer.

us with droll yet distressing scenes—the taking of the husband from the arms of his wife in bed, the searching for them when hid beneath the warm clothes, and, the better to prevent delay, taking them off naked, while the frantic partner of his bed, forgetting the delicacy of her sex, pursued us to the doors with shrieks and imprecations, and exposing their naked persons to the rude view of an unfeeling press gang." (Journal of Rear-Admiral Bartholomew James, 1752–1828, Vol. VI, [British] Navy Records Society.)

Coppering was only just coming into use, the first British man-of-war having been coppered in 1761. By 1778 perhaps half had been so treated; by 1785 practically all. Naturally the uncoppered ships suffered greatly in speed, through the rapid sea-growth on wood, and in destruction through the sea-worm. So dull and heavy in movement were the ships of the time that many hours were sometimes spent in forming a line, and even then often without success. Says Captain Young, Rodney's flag-captain in 1780, in a letter to Charles Middleton (later Lord Barham), Controller of the Navy: "Your attention to the coppering reflects the greatest merit on you. It is impossible for me to describe the advantages attending it, and indeed exceeds the expectations of everyone. The advantages from the helm alone is immense, as they feel them instantly, and wear in a third of the distance they ever did; it keeps them tight and covers the neglect in your dockyards from bad caulking; increases their speed in every situation, more particularly in light winds tending to a calm, which is no small advantage in this and every fair weather country. Its greatest effect is in sailing large; we have frequently made the signal for a line of battle ahead (the squadrons all pretty close to us) when going with the wind near aft, our topsails on the caps, the yards braced contrary ways, and the uncoppered ships with every sail they could set, and have not been able to form, though six hours at it, but obliged to give it up."[1]

To understand the unseaworthiness of the ships of the day, one has but to read the terrible account of the

[1] The Barham Papers, [British] Navy Records Society, Vol. XXXII, p. 67.

gale of September, 1782,[1] encountered some 300 miles southeast of Nova Scotia by the merchant fleet from the West Indies, of over ninety sail, under convoy of ten line-of-battle ships commanded by Admiral Thomas Graves, who was in the "Ramillies." Half the battle-ships went down with a loss of 3500 men. Among the ships lost were the lately captured "Ville de Paris" and two others of the prizes taken by Rodney in the battle of the 12th of April of that year. No doubt the great loss was due to laying to, through ignorance, on the wrong tack. The law of storms was not yet developed or even broached.

The wonder is that these great tublike hulks, usually but 170 feet long on the gun deck and 47 feet broad, (and none exceeding 190 feet by about 53), with their lofty freeboard of three or four decks, should ever have got anywhere in reasonable time even under the favorable circumstances of being coppered; and the wonder is still greater that they could be manœuvred as an effective coherent mass. And very frequently they could not. The diagrams of actions usually depict them in a beautiful and mathematically exact formation. We know, however, that a fleet of twenty or more battle-ships which should not under ordinary circumstances have formed a column of more than two nautical miles, frequently stretched as many leagues (and sometimes greatly more), owing to calms or light airs. It was such a condition which was fatal to De Grasse on the 12th of April, 1782, when, with a few ships, he became separated from the rest of his fleet and was thus over-powered by numbers. Historians have spoken of this as breaking the line. The fact is that with the vary-

[1] See Beatson, Naval and Military Memoirs, V, 497 *et seq.*

ing and light winds of the region natural in the situation, near to several islands, both fleets were scattered over leagues of sea and instead of a line being kept there were widely separated groups. De Grasse's line, so called, was broken by wind conditions under the high land of Dominica. His main body had sailed or drifted away and he was simply left unsupported.

Such conditions as existed,—blunt, short and broad hulls, some ships coppered, some not, the varying sizes of ships in the line of battle,—could not but work for great uncertainty of action and had gravest weight on the outcome of effort. Thus D'Estaing, sailing from Toulon the 13th of April, 1778, did not reach his objective point, the Capes of the Delaware, until the 6th of July. He was thirty-three days in getting to the Straits of Gibraltar and fifty-two thence to the Delaware, a delay which was fatal to the success of his campaign. Just half of his twelve ships of the line were coppered, but only two were good sailers. That he divided his twelve ships into five categories shows in itself how unequal his fleet was to concerted movement.

Admiral Byron who, on account of D'Estaing's departure, left Plymouth on the 9th of June with twelve ships of the line, to reinforce the British force at New York, was sixty-seven days in reaching the American coast. And when he did come in sight of Long Island on the 18th of August he was all alone, his fleet having been wholly scattered and much injured in a heavy gale of wind just encountered. In this condition he sighted the French fleet at anchor off Long Island, the greater number of which were under jury-masts, thus showing that they had suffered also. Byron headed for Halifax, which he reached eight days later, fearing, on account

of the enemy, to attempt to go to New York or Narragansett Bay. Some of his ships had, however, already reached New York.

These experiences are but fair illustrations of the defects of the ships of the day.

For the benefit of the unprofessional reader, and as the ships of a century and more ago are as obsolete and as unknown almost even to the seamen of this generation as the ancient galley, it is well to state that a ship of the line was a vessel of a size and armament equal to taking a place in the line of battle. The modern equivalent is found in the shorter phrase battle-ship. Such ships varied materially in force much as the battle-ships do to-day. They ranged from those of 60 guns to 120; the latter, however, were rather rare exceptions. By far the larger part of a fleet was made up of the class known as seventy-fours. This was a "two-decker," *i.e.,* it had two complete tiers of guns, or two gun decks and an incomplete tier on the upper deck. The two-decker thus had guns really on three decks and the three-decker on four. Naturally the lower gun deck was not far above the water and the lee guns on this deck frequently could not be fought, as the ports would have to be kept closed on account of the heeling of the ship. The frigates had but one covered gun deck. They were the scouts of the period; the eyes of the fleet of heavy battle-ships. They had no place in the line of battle but repeated the commander-in-chief's signals. The sloop-of-war was a ship with guns only on the upper deck.

Though the information is readily available, it is not amiss to give some details of the construction and armament of the ships of the time, as being necessary to a reasonable understanding of the actions of the period.

For a good three-quarters of a century, or one may say well on to a full century, there was but little change in size, character and armament of ships. Thus the "Royal Sovereign" of 100 guns, launched in 1728, was 175 feet long on the gun deck; 140 feet 7 inches on the keel and 50 feet 3½ inches beam, with a tonnage of 1883 tons, equivalent to a displacement of about 3000 tons; the "Barfleur," of 90 guns, was 163 feet on the gun deck; 131 feet on the keel and 47 feet 3 inches beam, with a tonnage of 1565. The "Victory" of 100 guns (launched 1765 to replace a "Victory" lost in 1744), Nelson's flagship at Trafalgar, and which is still afloat, was 186 feet on the gun deck; 151 feet 3½ inches on the keel and 52 feet beam, with a tonnage of 2162. The 36-gun frigates were about 140 feet on the gun deck; 120 on the keel, and 36 feet beam, with a tonnage of 900 tons. Their displacement may be taken as about twice the measured tonnage.

The guns (by the establishment of 1743, which held for a long period) were, with slight variations as to length and weight, as follows:

	Length ft.	in.	Weight cwt.	Calibre in.	Service Charge lbs.	Windage in.
42-pounder	10	0	65	7.03	17	.35
32	9	6	55	6.43	14	.33
24	{9	6	50		11	
	{9		46	5.84		.30
18	{9	6	42	5.3	9	.27
	{9		39			
12	{9	6	36			
	{9		32	4.64	6	.22
	{8	6	31			

There were five classes of the 9-pounders, varying in weight from 28.5 to 23 cwt. with a charge of 4 lbs. 8 oz., and a windage of .22 inch.[1]   There were six of the six-pounders, varying from 9 ft. to 6 ft. 6 in.   Their calibre was 3.67 in.; charge, 3 lbs.; windage, .19 in.   The 100-gun ship carried about 900 men; that of 90 guns, 800; of 80 guns, 700; the seventy-fours, 600; the sixty-fours, 500; the fifties, 350; the forty-fours, 280; the thirty-twos, 220.

By the strict wording of the "Establishment" the 100-gun ship carried twenty-eight 32-pounders on the lower deck; twenty-eight 24-pounders on the middle deck; twenty-eight 12-pounders on the upper (gun) deck; twelve 6-pounders on the quarterdeck, and four 6-pounders on the forecastle.   The class of seventy-fours carried twenty-eight 32's on the lower deck; twenty-eight 18's or 24's on the upper deck (as the size of the ship varied); fourteen 9's on the quarterdeck, and four 9's on the forecastle.   These figures are, however, only approximate, as the heavier ships usually carried from 8 to 10 more guns than the number rated.

Carronades, invented as early as 1752 by a General Melville, and which took their name from the foundry at Carron in Scotland where they were made, did not come into use until the period of our Revolution.   They were short guns of heavy calibre but of much less weight for the same calibres.   Their powder charge was comparatively light and their ordinary range but 300 yards.   As the actions of the day were usually at close quarters, however, ships often being in actual contact, the new invention was, for mixed batteries, a valuable one, as it gave a much greater weight of fire in close

---

[1] That is, the ball was that much less in diameter than the bore.

action.[1] The guns and gun mountings were in general character practically those carried in broadside down to the time of our Civil War. Mountings, sights, and methods of training and elevation were exceedingly primitive and continued so with but little change for generations. Neither sights nor locks were much used until after 1780:[2] guns were trained or elevated by guesswork. As actions were frequently fought with ships, as mentioned, in actual contact, such defects were not in the long run as serious as might be thought. Lateral train was of course comparatively accurate; the elevation was of secondary consideration, as at the close range at which actions were usually fought, if the shot missed the hull it was pretty sure to cut something in the towering mass of rigging which offered a target about 180 feet square. Notwithstanding the crudity of the means of handling, loading, pointing and firing guns, an amazing number of shots were fired. Thus the "Sandwich," Admiral Rodney's flag-ship, in the action with the French fleet under Guichen off Martinique, on April 17, 1780, fired 3288 round-shot, using 160 barrels of powder. She had herself eighty shot in the hull and a mast shot away.[3]

[1] Their real use was, however, as auxiliaries to the longer gun. Their short range was fatal to the Essex in the action in 1814 with the Phœbe and Cherub near Valparaiso. The Essex carried 40 thirty-two-pounder carronades and six long 12's. The Phœbe had 30 long 18's and 16 thirty-two-pounder carronades. Captain Porter, it must be said, protested against the armament before leaving the United States. The British ships had only to stand off at long range and pound the Essex to death, and this too within a half mile of the shore just north of Valparaiso.

[2] They were flint locks. "The detonating lock and percussion tube came in 1842." (Robinson, The British Fleet, p. 254.)

[3] Mundy, Life of Rodney, I, 287, note.

All rigging was of hemp, and this on account of its tendency to stretch in heavy weather was liable to give wholly insufficient support to the masts, which in the large ships towered from 175 to 190 feet above water, with an immense weight of yards and canvas. The ironwork (chain-plates) supporting the lower dead-eyes was often inferior and gave way under severe stress. Fleets were thus frequently disabled by the loss of masts when only a few days out of port.

While the masts and spars were so at the mercy of the gale, they suffered equally in action. It would seem that one had but to fire a gun and a mast went by the board. The cutting of a few shrouds or stays might result in leaving the ship a helpless hulk. The battle pictures of a sea covered with floating masts and debris of yards and sails are in no degree, as a rule, overdrawn. Such was but the natural result of every severe battle.

Chain cables were unknown;[1] all cables were of hemp. Those of the three-deckers of 80, 90 and 100 guns were 22, 23 and 24 inches in circumference. The seventy-fours had cables of 21 inches.

The handling of such great ropes was a matter of extreme labor and difficulty and the means were of the crudest. One need not wonder that cables were cut when in a hurry, instead of spending hours in heaving in. The care of such a mass of water- and mud-soaked material was a serious matter.

The continuous "spar deck"[2] of more modern days was unknown. There was a deep "waist" between the

---

[1] These were not used until about 1811.

[2] This name came from the use of the upper deck for the stowage of the immense mass of spare spars, such as yards, topmasts, etc., carried there, forward of the mainmast. The quarterdeck was a real quarter of a deck; forecastle needs no explanation.

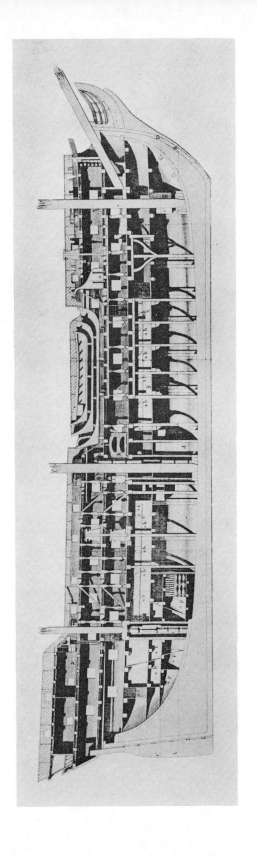

Plan de la Coupe Verticale-Longitudinale
d'un Vaisseau de 74 Canons

quarterdeck and forecastle, uncovered but for spare spars and boats, all of which were stowed on thwart-ship beams, boat davits being unknown. Bright yellow sides with upper works of blue and broad strakes of black at the water-line, and nearly all inboard a dull red, was the fashion in paint throughout the eighteenth century. It was Nelson who introduced the black sides with yellow port strakes which later were changed to white and so continued throughout the era of wooden ships.[1]

All ships of the period were very low between decks. Ventilation was thus of the slightest, and of hygiene there was but little thought. The water was carried in wooden casks. It was often impure when taken on board, and naturally did not improve by so keeping. As a rule, the health of ships' companies was thus almost incredibly bad, though there were some captains who kept healthy ships. "The 'Stirling Castle,' 64, Captain Samuel Cornish, arrived at Portsmouth [in 1756, after a few months only of Channel service] with 480 men, of whom 225 were the pressed refuse of gaols and scum of streets; she was full of fever and other illnesses, and when the sick had been sent ashore but 160 men remained for duty." Later, going to New York and the West Indies, her new captain writes from Antigua: "I officiate as Chaplain and bury eight men in a morning."[2] Of the 175,990 men raised from September, 1774, to September, 1780, 18,541 died from disease; only 1243 had been killed, 42,069 had run.[3]

[1] Cf. Robinson, The British Fleet, pp. 248, 249, for fuller details of painting.
[2] Clowes, The Royal Navy, III, 23.
[3] Ibid., III, 339.

The habit of systematically carrying women to sea, which, toward the end of the seventeenth century, was in the proportion of so many per company of marines, lasted in some degree throughout the eighteenth, as one finds frequent mention of them. Of what we call "morals" there was but little; Captain Thompson, writing in the middle of the eighteenth century, after describing the unsavory persons and dwellings of the negroes of Antigua, goes on:

"But bad smells don't hurt the sailor's appetite, each man possessing a temporary lady, whose pride is her constancy to the man she chooses; and in this particular they are strictly so. I have known 350 women sup and sleep on board on a Sunday evening and return at daybreak to their different plantations."[1] I have been told of similar things in our own service as existing in the "forties" of the last century, my informant being Captain Patterson, who was later head of the Coast Survey. It is evident that in other times there were other manners.

It is clear that Smollett in "Roderick Random" scarcely overdraws the picture of sea-life in his own time (1760). But the period was a coarse one both afloat and ashore. The life of the sea was but a reflex of the other. Both have changed together in immense degree, in sanitation, morality, temperance, culture and manners. In all these, navies have much more than kept pace with their shore-dwelling brethren. I have no hesitancy in giving it as my opinion, after an acquaintance of nearly fifty-five years with naval life, that the naval officers of every period have typified the best men of that period, and never more than to-day. I quite

[1] Clowes, The Royal Navy, III, 23.

agree with the remark to me of a well-known British Admiral: "The best men I meet in every country are the naval officers." It stands to reason that they should be. For no men have higher or heavier responsibilties, in command, in diplomacy and in all that calls for man's best efforts. The sea does not brook inefficiency. It is not for the weakling to meet Nature in her stormiest moods nor for such to deal in diplomacy or war with men of all degrees and all races. Naval life is of so stern an exigence that of necessity the unfit must disappear. The life of the sea is thus a great democracy which respects man's ordinary social status not at all. The great reward goes only to the man of whom it can, in all truth, be said: "Well done."

Some time before the outbreak of our Revolution, tactics and signals had begun a new development. The British "Fighting Instructions," which had long obtained and in the main long continued in the letter, were hidebound and forbade anything like originality. Deviation from them, if thereby any disaster occurred, was fatal to the standing of a commander-in-chief, and, as mentioned in the case of Byng, to life. Scarcely any captains dared to deviate from what was laid down. There was no initiative. Thus through scores of years there had never been a really decisive fleet action. The French were the first to develop anything like an efficient system of tactics. The work of Vicomte de Morogues, published in 1763, was the leading book of its period on the subject. He wisely advised large ships and heavy guns as thereby a fleet could be less numerous without being less powerful: "Its movements were more prompt, signals better received, formation more exact." Kempenfelt wrote Middleton (the Controller of the Navy), in August, 1779: "That we have no regular system of tactics you know; also that tactics are as necessary for fleets as armies." And in January, 1780: "I believe you will with me think it is something surprising that we who have been so long a famous maritime Power should not yet have established any regular rules for the orderly and expeditious performance of the several evolutions necessary to be made in a fleet. The French have long set us the example. They have formed a system of tactics which are studied in their academies and practiced in their squadrons. . . . We should therefore immediately, and in earnest, set about a reform."[1] Well had it been for British success in our Revolutionary period had Kempenfelt been listened to when he first pressed the subject. Kempenfelt urged a translation of the French tactics, and even went to France to study the subject.[2] Morogues, as mentioned, favored throughout the fleet composed of fewer big ships rather than of a greater number of smaller ones. "The shortened line was the method of his choice."[3] "Summing up his theory of naval warfare in general and tactics in particular, it is this: Firstly, that the paramount means of securing the end of warfare is a crushing decision against the enemy's fleet. Secondly, that, given the gun as a basis of tactics, and given the ease of avoidance at sea, such a decision can only be gained by superior concentration of fire and superior mobility. But here a dilemma is involved. Superior concentration can best be obtained by close order, but close order means loss of mobility. The dilemma, however, is not

[1] Signals and Instructions, Navy Records Society, Vol. XXXV, pp. 2, 3.
[2] *Ibid.*, Introduction.
[3] *Ibid.*, 12.

insoluble. The way out is to use big ships and big guns whereby you can secure at the same time both superior concentration and, having fewer units, superior mobility."[1] We have here the theories of to-day enunciated in 1763. Concentration against a portion was also held by Rodney to be the true object rather than to follow the rule of generations which required a careful formation parallel to the enemy's line and then each ship engage its opposite. In a note to Clerk's "Tactics" he said: "It is well known that attempting to bring to action the enemy, ship to ship, is contrary to common sense, and a proof that that admiral is not an officer whose duty it is to take every advantage of an enemy by which he will be sure of defeating the enemy and taking the part attacked, and likewise defeating the other part by detail unless they make a timely retreat. During all his commands Admiral Rodney has been entrusted with he has made it a rule to bring his whole force against part of the enemy's, and never was so absurd as to bring ship against ship."[2]

We have here in 1779 the beginning of the departure from the ancient ship-to-ship rule, a departure attempted by Rodney in his action with Guichen on April 17, 1780, off Martinique, but rendered abortive by an ambiguous signal combined with the authority of the old "Fighting Instructions," which throughout their careers had been stamped upon the minds of the captains. One can readily understand the confusion that would result from such a misunderstanding in a fleet of twenty ships in the close order of one cable distance,[3] which even

[1] Signals and Instructions, Navy Records Society, Vol. XXXV, p. 11.

[2] *Ibid.*, 14.

[3] The old cable was 120 fathoms = 720 feet.

thus stretched about three and a half nautical miles, in action with one of twenty-two ships, with a line, by Rodney's estimate, of four leagues (twelve miles) in length, as occurred in his action with Guichen. The British captains in the van pressed all sail to reach the head ships of the French line, and the concentration of the compact British line upon the rear of the much extended French was thus rendered abortive. Hence much acrimony and ill-feeling, courts-martial and a most harsh report home from the commander-in-chief, whose own insufficient clarity in signals was chiefly responsible. Something of the same kind was to happen in Graves's encounter with De Grasse, by which the battle was lost, and, with the battle, America.

A great deal which is more or less nonsense has been written about "breaking the line." There were generations of controversy over Rodney's action in this respect on April 12, 1782, when De Grasse was defeated and his flagship, the "Ville de Paris," taken. Rodney in reality broke no line in this action because there was none to break. The French fleet was so affected by the light airs, calms and currents which prevailed in the immediate vicinity of the islands near which they were, that any careful reading of the narrative shows the impossibility of any real formation on their part. The battle ended with both fleets divided into widely scattered groups, miles apart; the French flag-ship with five others formed the central group; there were some dozen ships two miles to windward of her and the rest four miles to leeward. The British were in no better formation, but Rodney was fortunate in having a superiority near De Grasse's group. The result was the capture of the French flag-ship and her immediate com-

panions, and the escape, through Rodney's unwilling-
ness to pursue, of nearly all the others. The net loss
to the French, it may be said, was six line-of-battle ships
taken, two destroyed and a demoralization which ended
their naval efficiency in the West Indies. It was this
demoralization of the French, and not the capture of a
few ships, which gave the battle its great importance.

Returning to the formerly much-vexed question of
breaking the line, the matter is thus summed up after
an extended examination by Mr. Corbett, in his volume
of "Signals and Instructions, 1776-1794": "We are
brought to the incontestable conclusion that by the end
of 1781, there was a signal for breaking the line on
every principal station except that which Rodney commanded";[1] and one of its chief exponents, in theory at
least, was the admiral who lost the battle against De
Grasse off the Capes of the Chesapeake.

With this somewhat long beginning, we turn to the
actual events which led to the overthrow of British
dominion over the thirteen colonies. In dealing with
these it seems fitting that some general account of
French naval effort on our coast should be given.

The surrender of Burgoyne at Saratoga, on October
17, 1777, made the eventual independence of the United
States so likely that France, wounded to the heart by
the treaty of 1763, and ready to deal an avenging blow
to Great Britain, signed, on February 6, 1778, an alliance with the United States. Her sympathy and aid had
already been strongly shown, but now, on April 13,
1778, the Comte d'Estaing[2] sailed from Toulon with a

[1] Navy Records Society, XXXV, 57.
[2] Charles Henri Theodat d'Estaing du Saillans, born at the Châ-
teau de Reval (Puy-de-Dome), November 28, 1729; beheaded April

fleet of twelve ships of the line, two of which were of
80 guns, six of 74, three of 64 and one of 50. There
were also five frigates of 26 guns each. He carried
with him M. Gérard de Rayneval, the first envoy from
France to the United States.

Unfortunately D'Estaing was not a seaman. His career to the age of thirty-four had been in the army. He
was transferred to the navy in December, 1763, with
the rank of vice-admiral, and was now, in his fiftieth
year, in the most important command afloat which the
King of France had to give. The situation in America
was made to hand for an enterprising officer. General
Howe had, at the moment when he should have been
assisting Burgoyne's expedition to the utmost, transferred the main British force to Philadelphia. Clinton
was slow in moving to Burgoyne's support with the
remainder. The result was that he was too late, Burgoyne being forced to surrender the day Clinton's force
reached and burned Kingston on the Hudson. Howe
was still at Philadelphia, but was about beginning a
retreat across New Jersey to Sandy Hook and New
York. His brother, Vice-Admiral Lord Howe, who
was to come to high distinction, was in the Delaware
with six sixty-fours awaiting the preparation of the
large number of transports which were to carry the
army impedimenta. On June 18 the army crossed the
Delaware; the next day the transports moved down the
river, but did not get to sea until June 28. D'Estaing
had been at sea seventy-six days. He did not reach the
Delaware until ten days later, July 8. D'Estaing is
credited with the apothegm: "La promptitude est la

28, 1794, during the Terror. (Lacour-Gayet, p. 139. Genealogy in
Doniol's Participation of France, etc., Vol. III, chap. v.)

première des armes; étonner, c'est presque avoir vaincu."[1] Rarely has the observance of the precept been more necessary and seldom has it been more completely ignored. D'Estaing was thirty-three days to Gibraltar, a distance of but about 750 nautical miles. His average daily run was thus at the almost inconceivably slow rate of twenty-three miles a day. Passing Gibraltar, where of course he was observed, and whence he was followed for fifty leagues by a British frigate which carried the news of his westward destination to England, he was to be yet fifty-three days in reaching the Delaware, though with the Straits as his point of departure he was most favorably placed for making a good passage. As mentioned, his quarry by the time of his arrival had flown.

The meaning of the foregoing is that had D'Estaing arrived ten days earlier—and by all reasoning he could have done so by devoting his efforts wholly to a quick passage, towing his slower ships as De Grasse did later in his passage from Brest to the West Indies, thus making the passage from Brest to Martinique in five weeks —he would have captured Lord Howe's much weaker force in the Delaware, with all the British transports, New York would have been defenseless and must have fallen, and with this capture would have come an end of the war, certainly so far as it concerned America.

D'Estaing's next move was of course to appear off New York. But Howe, who was inside of Sandy Hook on June 30, had shown every energy in preparing a defense. A five-gun battery was established on the Hook, commanding the channel; seven ships were echelonned

[1] Lacour-Gayet, La Marine Militaire de la France sous la Règne de Louis XVI, p. 143.

[xxxix]

in the channel with springs and separate anchors. By veering on the cables, their broadsides would present to the east; and echelonned as they were, each ship would fire clear of the other. Several other ships were utilized independently of these, the whole being six sixty-fours, three fifties and six frigates. D'Estaing anchored off the Hook on July 11. The New York pilots declared it impossible to take the heavy French ships over the bar, though Admiral Arbuthnot states in a letter of October 8, 1779, to the Admiralty, that "at spring tides there is generally thirty feet of water on the bar at high water." How much of the pilots' action was the result of disloyalty, how much fear, one can only surmise. Their cupidity was tempted by an offer of 150,000 francs without avail, and it is fair to suppose that both disloyalty and fear must have contributed to defeat such a temptation. Under the circumstances it required a Farragut or a Suffren (who, by the way, commanded the "Fantasque," 64, of D'Estaing's fleet). D'Estaing was neither. In any case he gave up the attempt, though on July 22 everything conspired to give every advantage; for on that day there was a fresh northeast wind and a spring tide. "At eight o'clock," wrote an eye-witness in the British fleet, "D'Estaing with all his squadron appeared under way. He kept working to windward, as if to gain a proper position for crossing the bar by the time the tide should serve. The wind could not be more favorable for such a design; it blew from the exact point from which he could attack us to the greatest advantage. The spring tides were at the highest, and that afternoon thirty feet on the bar. We consequently expected the hottest day that had ever been fought between the two nations. On our side all was at stake. Had the men-of-war been defeated, the fleet of transports and victuallers must have been destroyed, and the army, of course, have fallen with us. D'Estaing, however, had not spirit equal to the risk; at three o'clock we saw him bear off to the southward, and in a few hours he was out of sight."[1]

Thus ended d'Estaing's second great opportunity. He was to have one more, which, though not comparable in importance with either of the others, would, if successful, have been a momentous event. This was the possible capture of the 6000 British and Hessians, with a naval force of five frigates and some smaller vessels and transports, at Newport and the lower part of Narragansett Bay.

It had been concerted with Washington that should the attack on New York not be ventured, D'Estaing should go to Newport, in the vicinity of which was already General Sullivan with a small force, shortly to be added to by 2000 men under Lafayette, sent from Washington's main force on the Hudson. General Nathanael Greene was also sent to command one of the three divisions into which the American investing army was to be formed. Sullivan was hoping to raise his force to 10,000 men, but militia are a very uncertain quantity, and it was the slowness of their coming in from Rhode Island and the neighboring States, and Sullivan's request to await their coming, which was the chief element in the miscarriage of this most promising opportunity.

D'Estaing anchored off Brenton's Reef on July 29. There was every reason for haste, for it was known that Vice-Admiral Byron, who had sailed from England on

[1] Clowes, The Royal Navy, III, 401.

June 9 with thirteen ships of the line, was now due in America. This fleet, scattered by heavy gales, was soon indeed to begin to reach port, the flag-ship, for reasons already mentioned, going into Halifax. The situation thus offered a dangerous potentiality. Sullivan, at once boarding the French flag-ship, in company with Lafayette, explained his own situation and asked for a little more time to collect his troops. Delay was fatal. It not only gave opportunity to the British general, Pigot, who commanded the army, and to Captain John Brisbane, the senior naval officer in command of the ships, to take measures for defense, but, what was of much more importance, it brought, after a delay of nine days, the British fleet under Howe, which caused D'Estaing unwisely to leave the bay to meet them, and eventually sent him to Boston with his ships much damaged by a heavy gale, and without bringing the British fleet to action. War is not a game in which success is to be subordinated to an ally's vanity. Every element of the situation demanded the disregarding of General Sullivan's request at least to the extent of entering the bay at the earliest moment and taking advantage of a surprise.

D'Estaing the day after his arrival had sent two of his ships of the line under Suffren into the channel west of Conanicut Island, and two frigates and a corvette into Sekonnet River, where the British now destroyed a sloop of war and an armed galley. On August 5 Suffren anchored north of Conanicut and two other ships took his place in the West Channel. It was now that the five British ships were destroyed by Captain Brisbane. Two were sunk south of Goat Island in the channel leading to the inner harbor, and five transports were sunk between Goat and Coasters Harbor Islands. The 1500 Hessians on Conanicut Island were withdrawn to Newport, and the batteries built on Goat Island and at other points on the water-front were manned by the seamen of the sunken ships.

On August 8 the other eight French ships of the line, coming in at the main entrance, ran past the batteries without damage and anchored north of Goat and Rose Islands, where they were rejoined by Suffren with his two ships, the two in the west passage being ordered to cruise outside. On Sunday morning, August 9, at 7 A.M., D'Estaing landed on Conanicut Island such of the thousand soldiers as the prevailing scurvy and general ill-health had spared, and 2000 armed seamen. Some fifteen flatboats had been provided by the Americans for the landing and for the transport next day to the northern part of Aquidneck Island (on which is Newport). It was while the landing upon Conanicut was in progress that news came that General Sullivan, anticipating the plan agreed upon for next day (the 10th), had already crossed to the upper end of the island with between two and three thousand men, but without artillery and but little of his munitions. He desired assistance. Too much appears to have been made by the French officers of this breach of arrangement, which after all was vastly better than tardiness. But whatever the weight of the point of etiquette involved, it was as nothing to what now happened. D'Estaing had scarcely more than given orders to comply with Sullivan's request for an immediate transfer of his landing force to Aquidneck Island, when word was brought that Lord Howe's fleet was seen, in the interval of lifting of the fog, at anchor off Point Judith, which is seven miles south of the entrance to Narragansett Bay. He had with him one seventy-four, seven sixty-fours, five fifties, six frigates and some smaller vessels, but his exact force could not be absolutely determined.

The men were at once recalled aboard, a council of war called and steps taken to dispose the ships of the fleet for defense against attack in the bay, by anchoring in close order on an east-and-west line between Gould Island and Conanicut; there they should have remained. The afternoon and night was squally with the wind from W.S.W. to N.W., with intervals of calm. At daylight of the 10th the weather was overcast, with a light W.N.W. wind, almost calm. Many of the ships were kedging into position. At 7 A.M., the wind, now stormy, suddenly hauled to the N.N.E. and D'Estaing determined to profit by its direction, which was fair to go to sea and seek the enemy. Well would it have been had he and his people been more weather-wise, for the description in the journal[1] kept by the Comte de Cambis aboard the "Languedoc" flag-ship, and which has been largely used in this account, is an exact premonition of what is locally known as the "August gale," which has its origin in a West Indian hurricane. Any reference to local knowledge would, or at least should, have kept D'Estaing in harbor; any fisherman could have told him what was brooding; the British fleet, driven off by the furious tempest about to break, could not have returned for some time; the situation of the army in Newport was desperate, and it must have surrendered on the first attack; Lord Howe himself, after communicating with the British army and navy commanders in Newport, "was of opinion that it was impracticable for him to

[1] Doniol, III, 374 *et seq.*

afford Sir Robert Pigot any essential relief."[1] But the fates were against D'Estaing and at 7:30 A.M. (August 10) he gave orders to prepare to get under way. The flatboats were sent back to Sullivan with a promise to return with the fleet; and at 8:30 signal was made to get under way, cutting the cables, and leaving behind their boats and the four frigates. By 10:30 the fleet had passed out of the harbor entrance, suffering no injury of any moment from the fire of the British batteries. Once outside, it was seen that Howe was also under way, he having also cut his cables, and for the moment at least refusing action. In this he was entirely justified, seeing that his force in guns was but as 672 to 782, and that he was wholly outclassed as to ships, the French having two eighty-gun ships and six seventy-fours, whereas but one of the British was even of the latter force. There is no need to go into the manœuvres for position during that day and part of the next, or into any account of the difficulties to come through the rising gale. By the evening of the 11th this had so increased that engagement was out of the question; it became a matter of safety. The upshot was the scattering of the two fleets and severe injuries to both, though much greater to the French. The "Languedoc," flagship, lost all her masts, her bowsprit, and broke her tiller. In this unmanageable condition she was attacked by two of the British ships, and would have been captured but for the happy advent of some of her less injured consorts. All of the French fleet, but two, gathered together and on the 15th of August were at anchor twenty-five leagues east of Cape May. Here they were seen by Admiral Howe, who, with his fleet separated,

---

[1] Beatson, IV, 345.

was alone in the "Centurion." On the 18th, on their
way again to Newport, the French were seen south of
Long Island by Admiral Byron, who, in his flag-ship,
the "Princess Royal," was all alone, his own fleet scattered to the winds. Byron was now sixty-seven days
from Plymouth, and fearing in his damaged condition
to attempt to get into New York, with the French fleet
at hand, put for Halifax, where he also found others of
his ships, though some had reached New York. One,
the "Cornwall," had arrived there on July 30th and had
taken part in Lord Howe's expedition to Newport, the
only seventy-four of his fleet. Such in that day, and for
generations later, were the uncertainties of the sea.

D'Estaing, though his officers were of one mind
that they should proceed under orders, which were
explicit to go to Boston to refit or take refuge if threat-
ened by a superior force, held loyally to his promise to
return to Newport, an action for which he should have
every credit; with his flag-ship towed, he arrived off
Newport on August 20. Here he communicated with
General Sullivan, who sent Generals Nathanael Greene
and Lafayette aboard the "Languedoc" to press for an
attack. Both of the reasons given in his orders were
now active, but D'Estaing offered to land the 1500
troops and marine infantry with the fleet, if they would
guarantee to reduce Newport in two days. This the
American officers felt unable to promise. D'Estaing
called a council of war; his captains were unanimous
that the fleet should go at once to Boston, and on August
22 it sailed. It arrived at Boston on August 28, and was
busied with repairs and looking after the defense
against the British fleet, which appeared but three days
after under Byron, Howe having now resigned his com-

mand. It did not attack. During most of the time at Boston relations between the French and the populace were strained. A riot even occurred in which a French officer was killed. The feeling over the Newport failure ran high, aided much by the indiscreet action of Sullivan, who did not recognize how far his own delay had gone to produce failure. He wrote a wholly uncalled-for letter upbraiding D'Estaing, and in a general order to his now rapidly dwindling army (3000 had left in one day) criticized our allies so severely that a duel was imminent between himself and Lafayette. To endanger thus our alliance with France was an astonishing error which it required the ever wise Washington to repair.

On November 3, 1778, D'Estaing sailed for the West Indies. Arriving at Martinique December 9, he entered upon a year of varying fortune. He was reinforced in February by a division of four line-of-battle ships under De Grasse, by two under Vandreuil in April, and five more under La Motte-Piquet in June. He had under his command twenty-five of the line. One must look elsewhere for the happenings in the West Indies. The occupation, however, by the British of Savannah in December, 1778, caused loud calls for naval aid from the United States. The success of the French in taking all the Windward Islands except St. Lucia emboldened D'Estaing to disregard for a time his orders to return with his own particular command to France, and attempt the relief of Savannah. On August 31 he anchored off Savannah River, with twenty-two of the line, with the idea of even continuing a career of conquest as far as Halifax, after taking Savannah. Things were to be far otherwise. The attempt on Savannah by

the French under D'Estaing and the Americans under
Lincoln was wholly unsuccessful; the two weeks proposed for the capture lengthened into two months, until
on October 28, the fleet, anchored in an open roadstead,
was driven to sea and separated in a fierce gale. On
November 5 the flag-ship, with not an anchor remaining
aboard, was 250 leagues southeast of Savannah, and
alone. To gather the scattered fleet, which returned
ship by ship to the West Indies, was hopeless. D'Estaing stood for France, meeting the "Provence," which
gave him an anchor, and on December 7, 1779, reached
Brest.

D'Estaing's move against Savannah had had the important effect of causing the withdrawal on October 25,
1779, of the British from Newport to New York,
through fear of attack there. Had D'Estaing, instead of
Savannah, attempted New York, where Admiral Arbuthnot then had but five ships of the line, he might
have ended his campaign with all the brilliancy of his
utmost hopes. Again he had the chance of ending the
war. As it was, the American coast was left open for
the movement at will of the British ships, of which there
were twenty-seven of the frigate class, large and small.
The southern coast was open to freest occupation and
desolation; and though the eccentric policy now under-
taken by the British was, through almost fortuitous circumstances, to end unfavorably for them, it was not far
from conquering the country. For it delivered for a
time into their hands the whole region south of Virginia, in which the loyalists were as many and as active
as were the patriots.[1]

[1] On this subject see Van Tyne, The Loyalists in the American
Revolution.

[xlviii]

Le Comte de Grasse

Etched by H. B. Hall from an original miniature

Thus ended the first French naval expedition to the United States, from which so much had been hoped. It was pursued by misfortune from beginning to end: in the slowness of its passage, whereby Howe escaped from the Delaware; in the failure to be properly served by the pilots at New York, which not unnaturally disheartened a commander to whom and to whose captains the waters were totally unknown; and in the delay in attack at Newport, which resulted in such disaster. D'Estaing's force was such that an immediate attack must have been successful. He would have captured the 1500 Hessians upon Conanicut and the ships which the navy was given time to sink, and there would have been no time to build the batteries which he would later have had to attack with probably some loss. Whether he should not have remained in the bay on the appearance of Hood is a moot question. Beatson, an excellent contemporary authority, says that "Lord Howe was of opinion that it was impracticable for him to afford Sir Robert Pigot any essential relief." Almost certainly D'Estaing could have held his own in the bay and have reduced Newport, in so doing, easily. His choice as it turned out was a misfortune, and almost a fault, for even a defeat of Howe's fleet at sea would have left him with a much shattered force, which would shortly have again been faced by one much more powerful under Byron. In the circumstances, instant action on the first arrival at Newport was a necessity. The failure to act promptly must, as said, be laid chiefly at our own door, through General Sullivan's specific request for delay. To accede to this was courtesy but not war. Perhaps Suffren would have been more insistent and less polite. D'Estaing's failure was not far from wrecking the American cause. Perhaps Suffren was right in his estimate of his chief: "S'il avait été aussi marin que brave . . ."[1]

There seems to have been but one man of his time who recognized the situation clearly: Washington. His dictum, and it was an opinion expressed at various times and in various forms throughout the war, places him among the first who had a real recognition of the value of command of the sea, which goes back to Bacon's generalization. In a memorandum of July 15, 1780, which he sent to Rochambeau by the hands of Lafayette, Washington said: "In any operation, and under all circumstances, a decisive naval superiority is to be considered as a fundamental principle, and the basis upon which every hope of success must ultimately depend." A hundred years were to pass before this was to have a world-comprehension through the genius of the American naval historian, Mahan.[2]

The years 1779 and 1780 were years of deepest gloom to the American cause. Actually we had no government. On the same day, June 10, 1776, that there was appointed a committee to draft the Declaration of Independence, another was formed to draw up the "Articles of Confederation." This committee first reported on July 12, 1776, but it was not until November 15, 1777,

[1] For further accounts of this first French effort, see Doniol, Participation de la France à l'Établissement des États Unis d'Amérique.

[2] A little-noticed writer who advanced the theories later so forcibly inculcated by Admiral Mahan was the Frenchman Deslandes. In his Essai sur la Marine et le Commerce (printed at Amsterdam, by François Changuion, in 1743) he proclaimed that "from the beginnings of history the marine had been a decisive factor in the rise and fall of states." The only copy I know of is in the Yale University Library. —Editor.

that their report was adopted, and even then it was not until March 1, 1781, that the last colony, Maryland, signed it, and it came definitely into the ineffective operation of which only it was capable. Probably no more impotent system of government was ever attempted. Appropriations could be passed, but they were only advisory, as the several States could be appealed to only to furnish their quota. There was no such thing as a command by Congress; it could only request; any State could withdraw at will, for there was no means of forcing it to remain in the Confederation. Each State had entire independence as to fiscal arrangements. This is no place to enlarge upon this subject, but the situation is well expressed by the phrase: "The States were independent sovereignties, united in a league of which the first object was, not to guard against Great Britain, but against each other."[1] Interest gradually fell away until the actual attendance rarely rose to thirty of the ninety delegates. Even the definitive treaty of peace could not be ratified until January 14, 1784, because it had been impossible to bring together the representatives of the necessary nine States. The army in 1779 and 1780 was famished and in rags. Washington marveled that there had not been a "general mutiny and dispersion," and he marveled equally at the "incomparable patience and fidelity of the soldiery," notwithstanding the fact that during the winter of 1777–1778 "twenty-three hundred deserters went into Philadelphia and joined the British Army."[2] They were simply driven by hunger to the plentiful food which a sound

[1] Encyclopedia Americana: Confederation, Articles of.
[2] Van Tyne, The American Revolution, American Nation Series, Vol. IX, p. 237.

currency could buy and an utterly discredited currency could not.

One who lifts the screen of laudation and glamor woven in later generations can only marvel at our success. There was in fact but one reason for it—Washington, who was the Revolution embodied. Ever firm and constant, neither over-depressed nor elated, he dominated events as no other man in history has done, the nearest approach to his incomparable firmness and tenacity being found in Frederick the Great in the Seven Years' War.

Once again the French fitted out an expedition to operate on the American coast. On May 2, 1780, the Chevalier de Ternay, with seven ships of the line and three frigates convoying thirty-six transports carrying some 5000 troops under the Comte de Rochambeau, left Brest for Newport, Rhode Island. It arrived on July 11. For a whole year this very considerable force was to effect nothing for want of anything like the naval superiority which Washington so truly announced as a principle in his first communication to Rochambeau, and emphasized later to De Grasse: "Whatever efforts are made by the land armies, the navy must have the casting vote in the present contest."

Rodney, leaving the West Indies with ten ships of the line, had reached New York on September 14 and had assumed general command over the naval forces under Arbuthnot without any specific authority from the Admiralty and despite the very proper indignation and protests of Arbuthnot.[1] He started on his return to the West Indies on November 16, having done nothing except create ill-feeling, though with the twenty-one

---

[1] Rodney was, however, upheld by the Admiralty.

sail of the line then in the combined squadrons at New York he might have annihilated the French squadron at Newport. Rodney's departure left Arbuthnot with but ten of the line, including the six which had arrived on July 13, 1780, under Graves. In September the treason of Arnold had come to add to Washington's heavy burdens. On September 15 De Ternay, who saw no hope for America, died at Newport,—"of chagrin," says Lafayette. He was clearly unfitted for his post. Said an officer of Rochambeau's command: "I have never seen an admiral more cast down or less enterprising."[1] He was succeeded for the moment by the next in command, the Chevalier des Touches.

On December 20 a British force of 1500 men under Arnold sailed for Virginia to create a diversion for Cornwallis, then in North Carolina, whence adverse conditions were soon to cause him to move to Virginia. In Virginia was Lafayette, who, with De Kalb, was unable, despite unsparing energy, to prevent the ruthless devastation of the State. It would now have been good strategy to meet Washington's views by making a diversion from the West Indies with a few of the French fleet under Monteil, who was left in command after the departure in 1780 for France of Guichen, De la Motte-Piquet and De Grasse, and who, says the French historian Lacour-Gayet, did "almost nothing." "His correspondence abounds in documents, reports, memoirs, but in all this mass one cannot glean a single fact of a truly military character. He was at the Cape [Haitien] and he did not budge from Santo

---

[1] Colonel le Vicomte de Charlus, Journal de mon Voyage en Amérique (Lacour-Gayet, p. 254).

Domingo, or he was at Havana and he did not budge from Cuba."[1]

De Ternay had written Guichen for the aid of four of his ships, but his letter arrived after Guichen's departure, and, Monteil not having the cipher, De Ternay's request, through Monteil's failure to make it out, had no effect. Des Touches limited his first efforts to the despatch of a ship of the line, two frigates and a cutter to the Chesapeake in February. This squadron effected nothing beyond the capture of a British forty-four and eight transports. Finding Arnold's force afloat supported by land batteries, the French ships returned to Newport. In March Des Touches tried again with his whole force of seven of the line and three frigates. But this time he found within the Capes of the Chesapeake Arbuthnot, who from his base in Gardiner's Bay, Long Island, had been keeping close watch upon the movements of the French, and had left almost at the same time, arriving at the Capes before Des Touches; it was but another instance of the general superior capacity of the Anglo-Saxon as a seaman. Arbuthnot came outside the Capes, a futile action was fought on March 16, 1781, and Des Touches returned to Newport with nothing accomplished. Meanwhile, as said, there were in the West Indies fifteen French ships of the line doing nothing. As affairs turned out, any discussion pertaining to these items of history is purely academic, but they are, notwithstanding, necessary parts of the account of the events which led finally to the great success. All mistakes may be said to have been providential, for all led to Yorktown.

De Grasse, on his return to France in 1781, was se-

[1] Lacour-Gayet, p. 345.

lected for the command of the new fleet fitting out for the West Indies. He sailed from Brest on March 22, 1781, with twenty sail of the line.

Born September 13, 1722, De Grasse was now in his fifty-ninth year. He had only returned in January, 1781, from the West Indies, where he had served under D'Estaing and Guichen. Four days after De Grasse, the Comte de Barras, named as the successor of De Ternay, sailed in the frigate "La Concorde" for Boston, where he arrived May 6, and at Newport on the 10th. On May 20, Cornwallis arrived at Petersburg, Virginia, having moved from North Carolina, and there he took over the command from the traitor Arnold, who had but just succeeded to the command of the force under General Phillips, who died on May 13. Arnold returned to New York. Clinton, with between ten and eleven thousand men at New York, was apprehensive of attack, and was desirous that Cornwallis should send back to New York some of the 7724 troops sent to Virginia between October, 1780, and June, 1781. Cornwallis, who had now moved to Portsmouth, Virginia, declared, however, that it was impossible to hold his own in Virginia with less than the force he had with him, which now, with a late reinforcement of 1700, amounted to over 7000 men. The selection of a *point d'appui* was ordered, Old Point Comfort being specially named. The engineer and naval officer who inspected the position declared against it, and the main body of Cornwallis's force finally left the vicinity of Norfolk for York River on July 30, and the whole were at Yorktown and Gloucester by August 20. All this, of course, was subsequent to the Wethersfield meeting and could have no bearing in any decision there.

Barras carried a letter from the Minister of Marine to Rochambeau stating that De Grasse would inform him when he could leave the West Indies for our coast. Said the Minister: "[As De Grasse] is master of his own movements, with authority to unite or separate his forces, I trust he may control the American coasts for some time to come, and that he may coöperate with you if you are projecting any enterprise in the North."[1] With this knowledge and also with the information from despatches of the British Minister of War, dated February 7 and March 7, 1781, captured and sent in by a privateer, that it was the purpose of the Government to occupy the Southern States and carry thence their conquest North, the meeting of the two commanders for consultation took place at Wethersfield on May 21. The arrival of Cornwallis in Virginia from North Carolina was yet unknown. The conclusions reached are shown in the formal question of Rochambeau and the reply of Washington. The former was: "If the fleets from the West Indies should arrive in these waters, an event which will probably be announced beforehand by a frigate, what operations will General Washington have in view, after a juncture of the French troops with his own?" Washington's reply was to the effect that, the enemy at New York having been reduced by detachment to less than half the force which they had in September, 1780, it was advisable to unite the French and American forces on the North River and move to the vicinity of New York "to be ready to take advantage of any opportunity which the weakness of the enemy may afford. Should the West Indian fleet arrive on the coast

[1] MS. Letter Books of Rochambeau, Library of Congress, quoted by Tower, Lafayette, II, 283.

. . . either proceed in the operation against New York" or "against the enemy in some other quarter as circumstances should dictate." The difficulties of a move south were dwelt upon and the preference for an operation against New York "in the present circumstances over an attempt to send a force to the southward," reiterated.

With this understanding Rochambeau returned to Newport.

On May 28, Rochambeau, now assured of the intention of the French Government that De Grasse should at least at some time appear on the coast, wrote a letter to the admiral to go by "La Concorde" from Boston, saying: "The enemy is making the most vigorous efforts in Virginia. Cornwallis is marching from Wilmington near Cape Fear to join on the Roanoke at Halifax with the corps of Phillips and Arnold, which goes to make up an army of 6000 men at Portsmouth, Virginia, . . . whence with his small armed vessels he ravages all the rivers of Virginia. . . . General Washington is certain that there remain at New York but 8500 regular troops and 3000 militia. He has pressed the Comte de Barras to go with the French troops to Chesapeake Bay. M. de Barras has shown the impossibility of this. He then pressed for the junction of the French army with his own, on the North River, to conjointly menace and perhaps attack New York. M. de Barras says that as soon as the army leaves he will go to Boston, following out his orders. There will remain at Newport 500 American militia to hold the works, which the enemy does not appear to be in a position to attack.

"Some days since the English squadron cruised off here five or six days. Four of them stood to sea, it is supposed to return to New York or towards the Chesapeake to assist the offensive operations in the South. There are seven ships of the line; one of three decks, three 74's, three 64's, two 50's, four 44's and many frigates. These last are not always with the squadron; they spread themselves about in support of their different movements.

"This is the state of things and of the severe crisis in which America finds herself and particularly the States of the South at this moment. The arrival of the Comte de Grasse can save it; all our means at hand can do nothing without his assistance and the naval superiority which he can bring.

"There are two points at which to act offensively against the enemy: the Chesapeake and New York. The southeast winds and the distress of Virginia will probably cause you to prefer the Chesapeake Bay, and it is there where we think you can render the greatest service; besides, it would take you only two days to come to New York. In any case it is essential to send us, well in advance, a frigate to forewarn the Comte de Barras as to the place at which you will land, as also General Washington, in order that the first may join you and the second may support you with the land forces."

Rochambeau added a postscript three days later informing De Grasse that Barras had decided to remain at Newport. This decision was the result of a council of war of officers of both army and navy.

On June 10 the ship of the line "Sagittaire" arrived at Boston, bringing a letter dated March 29 from De Grasse himself to Rochambeau: "His Majesty, Monsieur, has confided to me the command of the naval forces which he has destined to protect his possessions in southern America [the West Indies], and those of his allies in the North. The forces I command are sufficient to execute the views as to the offensive which it is in the interest of the allied powers to carry out in order to bring an honorable peace. . . ."

He requested to be informed at Santo Domingo, "where I shall be at the end of June," of the British naval forces north; that word be sent by several despatch vessels, and ended by saying that it would be toward the 15th of July, at the earliest, that he could reach our coast; "but it is necessary," he added, "seeing the short time I can stay in the country, which in any event the season will force me to leave, that everything which can serve in the success of your projects shall not delay action a moment."

Rochambeau replied the day of the reception of the letter, June 11, informing De Grasse that Washington had written him four letters since his previous writing on May 28, pressing him to move; that he expected to join in five or six days and try, in menacing New York, to make a diversion in favor of Virginia. He continued: "I cannot conceal from you that Washington has not half the troops he counted on having, and I believe, though he is reticent on this, that he has not at present 6000 men; that M. de la Fayette has not 1000 regular troops, including the militia, to defend Virginia, and about as many more on the way to join him. . . . It is then of the greatest consequence that you take aboard all the troops you can, 4000 or 5000 would not be too many," to attack the force at Hampton Roads and then to force the Hook, the land troops taking possession of Sandy Hook, which would facilitate the entry of the fleet over the bar. "We are sure that the 'Sandwich,'

Rodney's flag-ship, in September, and the 'London,' Graves's flag-ship, more lately, have entered and gone out; finally in order to aid us after the siege of Brooklyn, supposing we are able to establish ourselves with 8000 men at this point of Long Island, keeping 5000 or 6000 at North River to mask King's Bridge,—*voilà,* Monsieur, the different objects you can have in view and the actual and grievous picture of affairs in this country. I am sure you will bring there a maritime superiority, but I cannot too often repeat to bring also troops and money."

He repeated also the necessity of forewarning Barras and Washington, and added a postscript: "I observe by a letter which the Chevalier de la Luzerne has written you that M. Washington appears to wish you to land first at the Hook, in front of New York, in order to cut off Arbuthnot's squadron from anchoring there. I subordinate my opinion to his as I am bound to do; but our latest advices indicate that the enemy's squadron, after having anchored for several days outside the Hook, has put to sea and gone toward the south."[1]

"This letter," says Tower, "and the one which General de Rochambeau wrote in the last days of May are, with regard to their results, among the most important historical documents of the Revolution; for they laid the basis upon which was established the coöperation of the allied forces in the Yorktown campaign."[2]

This correspondence and the minutes of the Wethersfield meeting, May 21 and 22, show very clearly the

[1] For this correspondence, see Doniol, Correspondance du Comte de Rochambeau, V, Appendix. The advices regarding the British fleet were in error.

[2] Tower, Lafayette in the American Revolution, II, 400.

minds of both the American and French commanders.
It was not until July 13 that Washington was able to
inform Rochambeau that by information received on
the 3d Cornwallis was between Richmond and Fred-
ericksburg, "free, from his superiority of force, to go
where he would." It is clear from the conference of
July 19 that even at that date Washington regarded
New York as the most important objective for the fleet,
if all conditions of time of arrival, length of stay, etc.,
should be favorable.[1] In these last words lay the crux
of the situation. Washington wisely held that the decision should rest upon the turn of events, and of these the
time of De Grasse's arrival was of supreme importance.
His own preference for the Chesapeake and his delay
from the earliest mentioned date, July 15, to the actual
August 30, were the deciding factors. One has only to
piece together the happenings of July and August to see
how fully Washington's hopes against New York would
have been realized. On July 21 Graves had left New
York with his whole force of battle-ships for a cruise
to the eastward, leaving the place, from a naval stand-
point, wholly defenseless. He did not return until
August 16. At any time in this interval, had De Grasse
appeared, he had but to enter the bay and New York
would have been his, and the main part of the British
army in America prisoners. Even after August 16
Graves had no force but five of the line to resist him,
two of his ships having been sent on August 17 to the
dockyard for repairs. And had De Grasse arrived at
any time before August 30, Hood's fleet, unless the latter might have escaped by some extraordinary good
fortune, must have been at his mercy. It is thus in no

[1] Minutes of Conference, Doniol, V, 516, Appendix.

[lxi]

sense derogatory, but far otherwise, to Washington's judgment that he was first inclined to a naval attack against New York, which was a certain prey at any time before August 31.

Some, including Doniol and the present (1916) honored French ambassador to the United States, have raised the question as to the initiator of the move against Cornwallis. They have not recognized that they are doing an injustice to Rochambeau's memory in supposing him to press an overhasty advocacy of a transfer of the allied armies to the South. It is an unnecessary and futile claim. It was a matter decided by the trend of events. Washington and Rochambeau worked indeed in finest accord and with absolute singleness of purpose. The noble self-effacement of Rochambeau deserves all praise. He placed himself entirely at Washington's command. In his own words, "Vous ferez de moi ce que vous voudrez."[1]

On June 18, 1781, a year less 23 days from its arrival in America, the French army, leaving some 430 artillerymen and all their siege guns to support Barras's squadron in case it should be attacked, started toward the Hudson to join Washington, who by July 4 occupied a line from Dobbs Ferry to White Plains. The French arrived and occupied the east end of the line on July 6.

The "Concorde" did not leave Boston until June 20. She had a swift safe passage to Cape Français. De Grasse had left Fort Royal, Martinique, on July 5. He arrived at Cape Français on July 26, where he found four ships of the line left there the year before by Guichen. On August 12 the "Concorde," carrying De

[1] Doniol, IV, 630.

Grasse's reply, dated July 28, reached Newport, and
two days later his letter was in the hands of Rochambeau and Washington. De Grasse announced his intention to leave on August 3 (it was two days later that he
sailed) for the Chesapeake, "the point which appears
to me to be indicated by you, Monsieur le Comte, and
by MM. Washington, De Luzerne and De Barras, as
the one from which the advantage you propose may be
most certainly attained." He had engaged at Havana
the 1,200,000 livres requested by Rochambeau, had embarked 3000 infantry, 100 artillerymen, 100 dragoons,
ten field-pieces, a number of siege guns and mortars,
part of the Santo Domingo garrison, all under the command of the Marquis de Saint-Simon. He announced
that he could remain upon our coast only until October
15, on account of operations planned by the allied
French and Spanish officers. He had acted wholly on
his own responsibility and could not venture to change
their arrangements by delay beyond the time set.

On August 5 De Grasse left Cape Haitien with
twenty-eight ships of the line and, going by way of the
Old Bahama Channel, anchored on August 30, in three
columns, just within the Capes of the Chesapeake. Barras, five days before, had left Newport with six ships of
the line, four frigates and eighteen French and American transports, and Cornwallis only eight days before
had completed the movement, begun on August 1, of
his force from Portsmouth to Yorktown, which position
he had taken under orders from Clinton, after having
made an examination of other likely points, including
Hampton Roads. He had some 7000 men, besides
about 1000 seamen belonging to several frigates and
smaller men-of-war, and a large number of transports.

Washington had broken camp on August 19, five days after the reception of the news of De Grasse's departure. He crossed the Hudson at King's Ferry on August 21. By the 25th both armies were across and the march south began with every caution against a revelation of destination, and with endeavor to give the impression to the British of a contemplated attack on Staten Island. Clinton was completely misled. The Delaware was forded at Trenton, and on September 5, the day of Graves's arrival off the Capes of the Chesapeake, the army reached Philadelphia, where Washington himself had arrived six days before. The march was continued thence to the Head of Elk.

The Continental army which marched south under Washington numbered only 2000 men. The French were 4000. Celerity was of the utmost importance, for if Lafayette failed to hold Cornwallis and he should escape to North Carolina, the situation would be of the most serious character. The aid of the 3000 troops under Saint-Simon brought from Santo Domingo, which De Grasse had at once, after communicating with Lafayette, sent into the James River, was now of greatest value. These, landing at Jamestown on September 2, effectually settled the question of Cornwallis's retreat southward.

Washington was at this moment still at Philadelphia, whence, on September 2, he had written Lafayette,— "distressed beyond measure to know what had become of the Comte de Grasse, and for fear that the English fleet [which he now knew had left Sandy Hook on August 31], by occupying the Chesapeake, toward which my last accounts say they were steering, may frustrate all our flattering prospects in that quarter. I am also not a little solicitous for the Comte de Barras, who was to have sailed from Rhode Island on the 23rd ultimo and from whom I have heard nothing since that time."[1]

Washington left Philadelphia on September 5 for the Head of Elk on the Chesapeake. His anxiety would have been still greater had he known that at that moment De Grasse was getting under way to leave the bay and fight a battle with Graves.

As to the British: On July 2, Admiral Arbuthnot sailed for England, leaving Rear-Admiral Graves in command. On the same day the latter wrote a letter to Rodney which he sent by the brig "Active," that intercepted despatches showed that a heavy reinforcement was expected from the West Indies to coöperate with De Barras's squadron at Newport in operations on the American coast. But Rodney was already informed, and on July 7, then at Barbados, he wrote the admiral at New York that he would send reinforcements.

Two days later Rodney received word that De Grasse had left Martinique. He then gave Sir Samuel Hood preparatory orders to leave for the North. Certain reports delayed Hood and these orders were not executed in detail, the outcome being that while on August 1 Rodney sailed for England, on leave of absence, taking with him four ships of the line, Hood, on August 10, sailed directly from Antigua for the Capes of the Chesapeake.

It is the "ifs" which count in war as in everything else, and there was a momentous one in the events of this period in Rodney's seizure of the Dutch island of St. Eustatius as one of the first acts of the newly de-

[1] Sparks, Writings of Washington, VIII, 150.

[lxv]

clared war with Holland. This island had been the
great base of supply of the United States whither not
only neutral ships carried their cargoes, but many English as well who did not disregard such chances to turn
a dishonest penny. In conjunction with the army under
General Vaughan, Rodney seized the island on February 3, 1781. The booty was immense, being valued at
over £3,000,000. It was Rodney's undoing. He became so entangled in the distribution and in the result-
ing lawsuits that worry brought on his old enemy, the
gout, which made such serious inroads on his health
that he decided to go to England to take the waters of
Bath and to look after his interests, which had been so
severely assailed. St. Eustatius thus became a large
psychic element in determining the result of the war.
Had Rodney remained, had he himself gone to the
American coast, taking his available ships, it is not un-
fair to suppose another turn of events.

But all the gods of Olympus were, for the moment,
with the French and Americans. The "Swallow," sent
by Rodney, arrived at New York on July 27, but
Graves, with information from the Admiralty of a convoy from France for Boston, had sailed for Boston Bay
on July 21. Despatched thither, the "Swallow" was
forced ashore on Long Island and lost. The "Active,"
sent by Arbuthnot, reached Hood on August 3, was
despatched back to New York on the 6th, captured on
the way and carried to Philadelphia. Graves did not
return to New York until August 16, when he found a
copy which had been made of Rodney's despatch, but
this only notified him that a force *would* be sent, and
its course, not that it had started. He was still without
any word of Hood.

On August 25 Hood was off the entrance to the Chesapeake, and he now wrote to Graves: "Herewith you will receive a duplicate of the letter I had the honor to write you by Lieutenant Delanoe of the 'Active' brig, lest any misfortune may have befallen her in returning to you." This, carried by the "Nymphe," arrived at New York on Tuesday, August 28, 1781, and Hood's fleet, which Graves states never sighted the Capes of the Chesapeake, anchored off the Hook later on the same day.

The inability of Graves and Clinton to grasp the situation is shown in a letter from Graves to Hood written on August 28: "I have this moment received your letter by the 'Nymphe' acquainting me of your intention in coming here with the fleet under your command. It was not until yesterday that I had any information of your having sailed, which came privately from Lieutenant Delanoe, now prisoner at Philadelphia, taken on his passage to this place. . . . We have as yet no certain intelligence of De Grasse; the accounts say that he was gone to the Havana to join the Spaniards and expected together upon this coast; a little time will show us. I have sent up for pilots to bring your squadron over the bar, which should be buoyed to render it safe. To anchor without would neither be safe at this season of the year nor prudent, on account of its being quite exposed to an enemy as well as the violence of the sea.

"De Barras's squadron was still at Rhode Island by our last accounts, ready for sea. . . . All the American accounts are big with expectations and the army has lately crossed to the southward of the Hudson and appears in motion in the Jerseys as if to threaten Staten

Island. For my own part, I believe the mountain in labour; only now that you are come . . .

"My squadron is slender and not yet ready to move, or I should not hesitate upon your coming over the bar; as we are circumstanced it is a clear point. I met the General today at Denis, Long Island. . . ."[1]

On the reception of this letter, Hood pulled the long distance to Denis's in the afternoon of the 29th. He there told Graves that it was not right for him to go within the Hook: "for whether you attend the army to Rhode Island or seek the enemy at sea, you have no time to lose; every moment is precious." Graves promised to be over the bar next day. That evening word was received that Barras had put to sea from Newport with all his ships and transports.[2] In the afternoon of September 1,[3] Graves crossed the bar with his only five available ships, and the united armaments at once stood south. There were in all nineteen ships of the line.

At 9:30 A.M. of September 5 the fleet, now off the Chesapeake Capes, sighted the French fleet at anchor just inside Cape Henry. It had taken over three and a half days to come 240 nautical miles. Signal was now made, says the log of the "London," "for the Line of Battle ahead at 2 cables length [1440 feet]. At noon Cape Henry W. ½ S. 4 or 5 Leages."

De Grasse had sent four of his ships of the line into the bay to watch Cornwallis's movements, and he had now but twenty-four. About 9:30 A.M. on this eventful day of September 5, his outermost ships signaled a fleet in the east, and at 10:15 the lookouts aloft reported

---

[1] The Barham Papers, I, 121.
[2] Hood to Barham, The Barham Papers, I, 130.
[3] Log of London.

twenty-four ships, and at 11 the lookout frigate "Aigrette" reported thirty, the actual number being twenty-seven, made up of nineteen ships of the line, a fifty-gun ship, six frigates and a fire-ship. The French had gone to quarters and the admiral had signaled to get under way, without further signal, at noon, when it was expected that the flood tide which had set at seven would have slackened. At 12:30 the signal was made to form line of battle promptly without reference to particular stations.

The distance from Cape Charles on the north to Cape Henry is about ten nautical miles. The channel for heavy ships, however, is confined to a breadth of some three miles between Cape Henry and a large shoal known as the Middle Ground. In this channel were anchored the French ships in three columns. The tide, says the captain of the "Citoyen" (a name markedly indicative of the new French sentiment), was still setting strong on Cape Henry, and several of the ships had to tack to clear the cape. The "Citoyen" cleared the cape at 1:45, the "Ville de Paris" a little in advance. The former ship, through absentees on boat duty ashore, the sick and those who had died, was short some 200 men and five officers. There were not men enough to man the upper deck guns. Much the same may be said of the others of the fleet.

The two forces now to be opposed were—British: two 98's (three-deckers); twelve 74's (two-deckers); one 70; four 64's and seven frigates. These nineteen ships of the line carried nominally 1410 guns, though probably quite 100 more. The French were: one 104 (a three-decker presented by the city of Paris and so named, the finest ship of her day); three 80's; seventeen

74's and three 64's, with, nominally, 1794 guns, or probably nearer 2000. There were also two frigates. The odds were thus strongly against the British. But it is clear that under such circumstances as those just mentioned the French ships must have left the Capes in very straggling order, offering conditions which more than nullified the discrepancy of force. It was a great opportunity and had Graves had the initiative which was only now beginning to filter into the mind of the British service, so long hidebound by the old "Fighting Instructions," which required the formation of line ahead and each ship to engage her opposite, he would have at once stood down and destroyed the French van before the French line could have been formed.

At 1 P.M. Graves had formed his line on an east-and-west bearing, heading west, the distance between ships one cable (720 feet). On approaching the Middle Ground, he wore together (2:15 P.M.) and lay to in order to let the center of the French "come abreast of us" (the "London," flag-ship, being in the center of the British line). The van was signaled at 2:30 to keep more to starboard; the signal was repeated at 3:17 and at 3:30 the rear of the fleet was ordered to make more sail. At 3:34 the van was again ordered to keep more to starboard, and at 3:46 signal was made for line ahead, "the enemy's ships advancing very slow." Evening was now approaching and signal was made "to bear down and engage their opponents." The flag-ship filled the main topsail, bore down and at 4:03 repeated the signal, and at 4:11 hauled down the signal for "Line ahead" "so as not to interfere with the signal to engage close." Signals for the line ahead and for close action, which was begun at 4:20, were repeated at 4:22. At

6:30 all firing ceased and both fleets stood eastward, the lines being about three miles apart. The British had had 90 killed and 246 wounded; the French reported a total of about 200 casualties. But the damages to a number of the British ships were such that Graves did not again engage. The "Terrible," 74, was in sinking condition and five days later had to be burned. Nor did the French show any inclination to renew the battle. For five days the two fleets were more or less in sight, sometimes only from the masthead. On the 10th the French fleet bore, by the "London's" log, E.N.E. "five or six miles," though the journal of the French ship of the line "Citoyen" of the same day makes the British not visible, showing thus how widely scattered the ships of each fleet were. Cape Henry was N.N.W., distant "35 leagues."

It was now that the purpose for which they had come, and which seems, temporarily at least, to have escaped the minds of both commanders, came again into the consciousness of De Grasse, and he stood for the Capes, within which he again anchored on the 11th, taking off the Capes the British frigates "Iris" (formerly the American "Hancock") and "Richmond." De Grasse found Barras anchored in the bay. He had arrived on the evening of the tenth with all his fleet intact. The French had now thirty-six of the line, an overpowering force as against the British, even should we include a reinforcement of six ships of the line just arrived at New York under Admiral Digby; news which came near sending De Grasse again to sea in search of the enemy. It required the strongest protests of Washington to hold him to the real purposes of the campaign.

Thus both the French and British commanders

showed how little they comprehended the real strategy of the situation. Graves did his best, but it was a fatally bad best. He should, having a leading wind, have attacked the French as they made their exit, when they were necessarily in disorder and while but a portion were outside. Instead, after wearing at 2:15 and with his east-and-west line heading east, he "brought to in order to let the Central of the Enemy [where also was the commander-in-chief] come abreast of us."[1] An astonishing tribute to conservatism bred through the hard-and-fast rules of the "Fighting Instructions"! Following this, three successive signals were made between 2:30 and 3:34 for the van to steer more to starboard. At 3:46 signal was made for "Line ahead," followed by the signal, which certainly was not congruous with its immediate predecessor, "for the ships to bear down and engage their opponents." The admiral filled the main topsail and also "bore down to the Enemy." The signal to "bear down and engage" was repeated three minutes after the former and again at 4:11 when the signal for "Line ahead" was hauled down that it might not interfere with the signal to "engage close," having been up twenty-five minutes, the signal for "Close action" also flying. The van and center began action at 4:15. The signal for "Line ahead" was again hoisted at 4:22, "the ships not being sufficiently extended." This was again hauled down at 4:27 and the signal for "Close action" was again made; this was repeated at 5:20, upon which the rear (Admiral Hood) "bore down" (toward the enemy). The French rear, however, kept at such a distance that the British rear practically did not get into action at all. At 6:30 fire ceased on both sides.

[1] London's log.

That Graves desired "close action" by the whole line is sufficiently clear, and it is not comprehensible to-day why his orders, though marred by the signal "Line ahead," were not carried out. Sir Samuel Hood (later Lord Hood) was undoubtedly one of the most capable officers of his time. Though he did not do what was evidently the obvious thing, he was wise enough after the event, and expressed himself in a private letter to George Jackson, assistant secretary of the Admiralty, in terms which were an epitome, on this occasion, of good tactics and good sense.

It is impossible, however, to avoid the impression that Hood did not do his duty as, had he been in chief command, he would have expected a subordinate to do. Whether there was a temporary pettiness of mind, arising from an unconcealed contempt of Graves, or whatever the cause, he did not whole-heartedly aid his chief. The journal of the "Barfleur," his flag-ship, says at "31 minutes past 3 the Admiral made the Sigl. to the Fleet to Alter the Course to Starboard." The signal for "Close action" was flying, and this was Hood's opportunity. Instead he chose to consider that he was to hold the line and thus scarcely got into action at all. It was not until 5:20, when the signal for "Close action" was repeated (that for the line having been hauled down at 4:27), that Hood stood down, but the ships of the French rear bearing up also, he did not get near enough to accomplish anything. Certainly his conduct aided largely in the losing of the day for the British.

Graves says in one of the last paragraphs of his report of the action: "The fleets had continued in sight of each other for five days successively and at times were very near. We had not speed enough in so mutilated a state to attack them, had it been prudent, and they showed no inclination to renew the action, for they generally maintained the wind of us and had it often in their power."

This paragraph is curiously suggestive of the general "wooliness" of idea as to the duty of the British fleet. Its true strategy was to take advantage of the leading wind with which it approached the Chesapeake, and upon the straggling exit of the French fleet to have "worn together" and have stood in toward Cape Henry. With but the van of the French fleet outside, with the others in the disorder of exit against a flood tide, there was the assurance of victory for the British, the occupancy of the bay and the relief of Cornwallis. Everything favored such a course of action. Failing this, it should, from the British point of view, have been Graves who should, after the action, have gone into the Chesapeake and left De Grasse aimlessly sailing about. Whether the latter would have had the boldness to have then attacked New York, which was wholly undefended, is a question.

On the day of the action, September 5, Washington was standing on the river bank at Chester; "he waved his hat in the air as the Comte de Rochambeau approached and with many demonstrations of uncontrollable happiness he announced to him the good news" of De Grasse's arrival. Had he known that De Grasse was leaving the Capes at that moment to fight a battle, he would have been less joyous. But the fates were with the allies. It was an incapable British admiral that saved the situation and brought De Grasse back to a position he should never have left. As it was, by September 28 the combined armies were in front of Yorktown, partly transported from the head waters of the Chesapeake by French frigates sent to Annapolis, partly by the ordinary land route, and the loss of Cornwallis with his 7000 men, and the complete restoration of Continental authority in the South, a certainty. The surrender took place on October 19. On the same day Graves again crossed Sandy Hook bar, now with twenty-three ships, convoying Clinton with 7000 troops, bound for the Chesapeake. They arrived off the Capes on October 24. They there received word of Cornwallis's surrender. In any case the expedition was futile. The French were in fifty per cent. greater force and an attack could end only in disaster. The fleet and troops consequently returned to New York.

To show the low ebb to which we had fallen it should be mentioned that Washington marched south with but two thousand Continentals and four thousand French. This fact alone shows the supreme importance of the French fleet. Without it there had been no American independence.

A word as to Graves personally. The son of an admiral of the same name (Thomas), he was born (with some doubt as to the date) in 1725 and died in 1802. He accompanied his father in Vernon's expedition against Cartagena in 1741; was a lieutenant in 1743 at the early age of eighteen; a commander in 1754; a post-captain in 1755. In 1757 he was court-martialed for not making sufficient effort to discover the real character of a large French ship which Graves (commanding a sloop of but twenty guns) took for a seventy-four and thus did not engage. The Admiralty held that the French ship was but an Indiaman. The trial has a peculiar interest in that the sentence, rendered the same day as Byng's, shows that the court was, under the Articles of War, enabled to exculpate the latter also on the

[lxxv]

ground of error in judgment. Byng was found guilty of "negligence" under the 12th article; Graves was found guilty of "error of judgment" under the 36th.

Graves later commanded the "Conqueror," 74, one of the ships of Byron's squadron which went to North America and the West Indies in 1778. He was promoted to Rear-admiral of the Blue, March 29, 1779; was recalled home on this account and hoisted his flag as a subordinate commander in the Channel squadron. He was shortly ordered to command a reinforcement of the fleet in North America under Admiral Arbuthnot. He was made Rear-admiral of the Red, September 26, 1780. He took part under Arbuthnot in the latter's action with Des Touches on March 16, 1781, off the Chesapeake; relieved Arbuthnot in chief command on July 4, 1781, and occupied this post just long enough to ruin his reputation with posterity as a naval officer.

In the fall of 1781 he was ordered to the West Indies. He was there as a subordinate, a situation to which, after being commander-in-chief, he strongly objected. He had, however, lost no favor with the Admiralty and his request to be relieved was granted. He thus started from Port Royal, Jamaica, July 10, 1782, under orders from Sir George Rodney to convoy to England some ninety sail of merchantmen. He had with him ten line-of-battle ships, six of which (among them the "Ville de Paris") were the French prizes taken in Rodney's action of April 12, 1782. Caught in a heavy gale some three hundred miles south of Nova Scotia, the fleet lay to on the wrong tack (the law of storms not then being even heard of), with the result of one of the greatest sea-disasters on record. The "Ramillies," Graves's flag-ship, had to be abandoned; the crew, all saved, being

distributed among the merchantmen. The "Ville de Paris" and "Glorieux" foundered with all on board. The "Ardent" and "Caton" reached Halifax. The "Jason" was the only one able to continue to England. The loss of life, says Beatson, "may be safely computed" at "three thousand five hundred men."

Graves was promoted Vice-admiral of the Blue on September 24, 1787; Vice-admiral of the White on September 21, 1790; of the Red, January 2, 1793; Admiral of the Blue, April 12, 1794, and of the White, June 6, 1795;[1] was commander-in-chief at Plymouth and in 1793 was second in command to Lord Hood in the battle of the first of June, when he was badly wounded. For his services in this action he was made an Irish peer in 1794, receiving a gold medal and chain and a pension

[1] The following is given by Commander Charles N. Robinson in his book, The British Fleet, as the origin of the three ranks of admiral in each grade:

"In or about 1627 and probably at the time of the expedition against the Isle of Rhé, the fleet was divided into three squadrons, and each squadron was given a different ensign, the centre red, the van blue and the rear white; each flag having in the upper corner, next to the staff, a white canton charged with a St. George's cross. At the same time the squadrons were divided into three, respectively commanded by an admiral, vice-admiral and rear-admiral, carrying their distinctive flags on the main, fore and mizzen masts. As, however, the admiral commanding the centre was not only in command of the red division but of the whole fleet, he flew, instead of the red flag, the Union at the main, and thus it happened that there was no Admiral of the Red; nor was there any until November 9th, 1805, when, as a special compliment to the Navy after Trafalgar, this rank was instituted. The second in command flew a blue flag at the main and the Union at the fore; the third a white flag at the main and the Union at the mizzen."

All the ships of an admiral's command flew the ensign of his color.

The several grades of red, blue and white were abolished by order of August 5, 1864, when the white ensign was ordered for all ships of war; the blue became the Naval Reserve flag, and the red the merchant flag; the admiral's flag, white with a St. George's cross; the vice-admiral's, the same but with a small red disk (in heraldry, *torteau*) in the upper quadrant next the staff; the rear-admiral's, with a *torteau* in each quadrant next the staff.

of £1000 a year. On account of his wounds he resigned his command and saw no further service.

He married in 1771 and left a son and three daughters. He died February 9, 1802.[1]

In concluding, the Editor desires most gratefully to express his obligation to the Director of the Archives Nationales of France and M. Charles de la Roncière of the Bibliothèque Nationale in Paris, through whose courtesy the De Grasse papers were found and transcribed for the Society, and to Mr. Gaillard Hunt of the Library of Congress and Messrs. B. F. Stevens and Brown, for their assistance in collecting the despatches from the British Admiralty Records contained in this volume.

[1] Condensed from the British National Biography and Clowes's History of the Royal Navy.

THE GRAVES PAPERS

THE GRAVES PAPERS

REAR-ADMIRAL THOMAS GRAVES was ordered to a command in the Western (Channel) Squadron on September 2, 1779, his flag-ship being the "London." The usual delays in fitting his flag-ship for service occurred, and he was most of the time at the dockyard.

Early in 1780 it was decided that he should go to New York to reinforce the fleet of Vice-Admiral Marriot Arbuthnot, then in command in American waters. His orders to prepare for this service were issued on March 16, 1780, as follows:

[THE LORDS COMMISSIONERS OF THE ADMIRALTY TO
REAR ADMIRAL GRAVES[1]]

By &c.

Having Ordered the Captains of His Majesty's Ships named on the other side hereof at the places against each exprest, to put themselves under your command & follow your Orders for their further proceedings; You are hereby required & directed to take them & the said Ships under your command accordingly; & to cause the

[1] Admiralty Records, Orders and Instructions, 2, 108, p. 400.

utmost dispatch to be used (so far as the same may depend upon you) in getting them ready for the Sea, & then to hold yourself in readiness for sailing. Given &c. 16th March 1780.

SANDWICH [1]
LISBURN
R. MAN.

Thomas Graves Esqr. Rear Admiral
   of the Blue, &c.
     By &c. P. S.

[1] The First Lord of the Admiralty from January 12, 1771, to March 30, 1782, when he was replaced by Admiral Augustus Keppel. The latter held the office only until January 30, 1783, when Lord Howe came, to remain but a few months (until April 10, 1783). Keppel then again was appointed, but remained only until December 31 of the same year, when Howe again became First Lord until July, 1788. The latter was of saturnine temperament, gloomy and in a way inarticulate both in speech and writing but with strong character.

The initials P. S. where they occur in the documents stand for Philip Stephens. Stephens (later Sir P. S.) was secretary of the Admiralty from 1763 through the Revolution. Under the British system this official is the medium of communication to and from the Admiralty Board. His position is thus highly responsible and important.

Enclosure A

LIST OF SHIPS REFERRED TO (NOT ALL OF WHICH WENT WITH HIM).[1]

Capt. Graves	London	Spithead
" Tenny	Marlboro*	Do.
" Robinson	Shrewsbury*	Do.
Rt. Hble. Ld. Capt. Robt. Manners	Resolution	Do.
Capt. Cornish	Invincible*	Do.
" Burnett	Prudent	Do.
" Biggs	Amphitrite	Do.
" Sir Digby Dent	Royal Oak	Portsmouth
" Thompson	America	Do.

By &c.
P. S.

[REAR ADMIRAL GRAVES TO PHILIP STEPHENS]

Sir

I beg of you to represent to the Lords Commissioners of the Admiralty that the addition of eight cannon upon the large second rates without an augmentation of the compliment has made it necessary in quartering the people to reduce the lower Deck Guns to 11 men each which are too few to work a 32 pounder well; and like-

[1] The ships starred did not go on account of delays in fitting out, trouble with mutinous crews, etc. (the chief cause of which was delayed pay). The Bedford, 74, was substituted. The Amphitrite was a small frigate; the others, line-of-battle ships.

[3]

wise to reduce the middle deck guns to 9 men which are too few for an 18 pounder

I presume to hope that their Lordships will thinck it reasonable a Ship going on foreign service with 98 Cannon mounted should be augmented with 50 men, more than the ordinary establishment for 90 Guns. The London has now only two Guns less than a first rate, and at the same time has fewer men by 100—under both these considerations I hope their Lordships will be pleased to order an addition of fifty men to the compliment of the London.

I am Sir your most obedient

Humble Servant

London at Spithead   THOS. GRAVES.
 13th. March 1780—
  Philip Stephens Esq:—

Minute 16 Mar | let him know | that their Ldps | cannot consent to | the encreasg the | Complemt. of Ships of the | 2d. Rate

[THE LORDS COMMISSIONERS OF THE ADMIRALTY TO
REAR ADMIRAL GRAVES[1]]

By &c

You are hereby required and directed to proceed, with His Majesty's ships under your comand, without a moment's Loss of time, to No. America, in order to join and re-inforce the squadron under the comand of Vice

[1] Public Record Office, Admiralty 2, 1337.

Admiral Arbuthnot; proceeding, in the first place, to New York unless you shall sooner fall in with the said Vice Admiral or receive contrary Orders from him, And upon joining him, you are to deliver to him the inclosed pacquet; and, putting yourself under his command, follow his Orders for your further proceedings.

In case, upon your arrival at New York, you shall find that the sd. Vice Admiral is not returned from the Southward, or being returned, that he is gone to any other part of the Coast of America, You are to dispatch a Frigate immediately to him whereever he may be, to acquaint him with your arrival; sending by her, the abovementd pacquet and waiting at New York until the arrival of the said Vice Admiral, or you shall receive orders from him to quit that place & proceed elsewhere. Given &c 25th March 1780

SANDWICH
J BULLER
Thomas Graves Esqr   LISBURNE
Rear Admiral of the
Blue &c.   By &c. P. S.

Endorsed O.R.D. 25 Mar. 1780 / R. A. Graves.

[PHILIP STEPHENS TO REAR ADMIRAL GRAVES[1]]

A. O. 25th March 1780.

Sir.

Vice Admiral Lord Viscount Howe, late Comr in Chief of His Majesty's Ships and Vessels in North Ammerica having during such his Command estab-

[1] Public Record Office, Admiralty 2, 1337.

lished a Monthly Change of Signals for the Squadron employed on that Station which still continue in force, I am commanded by my Lords Commissioners of the Admty to send you herewith a Copy of those Signals for your Information and use; and to recommend it to you to keep the same as secret as possible and to give similar Injunctions to the several Captains & Commanders of the Ships and Vessels under your Command, or others, to whom you shall find it necessary to communicate them.

I am &c

Rear Admiral Graves.—   P. S.

Endorsed Lre. 25 March 1780 / R. Adml Graves.

[REAR ADMIRAL GRAVES TO PHILIP STEPHENS]

London at Spithead 5th. April 1780.

Sir

The badness of the weather the deficiency of Stores, and the great quantity of work to be done, has occasioned with every exertion of Sr. Thoms. Pye and myself, that only the seven sail of the Squadron under my command named in the Margin will be ready by the evening— The Resolution will I hope be forward in a day or two more

Prudent
Royal Oak
Shrewsbury
America
Invincible
London
Amphitrite

The vast demand of Beer and water for so great a number of Ships, as well as Provisons required to keep up the daily consumption of so great a Fleet as is here I find occasions more employment than the other necessary wants of the Port will admit the Craft to do; and the Ships unavoidably fall back to a considerable deficiency.

I therefore purpose to improve the first possible opportunity of pushing to the westward, with those Ships which will be ready, and of stopping at Plymouth, where we can be more easily kept complete—Giveing orders to the other Ships to follow as fast as possible, which I thinck will stimulate the Officers more than by any other method whatever—And unquestionably one of the two Ships will sooner get to the westward through the narrow part of the Channel than the Squadron kept together; yet shou'd the Ship which will first follow overtake me I shall proceed on according to their Lordships intentions— If not, I shall certainly have it in my power to sail from Plymouth with many winds that, wou'd shut up the Squadron at this place and prevent my carrying into execution their Lordships order so early as if I go to the westward.

Therefore Sir be pleased to acquaint their Lordships that, I purpose sailing to-morrow with those Ships named in the Margin, and do not doubt but their Lordships will approve of my intention.

I am Sir your most obedient Humble Servt.

THOS. GRAVES

Philp. Stephens Esq. Admy.—

As the wind is Westerly and looks dirty, and the Ships can hardly be so forward as to move to-morrow, there will be sufficient time for my receiving any directions if their Lordships shou'd not quite approve of my intention.

Endorsed   Read

[REAR ADMIRAL GRAVES TO PHILIP STEPHENS]

London at Spithead 7 April 1780

Sir

I have receiv'd the Lords Commissioners of the Admiraltys order to keep company with Comōdore Walsingham and his Convoy to a certain distance, if I am ready to put to Sea (with the number of Ships mentioned in their order of the 25 last month) when he sails—

Be pleased to acquaint their Lordships that I shall be happy to comply with their orders, But the want of Stores, to complete the Ships, added to the delay occasion'd from bad weather in fitting them up with Beer and water makes it impossible for me to fix the time of being ready.

The Resolution is yet to be paid, her Books being sent down last Wednesday, and the Commissioner haveing no day to pay her before Sunday, it will from the disposition of the Ships company who mutinied about the time they sailed last from Plymouth be impossible to get her to Sea before the People get their money.

There is a disposition in my Ships company to require Two months advance before they go to Sea.— But if it is not within the Rules of the Service I hope to be able to keep them within the bounds of their duty—

I am persuaded were ship Courts martial to be established, and punishment to follow close at the heels of offence,—there wou'd be a great deal of inconvenience prevented—

I am Sir your most obedient
Humble Servant
THOS. GRAVES

Phil. Stephens Esq. Admiralty.

Endorsed ℞ 8th. | Ansd. do.

[REAR ADMIRAL GRAVES TO PHILIP STEPHENS]

London at St. Hellens 9th. April 1780

Sir

I have this Moment receivd your letter of the 8th. April wherein you mention the very great importance of my sailing with Commodore Walsingham, even though it be with Six Ships of the Line only— Their Lordships will be acquainted by my letter of yesterday and to day of my own situation and endeavors to get the Ships forward, and that I shou'd have joined the Comdore if the Ships of my Squadron cou'd have followed me— When I had made the Signal and unmoored the Capts. of the Shrewsbury, America and Invincible came to acquaint me of the mutinous state of their Crews— I strongly recommended to them to Arm their Marines & Officers, and such people as wou'd join them, to force their men up into daylight; (they having shut themselves up betwixt Decks with the Ports all down;) to mark those by wounds who stood in their way as they proceeded from aft to the Bows opening the Ports as they went on— And if any man ventured to

[9]

oppose by violence to put him to Death—and when they had got the men upon Deck, to call them by name to their respective stations, and by that means it wou'd be in their power to bring proof against the disobedient— And in the first instance whoever was wounded betwixt Decks wou'd carry evidence of his disobedience about him & might be brought to Trial— This method succeeded with the Shrewsbury & she is now at St. Hellens, And an Officer came to inform me it had with the America, where the Mutineers had turned two of the Day Guns aft & had drawn a third for priming.— The Resolution was in much the same state & I advised and directed both the Com̃dore and the Captain to use the same means—for that in my opinion mutiny was to be suppressed at the instant though it might cost some lives, and justice wou'd then take her seal with propriety

With regard to the Stores I stated the case truely.— Sr. Thoms. Pye exerted every means in his power— The Cordage was taken off the hooks as it was made, the Ships in the harbor were stripped of rigging & boats—that every thing was done that a Commanding Officer cou'd do—the detail was to be carried on by the Captains I wrote to Sr. Thomas of the mutinous state of the Crews—and told the Captains they were not to content themselves with stateing difficulties; it was the province of an Officer to remove them and when they had failed in every exertion of their own, to acquaint thier Comānding officer with the point beyond which they cou'd not not go—he wou'd then apply the remedy and by such concurrence every thing wou'd advance and go on well.

The Amphitrite is at this moment Ten Tons short of Beer, which is a great thing to a Frigate.

[10]

I am satisfied their Lordships will thing I have done every thing in my power And I will sail immediately with the ship here and if I join the Convoy proceed on —otherwise stop at Plymouth.

I am Sir your most obedt.

Humble Servant
THOS. GRAVES.

at St. Hellens
London
Prudent   I have received your packet to be
Shrewsbury   opend off the Lizard
Amphitrite

Phil. Stephens Esq. Admiralty

Endorsed 9 Aprl. 1780 | St. Helens. | Rear Adml. Graves | ℞ 10th. at 9 A M | by Mr. Maxwell

[REAR ADMIRAL GRAVES TO PHILIP STEPHENS]

London in Cawsand Bay 30th. April 1780

Sir—

I have receiv'd your letter of the 26th. inst. accompanying a large pacquet not to be opened until I get off the Lizard—and their Lordships may depend upon my complyance with their directions—

I am Sir your most
Obedient Humble Servant

To   THOS. GRAVES.
    Philip Stephens Esq. Admiry.—Office

Endorsed   Read

[11]

[THE LORDS COMMISSIONERS OF THE ADMIRALTY TO
REAR ADMIRAL GRAVES]

By &c.

To put to sea
without waiting
for Commo. Wal-
singham.

Notwithstanding any former Orders, you are hereby required & directed to put to Sea with the Squadron under your command with the first oppor-tunity of Wind & weather without waiting for Como. Walsingham & the Trade under his Convoy, and pro-ceeding down the Channel, open the sealed Pacquets which have been sent to you, when you are off the Lizard, & carry into execution with all possible dili-gence the Instructions you will therin find for your further proceedings. Given &c 13th. May 1780

SANDWICH
J. BULLER
H. PENTON.

Thomas Graves Esqr.
Rear Adml. of the Blue &ca.
Cowsand Bay.

By &ca. P. S.

[REAR ADMIRAL GRAVES TO PHILIP STEPHENS]

Sir—

My letter of 7th. August may not probably arrive as soon as this, to acquaint the Lords Commissioners of the Admiralty of my arrival off Sandy Hook, the 13th. July with the Squadron[1] in pretty good health, except the Prudent whose people had suffer'd from feaver and Scurvey.

Their Lordships several pacquets were delivered to Vice Admiral Arbuthnot who was within the bar.

During our passage in Lat. 32°, 00′ W. we took the Farges, Capt. Mugny from the Mauritius and Bourbon of 900 tons, bound to L'Orient old France with Tea and Coffee and a few other articles. The Amphitrite Frigate was left in care of her nine days before our arrival, to conduct her to New York, where they both arrived soon after.

I prefer'd the Southern passage, which cost us eight weeks to preform the voyage and I am inclined to beleive the good weather we met with contributed greatly to the health of the People. In the London we experienced great benefit from the essence of wort which was constantly administered to the Scorbutick and effected a cure upon thirty of our men besides many more greatly recover'd in their health, in as much that we sent but fourteen to the Hospital.

The slow effects of medicinal opperations cannot be expected to influence Seamen to receive the Wort in exchange for Spirits, when experience teaches us that

[1] London, 98; Resolution, 74; Bedford, 74; Royal Oak, 74; Prudent, 64; America, 64; Amphitrite, 24.

they will run every kind of risque to get at Spirituous liquors. Wine is found to be as great an antiscorbutick as most, and certainly accelerates the cure—therefore to retrench the seamen from the use of it whilest under a course of wort wou'd be to co-operate rather with the disease I would thence wish to recommend the use of Wort as a Medecine, to be administered under the judgement and discretion of the Surgeon which is the method followed in the London and from its continued success will, I hope meet with their Lordships approbation.

I have inclosed a State of the Squadron as deliver'd at my arrival to Adml. Arbuthnot and likewise a return of the promotion and removal of Officers in the Squadron from my leaving St. Hellens to the time of my arrival at the Barr of New York which I hope will meet with their Lordships approbation.

I am Sir your most obedient Humble Servant

THOS. GRAVES.

London in Martha's Vineyard Sound | 24th August 1780.

Philip Stevens, Esq. Admiralty.

Endorsed 24 Aug 1780 | Martha's Vineyd | R. A. Graves | Recd. 25 Sepr.

On September 13, 1780, Sir George Rodney with twelve ships of the line unexpectedly appeared at Sandy Hook from the Leeward Islands and assumed command, much to the wrath, which was not at all unnatural, of Arbuthnot.[1]   The latter, who was at the time at Gardiner's Bay, Long Island, watching the French at Newport, made strong protests against Rodney's action, which Rodney based upon the necessity of a single control in American and West Indian waters.   Strangely enough, his action was upheld by the Admiralty, for he had a specifically defined command and his assumption of such, in the circumstances, over Arbuthnot was distinct injustice to the latter.   With the combined force, now amounting to twenty ships of the line, the French at Newport should have been an easy prey, but Rodney did nothing beyond issuing some useless orders which, in so far as the despatch of Graves to the West Indies was concerned, were not carried out, De Ternay not leaving Newport.   On November 19 Rodney sailed again for the West Indies (leaving three of his ships with Arbuthnot), having done nothing but create ill-feeling, but himself better off by several thousand pounds of prize-money from a rich prize taken while he was at New York, which would have been Arbuthnot's had he not come.   His action was in keeping with an unpleasant and overbearing character, aggravated too by severe attacks of gout.   The following were his orders to Graves, whom he found at New York:

[1] Rodney's fleet at Sandy Hook was: Sandwich, 90, Sir G. Rodney, Admiral of the White, Captain Walter Young; Russell, 94, W. Drake, Rear-Admiral of the Blue, Captain B. Haswell; Centaur, 74, J. N. P. Nott; Triumph, 74, Ph. Affleck; Culloden, 74, Geo. Balfour; Alcide, 74, Charles Thomb; Terrible, 74, Ja. Fergusen; Shrewsbury, 74, M. Robinson; Torbay, 74, J. L. Gidoin; Suffolk, 74, Ab. Crespin; Intrepid, 64, Hen. Herney; Yarmouth, 64, J. T. Duckworth; Fortunée, 42, H. C. Christian; Boreas, 28, John Rodney; Greyhound, 24, Wm. Fooks.

[15]

[ADMIRAL RODNEY TO REAR ADMIRAL GRAVES[1]]

By Sir G. B. Rodney Bt. Admiral of the White and Commander-in-Chief, &c. &c.

You are hereby requir'd and directed to put Yourself under My Command and follow such Orders and Directions as You shall receive from Me for His Maj's Service, for which this shall be your Order.

Given under My Hand on bd. His Majesty's ship Sandwich off New York 8th October 1780.

G. B. RODNEY.

To
R. A. Graves
&c. &c. &c.

By Command of the Admiral.
(Countersigned) Will Pagett.

Endorsed Copy of an Order to | R. A. Graves. (dated 8th October) |
In Sir G. Rodney's | 12 Octo. 1780.

[1] Admiralty, In Letters (Class 1), Vol. 311.

[ADMIRAL RODNEY TO REAR ADMIRAL GRAVES[1]]

By Sir George Bridges Rodney
Secret   Rear Admiral of the White and
Commander in Chief &c &c &c

Whereas I have directed Vice Admiral Arbuthnot in
Case Monsr. Ternay and his Squadron should escape
from Rhode Island to give you orders to follow him
with the Squadron under your Command.

You are therefore hereby required and directed to
proceed without a Moment's loss of time and cruize
with the Squadron under your Command to Windward
of Martinique in such a Situation as you may jude
most proper for the Intercepting Monsr. Ternay's
Squadron or any other Succors going to that Island.

You are to dispatch one of your Frigates to Barbadoes and St. Lucia for Intelligence, and with Orders
for all the Copper Bottom'd Ships to join you.

You are to take the Command of that station till
joined by me, which Junction you may hourly expect.

And whereas it will be highly necessary on my Arrival at Barbadoes I should be acquainted with the
Situation of Affairs, You are to send to that Island any
Intelligence that you think it proper I should be acquainted with—taking care that it is never left without
a Frigate of War.

And whereas it is of infinite Importance the Enemy
should make no impression whatever on the Island of
St. Lucia, You cannot pay too great attention to the
preservation of that Island.

[1] Admiralty, In Letters (Class I), Vol. 311.

You will give such Orders and directions as you think most necessary not only for the protection of His Majesty's Islands, but likewise for the Annoyance of his Enemies.

> Given under my hand on board His Majesty's Ship Sandwich, off New York 8th October 1780.
>
> (Signed)   G. B. RODNEY.

To Rear Admiral Graves
&c &c &c

By Command of the Admiral
(Countersigned)   Will Pagett.

Endorsed Copy of an Order | from | Sir G. B. Rodney Bart. | To | Rear Admiral Graves | 8th Octr. 1780 | 7 | In Sir G. Rodney's | 12 Oct. 1780.

[REAR ADMIRAL GRAVES TO ADMIRAL RODNEY]

London, at Sandy Hook, 2d July, 1781.

Sir:

I have the honor to forward to you by Lieutenant Delanoe, in the Active brig, his Excellency General Clinton's messenger; also my despatch, containing the latest intelligence here, as well as that from Europe. The importance of that obtained here, which was taken from an intercepted post, will shew you the apprehension of a considerable force, expected from the French Commander in Chief in the West Indies, in concert

with whom M. de Barras seems to act; and will demon-
strate how much the fate of this country must depend
upon the early intelligence, and detachments which
may be sent by you hither, upon the first movement of
the enemy.

I shall certainly keep the squadron under my command as collected as possible, and so placed as to secure
a retreat to New York, where our stand must be made;
and will keep cruisers to the southward.

The French have the addition of a fifty-four gun
ship. We are weaker by the absence of the Royal Oak,
now at Halifax heaving down; in lieu of which the
Warwick has arrived sickly, and is not yet fit for service.[1]

I have the honor to be, &c.

THO. GRAVES

Graves passed nearly a year as second in command
under Arbuthnot. On July 4, 1781, the command-in-
chief was turned over to him, as is shown by the following:

[REAR ADMIRAL GRAVES TO PHILIP STEPHENS]

London off Sandy Hook 4th July 1781.
Sir
Be pleased to acquaint the Lords Commissioners of
the Admirality that I received a letter from Vice Adml.
Arbuthnot of which the enclosed is a Copy, relinquish-

[1] Beatson, Naval and Military Memoirs of Great Britain, 1727 to
1783, V, 257.

[19]

ing the command of His Majestys Squadron in North America, into my hands this day.

I beg leave to assure their Lordships that in Zeal and assiduity no person shall go beyond me, and that my great ambition is to merit their Lordships esteem.

> I am Sir
> > Your most obedient
> > > Humble Servant.
> > > > THOS. GRAVES.

P.S. A cartel is just arrived from the Havanah in fifteen days, with the first part of the Garrison of Pensacola, the enclosed paper is all the news come to my hand.

> To
> > Philip Stephens Esqre
> > Admiralty Office
> > London.

Endorsed 4 July 1781 | Rear Adml | Graves | Rcd. 4th Augt | (2 Inclosures)

Minute 13 Octr | Own rect

Enclosure A

[VICE ADMIRAL ARBUTHNOT TO REAR ADMIRAL GRAVES]

(Copy)

Sir   Bedford off Sandy Hook 4th. July 1781.

Mr Stephens Secretary to the Admiralty having in his letter dated the third day of May last, signified the acquiesence of the Lords Commissioners of the Admiralty to my desire to resign the Command of the Squadron of his Majesty's Ships in North America, to any Officer immediately upon the spot, and my wish to return home, I enclose an Extract of the said Letter herewith, as also a list[1] & disposition of the Said Squadron, and a Schedule of the Papers and Intelligence necessary for Your guidance in the conduct of the Command.

I therefore hereby resign the Chief Command of the said Squadron into your hands, and wishing you all imaginable success and happiness

I have the honor to be

Sir

Your most Obedient

humble Servant

MT.[2] ARBUTHNOT

Rear Admiral Graves
&ca. &ca. &ca.

---

[1] The enclosures mentioned are not available. Arbuthnot's command before Graves's arrival was the Europe, 74; Russell, 74; Robust, 74; Defiance, 64; Adamant, 50. There were in addition five 44's, seven 32's, four 28's, six 20's and eleven sloops of 14 to 18 guns, three armed ships of 20, a bomb-ketch of 8, and a fire-ship of 8 guns. This force, except the five ships of the line kept at New York as a base, was distributed from Massachusetts to the Carolinas.

[2] Marriot Arbuthnot.

Enclosure B

[PHILIP STEPHENS TO VICE ADMIRAL ARBUTHNOT]

Duplicate.

Admiralty Office 26th June 1781—

Sir,—

My Lords Commissioners of the Admiralty having taken into their consideration your letters, acquainting them with your having superceded some of the appointments made by Admiral Sir George Brydges Rodney while he was in North America, and of your intention to supercede the rest of such appointments from time to to time, as the Ships to which the officers who had been so appointed, should join you: I am commanded by their Lordships to acquaint you that Sir George Brydges Rodney having found it necessary for His Majesty's Service to proceed with a part of his Squadron from the Leeward Islands to North America, and to take you and His Majesty's Ships employed in those Seas under his command, had a right to fill up all vacancies that happened in any of the Ships in those Seas during his continuance there; that their Lordships have therefore thought fit to confirm the commissions given by him to Captains Douglas & Laugharne (whom you have superceded) and will confirm such other commissions, and also such warrants as were granted by him upon regular vacancies, while he commanded in North America when laid before them for that purpose; that their Lordships will direct Captain Douglas and Laugharne, and likewise such other officers as may come to England under similar circumstances, to return to North America to resume their commands or employments. And it is their Lordships direction you cause them to be reinstated on their arrival, as the commissions and warrants, you may have given to dispossess them of such commands or employments, cannot be confirmed.

I have the honor to be

Sir

Your most Obedient

Humble Servant

(Sign'd)   PHIL. STEPHENS—

Vice Admiral Arbuthnot.

(Copy)

T. Graves.

Enclosure C

London off Sandy Hook 4th July 1781

Intelligence

The Angel de Guarda in 15 days from the Havannah, with Major McDonald and 87 of the Officers and Garrison of Pensacola, consisting of Eleven hundred and thirteen Men under the command of Genl. Campbell which surrendered on the 10th May last, after a seige of Nine Weeks. The enemy had before the place 23,000 Men and eleven Spanish and four French sail of the line, with four Frigates Commanded by Adml. De Solano and General De Galvez.—

[23]

It was said at the Havannah that the four sail of the French line & one Frigate were about to sail for North America.—

Endorsed Intelligence

On July 19, 1781, despatches dated May 22 reached New York advising of "large supplies of money, cloathing and military stores, which young Laurens was preparing to send for the use of the rebel army in North America. They stated that he would in all probability sail from France before the end of June, with a number of merchantmen, under the convoy of one ship of the line, another armed *en flûte,* and two stout frigates: that there was every reason to believe that this was one of the most important supplies which the French had ever sent to the rebels; and that it was considered by themselves as furnishing them with the only possible means of carrying on the war." The Lords of the Admiralty also gave their directions to the Admiral to cause a good lookout to be kept for these ships, but left to his judgment the course to be taken for intercepting them.[1]

This despatch was one of the "providences" for the American cause. Graves sailed from Sandy Hook on July 21, bound to the eastward, and did not return until August 16. Meanwhile the Swallow, bearing Rodney's despatch giving information of the reinforcement to be sent north, reached New York. She was sent east to look for Graves (a copy of Rodney's despatch being

[1] Beatson, V, 258. The despatch itself does not appear among the Graves papers.

retained at New York). Her captain, with more courage than discretion, chased and took a privateer, but the tables were almost at once turned by the appearance of three privateers which drove him ashore on Long Island, where the ship became a wreck. Graves thus knew nothing of Rodney's information until his return, having accomplished nothing. That his move, though directed and expected by the Admiralty, was ill-advised and ill-judged is shown by the care taken by Graves himself to be kept informed. It is clear that he expected reinforcement in any case from the West Indies. He stationed a lookout frigate from Navesink to Cape May; three off the Delaware; three frigates and two sloops in the Chesapeake, and three coppered ships were ordered to Charleston to cruise alternately "and to look out for the enemy then expected."

The destination of the apprehended French fleet was entirely unknown. It was thought much more likely to go to Newport and reinforce Barras, who was there with eight ships of the line, than to the Chesapeake. No apprehensions seemed to exist as to the safety of Cornwallis, Clinton being firmly convinced that the allies meant to attack New York. In this he was supported by intercepted despatches of such tenor, and by the movements of the allies. But the main fault, strategically, of Graves's easterly movement was that it left New York wholly unprotected. Had De Grasse arranged to come a fortnight earlier and to go to New York instead of to the Chesapeake, and had he arrived at New York before August 16, he would have been able to sail into New York Bay with as little resistance as on August 30 at the Chesapeake. Such are the chances of war.

[REAR ADMIRAL GRAVES TO PHILIP STEPHENS]

London off Sandy Hook 20th July 1781.

Sir:

By the Roebuck I had the honour to acquaint the Lords Commissioners of the Adm'ty that Vice Admiral Arbuthnot had proceeded for England in that Ship, and left the command of the Squadron in this Country to me.

I can add very little to the information carried by the Vice Admiral, other than, that the Adamant so long missing is returned, after having been upon the extent of all the various rendezvous, owing to their not observing a particular signal for the rendezvous off Sandy Hook.

The Amphitrite returned from Boston bay on the 8th inst. having lost a Mizen mast and Main topsail and brought with her one prize. The General Monk[1] from the same place, arrived on the 12th with three prizes, by whom we learn that the Assurance was gone for Halifax, with the loss of a Mizen mast, and Main mast sprung.

The Pearl and Iris[2] are returned from a long cruize off Bermuda with only two prizes, one of them a French Xebeck from Cape Francois which I hope will enable us to accomplish an exchange for most of the

[1] A captured American privateer, General Washington, of 18 guns. She was taken in Delaware Bay, April 8, 1782, by the Hyder Ally of like force, Captain Joshua Barney, after a brilliant action.

[2] This was the Continental frigate Hancock, 34, Captain Manley, captured July 7, 1777, by the Rainbow, 44, Commodore Collin. She was recaptured by De Grasse's fleet on August 11, 1781.

Mentor's Ships company taken at Pensacola; the Port Royals is nearly effected, except for the Commission Officers, who will go to Europe by the first opportunity. The inclosed letter from Capt. Deans to Vice Admiral Arbuthnot will show his situation. I refer their Lordships to Captain Kelly for the terms of Capitulation.

The assembling of an Army upon the White Plains: —the attempt of the Enemy upon Lloyds Neck in the Sound, and the operations in the Chesapeake will come more correct and with greater propriety from head quarters.—

The Squadron has been kept constantly before the Hook to second any Army Operations which the General had to suggest; it will not be prudent to keep them much longer in so exposed a situation, as the time approaches which will make it necessary to attend to the appearance of Squadrons which the Hurricane Season may occasion to depart from the West Indies. I shall put them into safety the moment the Army detachments have done moving upon the Coast.

I beg leave to call their Lordships attention to the Agent Victuallers of the state of Provisions on the 5th inst. of which the inclosed is a copy and I will send a similar one to the Commissioners for Victualling His Majesty's Navy.

The state of stores at the Yard seems very low; of Slops[1] a slender quantity, and of Marine clothing none. As the winter approaches those deficiencies will be most severely felt—whatever is purchased in this Country is at immense expense. But of all other wants, the want of Provisions is the least to be contended with.

Yesterday arrived here His Majesty's Sloop Hornet

[1] In nautical language, clothes, etc., drawn from the paymaster.

with their Lordships intelligence and dispatches of the 22nd May, which I shall pay every possible attention to.

I am, Sir,

Your most Obedient humble Servant,

THOS. GRAVES.

Endorsed 20 July 1781 | Sandy Hook | Rear Adml. Graves | Rcd. 10 Sepr. | (2 Inclosures)

Minute 24 Sepr. Send Ext [thus | much] to Mr. Knox | for Ld. G. G. information | Own rect. | let him know it | let him also know | that a Supply of 6 Mo., | Provns. for 12,000 Men sailed | under Convoy of the Centaur | on the 5 July; that a like Supply is now embarked & will probably sail for | Spithd. in the Course of this Mo., | & that their Ldps have | orderd a further Supply of 4 Mo. Provns. for the | above-mnd. number of Men | to be shipped & dispatched | to No. America without | any delay.

Enclosure A

[CAPTAIN DEANS TO VICE ADMIRAL ARBUTHNOT]

Pensacola the 1st. of June 1781.

Sir:

After being embarkd., in Flags of Truce with the remains of the Crews of His Majestys Ship Mentor, and Port Royal Sloop agreable to the Capitulation at the Surrender of the Province of West Florida the 10th of

May 1781[1] I am orderd. to remain here, or to be carried I dont know where, no reason being given other than the disputes between the Spanish General Galvez and Major Gen'l Campbell. I send this to acquaint you that the Flag of Truce brings to your command Two Hundred and Ten effective Men, besides Officers under the direction of Capt. Kelly of the Port Royal Sloop and Lieut. Miller of the late Mentor both these Gentlemen are furnished with a copy of the articles of the capitulation and to them I beg leave to refer you. I have the Honor to be with the greatest respect Sir

Your most Obedient and most Humble Servant

ROBT. DEANS Capt. of the
Royl. Navy

To Vice Admiral Arbuthnot
or the Commander in Chief of
His Majestys Ships & Vessells &ca. &ca.

North America

Endorsed Captain Deans letter   In R.A. Grave's Lre of 26 July 1781[2]

Endorsed on first page   Recd. 24 Sepr. | Orgl. dated | the 20th recd. & Ansd.

---

[1] In the peace of 1763, the two provinces, East and West Florida, now constituting the State of Florida, had been ceded to Great Britain in exchange for Havana, captured by the British in 1762. A large body of Colonials arrived in the expedition. The Floridas were retroceded to Spain as the result of this surrender.

[2] Letter dated "26 July" does not appear in transcripts: it was evidently a duplicate of that of the 20th, mentioned in the endorsement.

Enclosure B

Account of Provisions and Victualing Stores Remaining on boar
Fleet employed in North America, under the Con

Bread in Pounds	Rum in Gallons	Beef in pieces of		Pork in pieces of		Pounds of		
		4 lbs.	8 lbs.	2 lbs.	4 lbs.	Flour	Currants	Raisin
128,800	4,000	29,900	"	41,756		83,000	9,640	61,98
{ Purchased	}	{ From	the Comm	issary Ge	neral }	Purchas	ed	

The above Provisions will serve Ten Thousa

Bread	Rum	Beef	Pork	Flour, Currants and Raisins as Beef
Days				Weeks
12	6	3	4	4

Pease		Oatmeal		Butter in pounds	Vinegr. in Galls.	Sour Krout Barrls.	Coals in Chalds.	Candles
Bushs.	Gall.	Bushs.	Gall.					
4,122	"	6,498	"	22,500 Purchased	1,746	240	3	" —

...en at whole allowance as under.

Pease	Oatmeal	Butter	Vinegar, Sour Krout and Coals as above
13	18	.3	

(A Copy)   Heny. Davies.

Endorsed A Copy of the Agent Victuallers | Return of Provisions remaining | in his Majestys Navy Victualling | Transports off New York the 5th. | of July 1781. | In R. A. Graves's Lre | of 26 July, 1781.

[31]

[REAR ADMIRAL GRAVES TO PHILIP STEPHENS]

London at Sandy Hook 20th August 1781.

Sir

My last dispatch acquainted the Lords Commissioners of the Admiralty of the arrival of the Hornet Sloop, after eight weeks passage from England.

Immediatly on the 21st of July I proceeded with the Squadron into Boston Bay, to be in the way of intercepting the Supplies from France to North America. The intence fog which prevailed without intermission as we approached St. Georges Bank, deprived us of all possibility of seeing, and soon convinced me how much the Squadron wou'd be exposed to accidents, and that the Fog Guns necessary to keep the Ships from separation wou'd give notice of our Situation. I therefore after having made Cape Ann, determind to withdraw, and we return'd to Sandy Hook the 18th of August, we retook a Brig being one of the Convoy from England, bound to Halifax, and burnt three small Vessels of little consequence.

The Royal Oak from Halifax joined the Squadron parted again in the Fog, and has since returnd to this place. She had taken soon after leaving Halifax, the Aurora Boston Privateer carrying 18 Guns and 120 Men.

The Cruizers before the Delawar have been more succesful, by taking the Bellisarius and Trumble,[1] the

---

[1] The Trumbull, built at Middletown, Connecticut. She was on her first cruise, had but just got to sea, and, dismasted in a gale, was met by the Iris and General Monk, both captured American ships.

first of 22 Guns 150 Men, the latter of 32 Guns 190 Men, and two small Vessels of a Convoy which were in motion for the West Indies, and had been forced to push back into the Delawar, by the Vigilance of the Medea and Amphitrite. The York Privateers have been succesful in taking more of the Convoy.

The Swift Brigantine 14 Guns and 60 Men on board, Richard Graves Commander, with dispatches from the Cheasapeke provd so leaky, that in order to bail at the Hatchways, they had taken their Lumber and Stores upon Deck, in so distresful a situation they found themselves attacked by the Holker Privateer carrying 18 Guns and full of Men; it was impossible to stand a Cannonade, they therefore with great spirit boarded the Enemy twice, but the Privateer having greatly the advantage in sailing, disentangled and made away, leaving their Enemy to pump and bail or drown, fortunately she arrived, and was hauled on shore, she had two Men killed and two wounded.

The Swallow Sloop Captn. Wills with dispatches from Sr. George Rodney, being sent after the Squadron into Boston Bay, on her return with a Privateer Brig of 14 Guns her Prize in Company, was attacked the 16th Instant, by four Rebel Privateers, and pushed on Shore upon Long Island 11 Leagues to the Eastward of this, Captain Wills burnt his Prize, but could not get all his People on Shore in time to burn the Swallow. The Privateers pillaged her, if she is not bulged, we shall endeavor to get her off, otherwise we shall set the wreck on fire. The dispatches were destroyed which has prevented my inclosing the Plan of Old Point Comfort.

The inclosed copies of Letters from Captain Hudson marked A & B. will show their Lotdships the state of

operations in the Cheasepeke, and at the same time
shew that one of my first attentions, was to secure the
best Naval Post in the Cheasepeke, as a place of retreat
during the Freezing Months for the Squadron, and at
the same time to shut the Door against the Enemys
Fleet.

The Robust is become so leaky, there is great reason
to apprehend that she must be hove down, to enable
her return to England.— The Europe is coming fast
into the same Condition, and I hope their Lordships
will see the necessity of relieving them as soon as possible. The wooden Bottoms in the Cheasepeke, and at
Carolina are eat up presently, there is nothing resists
the worm, but Copper.

The small Men of War upon the out posts here, are
so preforated by the Worm, we find a necessity of haul-
ing them frequently on shore to prevent their sinking,
this will oblige me to keep every thing upon Copper in
the Country, and to send home as Convoys all the
Wooden Bottoms, as well as the purchased Frigates, except a few of the most active, which may be employed
in places where they may be taken on Shore upon the
Tide and kept clean.

The Amphion, Britania and Ostrich and their Convoy[1] arrived safe, from Bremer Lee the 11th instant,
after 93 days passage, they had lost only 65 People, and
landed in good order.

The detachment of Troops with General Ried[e]sel
for Quebeck sailed the 27th of July under Convoy of the
Warwick, and Garland, and in their way were to take
up the Victualers from Halifax, which happened very

[1] Carrying part of the 29,867 troops hired in Germany and sent
during the war to America.

opportunely, as Governor Haldiman had been very Solicitous to get them.

The inclosure, Letter C, is a Copy of Sr. G. Rodney Intelligence.[1]

Inclosed are the Duplicates of my last dispatch, by which their Lordships will perceive the state of our Provisions to be very low at present.

Also a List of Captures so far as are come to my knowlege, since the departure of the Vice Admiral.

These dispatches will go by the Cartwright Packet.

Inclosed you will receive the State and Condition of the Squadron [not available].

I am Sir

your most obedient and

most humble Servant

THOS. GRAVES.

P.S. Captain Thompson of His Majestys Sloop the Beaumont, being in the last stage of Consumption, has my permission to return to England in the Packet. A change of Air being the only chance left to save his Life.

T. G.

Philip Stephens Esqre:

Endorsed 20 Augt. 1781 | Sandy Hook | Rear Adml. Graves | ℞ 24 Sepr. by the | Carteret Packet | (5 Inclosures)

Minute 13 Octo | Own rect & congratulate him | on the Success of | his Cruizers.

[35]

Enclosure A

[CAPTAIN HUDSON TO REAR ADMIRAL GRAVES]

Richmond in Hampton road 27th July 1781.

Sir—

I have had the honor of your order of the 12th inst. and every attention in my power shall be paid thereto. Earl Cornwallis as well as myself and other people are of opinion that Old Point Comfort is not a place equal to erect a Post at, or near it, for the protection of any of his Majesty's ships that may occasionally come here against an enemy of superior force. I herewith enclose you a plan of the above place taken by the Engineers which coincides with our opinion by which you will see it is not tenable and in consequence thereof the Earl as well as myself has come to a resolution to remove the troops that are now at Portsmouth and its vicinity to York and Gloucester river, where we apprehend a better Port can be established for the protection of the King's troops. This manoeuvre of course prevents Lord Cornwallis from sending any troops at present to York, and my forwarding the Charon and Loyalist to you, as every ship here will be necessary to assist and Co-operate with them on this service, which I hope you will approve of; and as soon as it is over I shall not only detach the ships that you directed to be returned to you but likewise keep a fast sailing vessel without the capes to give the earliest intelligence of an enemy's approach on this coast, and as soon as possible put the Richmonds orders into execution.

I have the honor to be

Sir

Your most Obedient and very

faithful humble servant

CHARLES HUDSON.

Rear Admiral Graves

    (Copy)

T. Graves

Endorsed Copy of a letter from | Captain Hudson of His Majesty's Ship Richmond | 27th July 1781 | A | In R. A. Graves | 20 Aug. 1781.

Enclosure B

[EXTRACT OF A LETTER FROM CAPTAIN HUDSON]

Richmond York river the 12th Augt. 1781.

Sir—

We sailed from Hampton road the 30 July with the Charon, Guadaloupe, Bonetta, Swift and Loyalist, and all the transports and as many troops as they could carry, in the whole about 4500 men. The Fowey and Vulcan I left for the protection of those that remained at Portsmouth.

We arrived here on the 2nd instant and the troops were immediately landed at York and Gloucester, and the Guadaloupe, Swift and Loyalist with the transports, returned to Portsmouth for the total evacuation thereof.

[37]

The Army having brought very little artillery with them by the first embarkation, the Earl requested that I would order guns on shore to Gloucester from the ship and the Charon (the only two now here) which I complied with, and that side is now tolerably well fortified.

Captain Robinson who I have a regular communication with by whale boats informs me that it will take ten days now to destroy the works at, and effectually to evacuate, Portsmouth. As soon as they arrive here I shall agreeable to your order dispatch the Charon and such Convoy and transports with troops as my Lord Cornwallis may think proper to send to New York, and as it will be absolutely necessary for the good of the King's service, that the Loyalist should remain in this bay, I have taken upon me to detain her here which I hope you will approve of, and I shall with this ship see the Charon and her convoy as far as the Delawar, where no exertions of mine shall be wanting to put the Richmond's orders into effectual execution.

The Bonetta I have stationed between the Horshoe and Lynnehaven bay to inform such friends as may come in, of the army's present situation, and prevent their going to Hampton road.

I have the honor to be, etc.

CHARLES HUDSON.

Rear Admiral Graves.

Copy

T. Graves.

Endorsed Extract of a letter from | Captain Hudson of His | Majesty's ship Richmond | 12th Augt. 1781. | B | In R. A. Graves | 20 Aug. 1781.

Enclosure C

[COPY OF THE INTELLIGENCE FROM SR. GEO. B. RODNEY]

Sir   Sandwich, Barbados 7th July 1781.

As the Enemy has at this time a fleet of 28 Sail of the Line at Martinique, a part of which is reported to be destined for North America, I have dispatched his Majesty's Sloop Swallow to acquaint you therewith, and inform You that I shall keep as good a look out as possible on their motions, by which my own shall be regulated.

In case of my sending a Squadron to America I shall order it to make the Capes of Virginia, and proceed along the coast to the Capes of the Delaware, and from thence to Sandy Hook, unless the intelligence it may receive from you should induce it to act otherwise.[1]

The Enemy's Squadron destined for America will sail I am informed in a short time, but whether they call at Cape François, I cannot learn: however, you may depend upon the Squadron in America being reinforced, should the Enemy bend their forces that way.

I have the honor to be &c &c &c

            G B RODNEY.

Copy

T Graves

[1] The copy of Rodney's letter forwarded by Graves omitted after the second paragraph the following (in Beatson, V, 261): "You will please to order Cruizers to look out for it, off the first mentioned Capes, giving orders to hoist a Dutch Ensign reversed at the fore-top-gallant-mast-head and an English Jack at the mizen-top-mast-head, and firing two guns, which will be answered by a Blue Flag pierced White at the main-top-gallant-mast-head, and three guns."

Endorsed Copy of the Intelligence | from Sr Geo. B. Rodney | 7'th. July 1781 | C | In R A Graves's | 20 Aug 1781.

[PHILIP STEPHENS TO REAR ADMIRAL GRAVES[1]]

25th Sepr. 1781

Sir

I received on the 10th inst. and immediately communicated to my Lords Commsrs. of the Admty your Letter of the 20th of July acquainting them with the occurrences of the Squadron under your Command since the Departure of Vice Admiral Arbuthnot, and enclosing a Letter from Captn. Deans late of the Mentor which was captured at Pensacola, received by the Flag of Truce which brought the Crews of that Ship and the Port Royal Sloop, giving an account of his Detention at that Place; And I am to inform you that my Lords have sent an Extract of so much of your Letter as relates to that Subject and a Copy of Capt. Dean's to Lord George Germain for his Information.

In answer to your observation of the State of Provisions for the Squadron; I am to acquaint you that a supply of Six Months Provisions for 12000 Men sailed under Convoy of the Centurion on the 5th of July, that a like supply is now embarked and will probably sail from Spithead in the course of this Month; and that their Lordships have ordered a farther Supply of four Months Provisions for the above-mentioned Number

[1] Admiralty 2, 573, p. 151.

of Men to be shipped, and dispatched to North America without any delay.   I am | &c

P. S.

Rear Admiral Graves, New York | By the Pacquet
  same day

Duplicate By the Pacquet 6th Octr. 1781.

Enclosure D

A list of prizes taken by his Majesty's Ships i
August 1781—so far as th

By what ship taken	When taken	Name of the Vessel	Master	To what nation belonging	Sort of Vessel
Pearl & Iris	6ᵗ July	Betsey	- - - - -	America	Ship
General Monk	6 "	Columbia	- - - - -	Do.	Ship priv.
Do.	7 "	Swallow } a recapture }	- - - - -	England	Brig
Do.	7 "	Recovery	- - - - -	America	Schooner
Charles town	7 "	Hero	- - - - -	Do.	Brig Privateer
Do.	8 "	Swift	- - - - -	Do.	Schooner Private
Orpheus	8 "	Tristm. Shandy	Jno. Brice	Do.	Ship
Pearl & Iris	10 "	Le Tinge	- - - - -	France	Xebec
Royal Oak		Aurora	- - - - -	America	Ship Privateer
Orpheus	24 "	Polly } a recapture }	N. Craddock	New York	Ship
Medea	30 "	Neptune	T. Seymour	America	Schooner
Squadron	2 Augt.	- - - - -	- - - - -	England	Brig
Medea	4 "	Belisarius	Monro	America	Ship Privateer
Genl. Monk	4 "	Mercury	- - - - -	Do.	Sloop Privateer
Do.	8 "	Liberty	- - - - -	Do.	Schooner
Do.	8 "	Experiment	- - - - -	Do.	Brig
Iris	9 "	Trumbull	Jas. Nicholson	Do.	Rebel Frigate
Orpheus	14 "	- - - - -	- - - - -	- - -	Brig
Do.	16 "	- - - - -	- - - - -	- - -	Schooner
Solebay	6th "	- - - - -	- - - - -	America	Do.
Medea	13 "	Maryanne	C. Whipple	Do.	Brig Privateer
Solebay	15 "	Amiable Elizh.	- - - - -	France	Lugger
Royal Oak	15 "	- - - - -	- - - - -	America	Sloop
Genl. Monk	14 Augt.	Magdalen	- - - - -	Do.	Do.

North America between the 6 July and 20th
Accounts have been recd.

From whence	Where bound	Lading	Tons	Men	Guns	In what Port arrived
hilidelphia	Hispaniola	Ballast		39	9	New York
rance	Boston	Bale Goods		50	16	Do.
ondon	New York	Do.	100	13	6	Do.
o. Carolina	New Providence	Salt & rum	40	7		Penobscot
alem	On a cruize	- - - - - -		41	14	Halifax
Do.	Do.	- - - - - -			2-6 Prs 10 Swivels	destroyed
enerief	Philidelphia	Wine and Salt		12	6	New York
ape Francois	Marseilles	Dry Goods		120	15	Do.
oston	On a cruize	- - - - - -		120	18	Do.
ew York	Tortola	Ballast		8	2	Do.
. Thomas	Philidelphia	Salt & dry goods	70	12	2	Do.
ngland	Halifax	Provisions	200	8		Do.
oston	On a cruize	- - - - - - - -	500	150	20	Do.
ew London	Do.	- - - - - - -	70	32	10	Do.
hiladelphia	Cape Francois	Provisions	60	12	4	Do.
Do.	Tenerief	Flour	60	10	1	Do.
Do.	Rhode Island	Flour & bread		190	32	Do.
- - - - -	- - - - -	- - - - -	- -	- -	- - - -	Do.
- - - - -	- - - - -	- - - - -	- -	- -	- - - -	Do.
ondon	On a cruize	- - - - - - -	- -	30	10	Do.
ovidence	Do.	- - - - - - -	87	47	12	Do.
Orient	Philadelphia	Silks, &ca.	140	40	10	Do.
oston	Rhode Island	Tobacco		12	6	Do.
erytown	Fish kill	Bread & cloth	60	9		

T. Graves.

[PHILIP STEPHENS TO REAR ADMIRAL GRAVES[1]]

Sir: 22d June 1781.

His Majesty having signified His Pleasure that Rear
Admiral Digby shall be appointed to Command His
Majesty's Ships and Vessels employed in North America; I have it in command from my Lords Comm'rs of
the Admty to acquaint you therewith. And their Lordships think it necessary I should likewise inform you
that the Squadron on the Jamaica Station having been
very much diminished from the effects of the late Hurricane, it is very probable you will receive Orders to
proceed in the London to reinforce the said Squadron.

                         I am, &c.   P. S.

Rear Adm'l Graves, New York, By the Centaurion.
Duplicate By the Prince George 7th July 1781.

The following documents include transcripts of all
the orders given by Rodney respecting the reinforcement of the British forces on the American coast.

[ADMIRAL RODNEY TO CAPTAIN WELLS OF
THE SWALLOW[2]]

By Sir George Brydges Rodney, Bart. &c. &c. &c.

You are hereby required and directed to proceed with
his Majesty's Sloop under your command to New-York

[1] Admiralty 2, 572, p. 46.
[2] Letters from Lord Rodney. London, Printed by A. Grant, No.
91 Wardour Street, Soho. MDCC LXXXIX.

without one Moment's loss of Time, and deliver the accompanying letter to the Commanding Officer of his Majesty's Ships at that Place. If before you arrive at Sandy-Hook you fall in with any of his Majesty's Frigates stationed to the Southward, you will give the Captain of such Frigate the sealed note you receive with this Order.

Given, &c., Sandwich, Barbadoes, 7th July, 1781.

G. B. RODNEY.

To
  Captain Wells of his
  Majesty's Sloop Swallow

[THE LORDS COMMISSIONERS OF THE ADMIRALTY
TO REAR ADMIRAL GRAVES[1]]

By &ca.

To proceed in the London to Jamaica, & to be under the Command of Vice Adml. Parker.

Whereas We think fit that you shall proceed in His Majesty's Ship the London to Jamaica in order to reinforce the Squadron of His Majesty's Ships on that Station, which has been very much diminished from the effects of the late Hurricane; you are hereby required and directed to proceed thither accordingly as soon after the receipt hereof as you possibly can; and, upon your arrival, to deliver the Pacquet you will receive herewith to Vice Admiral Sir Peter Parker, or the Commanding Officer of the said Squadron for the time being, and, putting

[1] Admiralty 2, 111, p. 139.

[45]

yourself under the Command of the said Vice Admiral, or such Commanding Officer (if Senior to yourself) follow his Orders for your further Proceedings.

In case Vice Admiral Arbuthnot shall have left the Coast of North America, on his return to England, and you shall, in consequence thereof, have succeeded to the Command of the Squadron of His Majesty's Ships on that Coast; you are hereby further required and directed to deliver to Rear Admiral Digby, who is appointed Commander-in-Chief of the said Squadron, and by whom you will receive this, attested Copies of all unexecuted Orders which may have been left in your hands by Vice Admiral Arbuthnot, and at the same time to furnish the said Rear Admiral with Copies of all Intelligence which you may have received, and with all particulars relative to the State and Disposition of the Squadron, which you may judge proper for his knowledge.

Given &c. 9th July 1781.   SANDWICH
                                        B. GASCOYNE.
Thomas Graves, Esq'r.   F. GREVILLE
Rear Admiral of the Red &c.
    North America.
    By Vc. P.S.

[ADMIRAL RODNEY TO REAR ADMIRAL HOOD]

By Sir George Brydges Rodney, Bart. &c. &c. &c.

Whereas I have received intelligence that a very considerable Squadron of the Enemy's Line of Battle

[46]

Ships are intended to reinforce the French Squadron in America, and it being absolutely necessary that a Squadron of his Majesty's Ships should reinforce his American Squadron:

You are hereby required and directed to proceed without Loss of Time with the Ships named in the Margin,[1] to the Road of St. John's, Antigua, where you are to use every Endeavour to compleat them with all possible Dispatch, with Masts, Cordage, and Sails for a foreign Voyage, and as much spare Cordage as the Ships can stand without Inconvenience.

. . . .

Given, &c. 9th July, 1781.

G. B. RODNEY.

To
Sir Samuel Hood, Bart., &c. &c. &c.

[ADMIRAL RODNEY TO REAR ADMIRAL HOOD]

By Sir George Brydges Rodney, Bart., &c. &c. &c.

Whereas the great Force the Enemy has to Leeward makes it necessary as much as possible, to secure the valuable outward bound Convoy for Jamaica, and the Addition of such of his Majesty's Ships as can be sent to North America, will in all Probability be wanted there for the furthering of his Majesty's Service and counteracting the Schemes of his rebellious Subjects: In order as far as possible to answer both those desirable Ends,

[1] Alfred, Alcide, Invincible, Barfleur, Monarch, P[rince] William, Resolution, St. Monica.

You are hereby required and directed, as soon as ever the said Convoy shall arrive with the two Ships I have directed you to send for, and protect them in their Passage from St. Lucia to St. Eustatius and St. Kitt's, to proceed with the Line of Battle Ships and Frigates named in the margin[1] taking whatever Trade, Transports, Victuallers, or Storeships, shall be then ready at either of these Islands, and see them safely toward Jamaica, as far as Cape Tiberoon; which having done, you are to direct the Senior Officer of the Ships you may leave to go quite through with the Convoy, to proceed to Port Royal Harbour, Jamaica, with the Trade bound there, and to the South Side, having at a proper time detached the Hydra or Ranger armed Ship, to see them to their respective Ports on the North Side of that Island.

Having seen the said Convoy in Safety as above, you are to make the best of your Way towards the Coast of North America with the Remainder of the Line of Battle Ships, together with the Saint Amonica, Nymph, Fortunée, and Pegasus Frigates, which you are to employ in such Manner, should you be Senior Officer on that Station (or until you come under the Command of such) as shall seem to you most conducive to his Majesty's Service, by supporting his Majesty's liege Subjects and *annoying his rebellious ones,* and in Counteracting such Schemes as it may be reasonable to conclude are formed for the Junction of the French Fleet from Cape François with that already there, or with the

---

[1] Barfleur, Alfred, Invincible, Monarch, Torbay, Alcide, Intrepid, Resolution, Centaur, Shrewsbury, Belliqueux, Pr. William, Montague, Terrible, Sandwich, Ranger, A. S., Nymph, St. Amonica, Fortunée, Pegasus, Hydra, Sandwich, A. S.

Forces of the Rebels in America. Having lately sent an Express to Admiral Arbuthnot or the commanding Officer on that Station by the Swallow, that the ships I might either bring or send from hence would endeavour first to make the Capes of the Chesapeak, then those of the Delawar, and so on to Sandy Hook, unless Intelligence received from his Cruizers (whom I desired might be looking out off the first Capes or Elsewhere) should induce a contrary Conduct; I think it necessary to acquaint you therewith, and to direct your sailing in Conformity thereto, unless Circumstances you may become acquainted with as you range along the Coast, should render it improper; which Service, although not only your general Experience and Skill as an Officer, but your particular knowledge of that Station, I make no Doubt will enable you with Reputation and Effect to perform. Having employed the several Ships and Vessels there during the Hurricane Months, you are to return with them immediately after the first full Moon in October to this Station, for the better protection of the Trade and Possessions of his Majesty's Subjects in these Seas; for which this shall be your Order.

Given under my Hand, the 24th July, 1781.

G. B. RODNEY

N.B. The Signals Established with the American Cruisers are . . .

To Rear Admiral Sir Samuel
   Hood, Bart., &c. &c. &c.
      By Command of the Admiral,
         Will. Pagett

[COPY OF INTELLIGENCE REFERRED TO IN THE ORDER TO
REAR ADMIRAL SIR SAMUEL HOOD]

A Mr. . . . arrived this Afternoon, the 31st
July, from Saint Thomas's reports, that he left that
Island on Saturday last;—six Days previous thereto,
a Fleet of Merchantmen arrived in nine Days from the
Cape where a French Frigate had arrived the Day before their sailing, with thirty Pilots for the Chesapeake
and Delawar, which together with a Number of North
Americans [vessels] Collected there and awaiting Convoy, to the number of Sixty or upwards, made it looked
on as certain, that the French Fleet, which was hourly
expected there from Martinique, would proceed immediately to America. He further adds, that a few days
before the fleet from Saint Thomas's left the Cape,
seven Spanish Men of War had arrived there from
Pensacola, which place had been taken by Storm with
great Loss: that the Spaniards afterwards attempted
Augustine, but could not get over the Bar; that the last
Advices there from the Continent were, that Lord
Cornwallis was 40 Miles above York-Town;—that
Washington had moved to the Southward;—the
French had abandoned Rhode Island, and taken possession of Washington's former Post at West-Point; but
that General Green had marched to the Southward,
and forced Lord Rawdon within his lines in South
Carolina;—but that the same Advices brought the Account of the Arrival of a Reinforcement of 3,500 Men
which it was supposed would oblige him to fall back
again: That the English Fleet were cruizing off Bos-

ton, at which place a Reinforcement of three Frigates had arrived with a Reinforcement, and Money for the Troops. Saint Eustatius, 1st August, 1781.

[ADMIRAL RODNEY TO CAPTAIN GIDOIN[1]]

By Sir George Brydges Rodney, Bart. &c. &c. &c.

You are hereby required and directed to take the Ships named in the Margin[2] under your Command and proceed without one Moment's Loss of Time, with the Trade bound to Jamaica, Arriving off the East End of the Island, you are to dispatch the Hydra with the Trade bound to the North Side of it; and having seen the Rest in Safety to Port-Royal, you are to make the best of your Way with his Majesty's Ship under your Command, and the Prince William to the Chesapeake, where you are to await further Orders.

To   Given under my Hand, &c., the 30th July, 1781.

Captain Gidoin, of his
Majesty's Ship Torbay.

[1] Note by Editor of the Rodney letters.—"Captain Gidoin was directed to see the Sandwich in Safety into Port Royal Harbour, with a letter to the Commander in Chief on that Station [Vice-Admiral Sir Peter Parker] to hasten the Torbay and Prince William, without a moment's delay to the Chesapeake;—and pressing him to add to their Force what Line of Battle Ships he could possibly spare from that station—the Admiral having undoubted Intelligence that the Enemy's Intention was certainly against the Chesapeake.

"N.B. The Torbay arrived at Jamaica on the 9th of August, where she found the Princess Royal of 90 guns, Hector 74, Albion 74, and Ramillies 74—and did not sail till the 24th from thence, and then with Convoy."

[2] Sandwich, Pr. William, Hydra, Ranger, A. S.

[51]

[REAR ADMIRAL GRAVES TO PHILIP STEPHENS]

London at Sandy Hook 30th August 1781.

Sir—

I beg of you to acquaint the lords commissioners of the admiralty, that the moment I knew of the fate of the Swallow I hasten'd out the Solebay and the Rover sloop to scour the privateers off, who I very soon learned had burned the Swallow before they left her. The Solebay returned soon after with a retaken vessel and the crew of a privateer brig, which she had taken, but which has since been retaken. The Rover unfortunately by missing stays and the fatal effects of a counter current got on shore near Shrewsbury inlet in the night, Captain Duncan used every possible means to get her off without effect, in which he had every kind of assistance from the Medea who saw her situation at daylight, the hull was burned the 26th so soon as the ship bulged, and all the people were saved and brought in here.

The 28th Sr. Samuel Hood arrived off the Hook with fourteen sail of the line, four frigates one Sloop and a fireship from the West Indies I was at that moment settling a plan with Sr Henry Clinton for attempting the French squadron in Rhode Island, as the French troops were mostly with General Washington in the Jerseys, we had only waited for the repair of three of the Squadron and the troops were ordered to embark, but the same evening intelligence was brought that Mons Du Barras had sailed the Saturday before, with his whole Squadron. As Sir Samuel Hood had brought intelligence from the West Indies that all the French fleet from the Cape were sailed, I immediately determined to proceed with both squadrons to the Southward, in hopes to intercept the one or both if possible. We only wait for a wind to carry the North American squadron over the bar and in the meantime, I have detached frigates to the Northward and Southward to give information and to bring intelligence.

The Richmond came in the 29th from the Chesapeake in four days, where every thing was quiet, and I have had two frigates before the Delaware for some time past.

Whether the French intend a junction, or whether they have left the coast, is only to be guess'd at. I shall get to sea as soon as possible, and shall use every means to the best of my ability to counteract them.

The Robust is so defective from what yet appears, that it is expected they can only make her fit to go home, or to Halifax to heave down.

The Prudent has two new masts but has not yet got out of the East river.

Enclosed you will receive duplicates of my last dispatch by the Cartwright packet; Also the state and condition of the fleet under the command of Sir Samuel Hood.[1]

I am
Sir
Your most Obedient and
most humble Servant.
THOS. GRAVES.

[1] Not available.

P.S.

The inclosed french letter was
addressed to one of La Fayette's family
and seems to give the best plan of the
destination of De Grasse's great Fleet
of any which has come into my hands.
Philip Stephens Esqr.

Endorsed 30 Aug 1781 | Rear Adml. Graves | R 3
Nov. | A 31 Jany. 82 | (1 Inclosure)[1]

Enclosure

The following are the more interesting parts of the
letter to La Fayette. (Spelling and accents as in the
copy.) It was signed only by a rubric.

"Havre de Grace [Le Havre] Le 31 Mars, 1781
"J'ai reçu Monsieur et Bon ami, La Lettre dont vous
m'avez honoré en date du 19 8bre denier datée du Camp

---

[1] Clinton, though but so shortly before so exercised in mind as
to a probable attack on New York by Washington and Rochambeau that he had gone to the extent of ordering Cornwallis to send
3000 men thither (against which Cornwallis successfully protested),
had now become eager to attack Barras (who was left at Newport unsupported), and reoccupy Newport and take Providence. Both naval
and military preparations had been proceeding to this end since
Graves's return on August 16. Clinton was, however, not to be
balked of an easterly expedition and prepared a force against New
London under the traitor Arnold, escorted by a frigate and several
sloops of war. The story of the destruction of New London and the
massacre of the defenders of Fort Trumbull across the river at
Croton on September 6 (the day after the action between Graves
and De Grasse) makes a very dark page of history.

du General Washington prés Potowa [?] dans les jerseys, elle m'est parvenue dans les premiers jours de fevrier. Je me flatte que Les Lettres que je vous ai adresse par voie de L'Orient vous auront été remises. cependant je ne suis pas sans inquietude sur leur sort vû que vous m'en dites mot . . .

"M. de Grasse est parti le 22 de ce mois avec une flotte de 26 Vaisseaux 8 fregates, 30 transports et 300 Batimens a la hauteur des Canaries, 9 vaisseaux sous le commandement de M. De L' Espinousse et 2 fregates, le quitteront pour filer dans L'inde avec 2 transports et des Batimens marchands tres forts, on dit que M. De la Mothe Piquet va parter avec une division de 6 vais-seaux et des Transports pour une expedition, rien de Certain, on dit que e'st pour votre armee en outre de ce que M. De Grasse vous porte que vous mene t'il on l' ignore. Les Anglais étoient sortis le 13 avec 28 vais-seaux dont 10 a 3 ponts. avec une flotte considerable qui se separera apres qu on oura ravitaillé Gibraltar. Les Espagnols avec 30 vaisseaux et en outre 2 francois sont sortie des le commencement de fevrier pour attendre les Anglais. on s'attend de moment en moment a des Evene-mens bien interessant et qui font palpiter. Les Es-pagnols ont des injures grossieres a vanger et malgré cela une tache considerable a remplir. Dieu veuille être une fois catholique, en outre Dom Barcelo est a l'ouvert du detroit avec 4 vaisseaux et bon nombre de chébecs ainsi pendant un combat le Convoi Anglais ne pourroit filer sans risque de tomber dans le Griffes de ce vigilant chef d'escadre, l'honneur de sa nation. voila vous en conviendrés un moment bien Critique. La Josephine corsaire fregate de ce port, une des meilleures voilieres qu'il y ait a pris le 22 un Paquebot doublé en cuivre de 14 canons partant de Plymouth pour New York chargé des depeches du Gouvernement Anglais pour clinton et Arbuthnot notre corsaire est commande par le Brave capitaine favre quo vous connaissés cette fregate porte 30 canons de 12 et de 8. il a beaucoup d'officiers americains. Le Ministre qui venoit de Brest presser le depart de l'escadre de M. de Grasse a recû à L'Orient la mâle des mains du Capitaine favre.

"Le havre, mon bon ame ce n'est plus ce petit Paris vivant, remuant, et si curieuse a voir en 1779. c'est un desert, tout commerce y á cessé.

"La misere y est affreuse. vous sentés que La Bourse de votre ami s'en ressent evaillement. quand reviendront les heureux jours de la paix ils sont encore eloignés. tout le monde le pense puisse t' on se tromper jamais erreur de Calcul m'aura été plus à notre avantage."

Endorsed In R. A. Graves' | 30 Aug 1781

[REAR ADMIRAL HOOD TO PHILIP STEPHENS]

Barfleur, off Sandy Hook,
30th of August, 1781.

Sir:—

I beg you will acquaint the Lords Commissioners of the Admiralty that Sir George Rodney sailed from St. Eustatius on the 1st of this month with the Gibraltar, Triumph, Panther, Boreas, and two bombs, with the trade for England, having the day before given up the command of his Majesty's fleet at the Leeward Islands to me. On that evening I received the intelligence No. 1, and early the next morning Sir George sent me the letter No. 2, and recommended to me to recall the ships he had sent from Basseterre with Rear-Admiral Drake to St. Lucia, and to wait their joining me before I proceeded to this coast.

I instantly dispatched the Sybille on that service, with orders for their meeting me at St. John's Road, Antigua, for which place I sailed the next evening with ten ships of the line. In the night I fell in with La Nymphe, which Sir George Rodney had sent to reconnoitre Fort Royal Bay and St. Pierre, and being informed by her commander that he had seen four sail of large ships in Fort Royal Bay, but that the weather was so very hazy he could form no opinion of their force, but thought they were of the line, I instantly sent La Nymphe back with the letter No. 3 to Rear-Admiral Drake. Early the next morning I spoke with an armed brig from New York with despatches from Sir Henry Clinton and Rear-Admiral Graves addressed to Sir G. Rodney, of which No. 4, 5, 6, 7 and 8 are copies.

I sent the armed brig into Nevis Road to complete her water, and then proceed to St. John's Road. On the 6th she joined me, and, without waiting an hour, pushed away on her return to New York with my answers to the letters she brought.

Having embarked the 49th Regiment on board his Majesty's squadron under my command, at the desire of Brigadier-General Christie, to whom Sir Henry Clinton's messenger delivered the despatches he was charged with for General Vaughan, I put to sea on the 10th at dawn of day, not caring to wait for the St. Lucia ships, lest the enemy should get to America before me; but as I was running out Mr. Drake appeared with four ships of the line, being certain the French had no ships larger than a frigate at Martinique, and without delaying a moment I pushed on as fast as possible.

On the 25th I made the land a little to the southward of Cape Henry, and from thence despatched a frigate with the letter No. 9 to Rear-Admiral Graves, and finding no enemy had appeared either either in the Chesapeake or Delaware,[1] I proceeded off Sandy Hook. On the 28th, in the morning, I received the letter No. 10 in answer, and foreseeing great delay and inconvenience might arise from going within the Hook with the squadron under my command.

I got into my boat and met Mr. Graves and Sir Henry Clinton on Long Island, who were deliberating upon a plan of destroying the ships at Rhode Island. This was an additional argument in support of my opinion against my going within the Hook, as the equinox was so near at hand, and I humbly submitted the necessity which struck me very forcibly, of such of Rear-Admiral Graves's squadron as were ready coming without the Bar immediately, whether to attend Sir Henry Clinton to Rhode Island, or to look for the enemy at sea. My idea was readily acquiesced in, and Mr. Graves said his ships should be sent out the next day, but for want of wind they are still within the Hook.

Herewith I send you, for their Lordships information an account of the state and condition of his

---

[1] Graves strongly affirms in his letter of May 4, 1782, written at Port Royal, Jamaica, that Hood did not look into either the Chesapeake or Delaware, but came directly on to New York.

Majesty's squadron I brought with me from the West Indies. I am, Sir,

Your most obedient, humble servant,

SAM. HOOD.

Endorsed.—The 30th of August, 1781, Rear-Admiral Sir Samuel Hood.

Received, the 3rd of November.
Answered, the 10th of November.

On September 8, the frigate Pegasus, Captain Stanhope, arrived with a third despatch from Rodney, addressed to Arbuthnot or the commander-in-chief for the time being:

[ADMIRAL RODNEY TO VICE ADMIRAL ARBUTHNOT]

Gibraltar, at sea, 13 Aug. 1781.

Sir,

Herewith I have the honour to enclose you intelligence which I received from St. Thomas's the night before I sailed from St. Eustatius, and to acquaint you that I left Sir Samuel Hood preparing to sail with all possible dispatch with 12 Sail of the line, 4 frigates, and a fireship, for the Capes of Virginia, where I am persuaded the French intend making their grand effort. Permit me therefore to recommend it to you to collect all the force you can, and form a junction with Sir

[59]

Samuel there. You will I hope, ere this reaches you, have heard of his approach, by his fastest sailing frigate, which I directed him to dispatch for the purpose of looking out for intelligence off the Chesapeak and Delaware.

The French fleet under Monsieur de Grasse, when they left the Grenades to collect their convoy, consisted of 26 sail of the line and two large ships armed en-flûte; and I imagine, at least 12 of those ships, and in all probability of part of Mr. de Monteil's squadron, will be in America; and it is not impossible they may be joined by some Spanish Ships.

It is certain that the enemy intend to make an early campaign in the West Indies after the hurricane months; I have therefore directed Sir Samuel Hood to return immediately after the full-moon of October, and I must request not only that he is on no account detained beyond that period, but that you will add to his force what line of battle ships can possibly be spared from the service in America during the winter season.

Besides the squadron Sir Samuel Hood brings with him, two line of battle ships, which I sent to strengthen the convoy to Jamaica, have my orders to proceed thence through the Gulph, and join him at the Chesapeak without delay.

I have the honour to be &a.

G. B. RODNEY

It is extraordinary that this despatch was not sent Hood earlier. The news from St. Thomas reached Rodney on the night of July 31. He sailed for England the next day. Hood was in easy reach, as he did not leave Antigua, distant only 70 miles from St. Eustatius, on August 10. Rodney took the Pegasus with him and when in the latitude of Bermuda sent her with the despatch to Graves's fleet. She was 26 days in reaching Graves. Rodney may have thought that his earlier orders to Hood respecting De Grasse's destination and occupancy of the Chesapeake were definite, but they clearly were not.

The despatch also shows how great a stress was laid upon the preservation of the British islands in the West Indies. This anxiety was ever uppermost in the British mind, and cost Britain the United States. America was sacrificed for a few sugar islands, which, had Britain succeeded in suppressing the American Revolution, would have fallen to the British navy in any case.

[REAR ADMIRAL GRAVES TO PHILIP STEPHENS]

London at sea the 14th Septr. 1781.

Sir.

I beg you will be pleased to acquaint the Lords Commissioners of the Admiralty, that the moment the wind served to carry the ships over the Bar, which was buoyed for the purpose, the squadron came out, and Sir Saml. Hood getting under sail at the same time, the fleet proceeded together on the 31st August to the southward, my intention being to go to the Cheasapeak, as the Enemys views would most probably be upon that part.

The cruisers which I had placed before the Delawar

coud. give me no certain information, and the cruisers
off the Cheasapeak had not joined; the winds being
rather favourable we approached the Cheasapeak the
morning of the 5th Septemr. when the advanced ship
made the signal of a fleet. We soon discovered a number of great ships at anchor, which seemed to be extended across the entrance of the Cheasapeak, from
Cape Henry to the Middle Ground; they had a frigate
cruizing off the Cape which stood in and joined them,
and as we approached, the whole fleet got under sail
and stretched out to sea with the wind at N.N.E. As
we drew nearer I formed the line, first ahead and then
in such a manner as to bring his Majesty's fleet nearly
parallel to the line of approach of the Enemy; and
when I found that our van was advanced as far as the
shoal of the middle ground would admit of, I wore the
fleet and brought them upon the same tack with the
enemy, and nearly parallel to them, though we were by
no means extended with their rear. So soon as I judged
that our van would be able to operate, I made the signal
to bare away and approach, and soon after, to engage
the Enemy close. Somewhat after four the action began
amongst the headmost ships pretty close, and soon became general as far as the second ship from the center
towards the rear. The van of the enemy bore away to
enable their center to support them, or they would have
been cut up, the action did not entirely cease until a
little after sunset though at a considerable distance, for
the center of the Enemy continued to bear up as it advanced, and at that moment seemed to have little more
in view, than to shelter their own van as it went away
before the wind.—

His Majesty's Fleet consisted of nineteen sail of the

line, that of the French formed twenty four sail in their line. After night I sent the frigates to the van and rear to push forward the line and keep it extended with the enemy, with a full intention to renew the engagement in the morning, but when the frigate Fortunée returned from the van I was informed that, several of the ships had suffered so much they were in no condition to renew the action until they had secured their masts. The Shrewsbury, Intrepid, and Montagu unable to keep the line, and the Princessa in momentary apprehension of the maintopmast going over the side: we however kept well extended with the Enemy all night, and in the morning, saw they had not the appearance of near so much damage as we had sustained, though the whole of their van must have experienced a good deal of loss.

We continued all day the 6h. in sight of each other repairing our damages. Rear Admiral Drake shifted his flag into the Alcide until the Princessa had got up another maintopmast. The Shrewsbury, whose Captain lost a leg and had the first lieutenant killed, was obliged to reef both topmasts, shift her topsail-yards, and had sustained very great damage. I ordered Captn. Colpoys of the Orpheus, to take the command of her and put her into a state for action.

The Intrepid had both topsail yards shot down, her topmasts in great danger of falling, and her lower masts and yards very much damaged; her Captain having behaved with the greatest gallantry to cover the Shrewsbury. The Montagu was in great danger of losing her masts, the Terrible so leaky as to keep all her pumps going, and the Ajax also very leaky from old complaints aggravated. In the present state of the fleet, and being five sail of the line less in number than the Enemy, and they having advanced very much in the wind upon us during the day, I determined to tack after eight, to prevent being drawn too far from the Cheasapeak, and to stand to the Northward.

Enclosed is the line of battle with ye numbers killed and wounded in the different ships and their principal damages during the action, marked A. The ships in general did their duty well and the officers and people exerted themselves exceedingly.

On the 8 it came to blow pretty fresh, and in standing against a head sea the Terrible made the signal of distress, I immediately sent the Fortunée and Orpheus frigates to attend upon her, and received the enclosed state of her complaints marked B.

At night about an hour after the fleet had been wore together, the Intrepid made the signal to speak with the Admiral, upon which the fleet was brought to, and I was soon informed that her main topmast was gone over the side and they expected the fore-yard would go every moment. These repeated misfortunes in sight of a superior enemy who kept us all extended and in motion, filled the mind with anxiety and put us in a situation not to be envied.

I have enclosed the state and condition of the ships letter C, by which their lordships will perceive the state of the fleet. To this I must add, that the Pegasus joined the fleet from New York with an account that after separating from Sir George Rodney in latitude 29° .55′ Longitude 59° .33′, having six victuallers and a storeship under convoy for New York, had fallen in with the French fleet and lost every ship, though the captain seems to have used every prudential means for their preservation.

[64]

It may not be improper to add that we are without resources at York, there having been neither stores nor provisions but what has been purchased, for many months past, and a very slender quantity even of that.

Several of the Squadron from the West Indies being bare of water and provisions, particularly bread, obliged me to supply them from other ships. It being determined in a council of war held on the 10th to evacuate the Terrible and destroy her, I took the first calm day to effect it, and at the same time distributed the water and provisions which were wanted. This took up the whole of the 4th, the wreck was set fire to, and I bore up for the Chesapeake about nine at night.

The Fleets had continued in sight of each other for five days successively, and at times were very near. We had not speed enough in so mutilated a state to attack them had it been prudent and they shewed no inclination to renew the action, for they generally maintained the wind of us, and had it often in their power.

The paper marked letter D will shew their lordships Captain Duncan's report of the state of the Chesapeake, when I sent him to look in, the day after the action.

The above-mentioned delay occasioned our losing sight for the first time, of the French fleet. I therefore sent Captain Duncan to reconnoitre the Chesapeake who brought me on the morning of the 13th, the information which occasioned the Council of War marked letter E; and I sent him again to take a better view, which confirmed the report of the French fleet being all anchored within the Cape, so as to block the passage. I then determined to follow the resolution of a Council of War for securing the fleet if possible before the Equinox at New York, and I immediately despatched the Medea with this pacquet for their Lordships information.

I am

Sir,

Your most Obedient and

most humble Servant,

THOS. GRAVES.

P.S.

Enclosed you will receive a duplicate of my last letter. I beg leave to recommend the necessity for the immediate return of the frigates which may be sent from this country, the want of the Roebuck has been much felt.

T.G.

Philip Stephens, Esqr.

Endorsed No. 7 | Rear Adml. Graves | Letter to P. Stephens Esq. | 14 Sept. 1781. | ℞ 13th Octo. at Night.

Enclosure A

THE LINE OF BATTLE

With an account of the numbers of the Killed & Wounded, and the damages sustained by the Fleet under the command of Rear Admiral Graves, in an action with the French Fleet off Cape Henry on the 5th Septemr 1781.

[66]

Line of Battle

The Alfred to lead with the Starboard and the Shrewsbury wh. the larbd.
tacks on board

Frigates	Rate	Ships	Commanders	Guns	Men	Divisions
	3	Alfred	Captain Bayne	74	600	
	"	Belliqueux	" Brine	64	500	
	"	Invincible	" Saxton	74	600	Sr. Samuel Hood Bart.
anta Monica } to repeat	2	Barfleur	{Rear Admiral Hood} {Captain Hood}	90	768	Rear Admiral of ye Blue &ca. &ca. &ca.
ichmond	3	Monarch	" Reynolds	74	600	
	"	Centaur	" Inglefield	74	650	
	3	America	Captain Thompson	64	500	
	"	Resolution	" Lord Rt. Manners	74	600	
alamander fireship	"	Bedford	" Graves	74	600	Thomas Graves Esqr.
ymphe repeat	2	London	{Rear Admiral Graves} {Captain Graves}	98	800	Rear Adml. of the Red
	3	Royal Oak	" Ardesoif	74	600	Commander in Chief
lebay	"	Montagu	" Bowen	74	600	
damant	"	Europe	" Child	64	500	
	3	Terrible	Captain Finch	74	600	
	"	Ajax	" Charrington	74	550	Francis Samuel Drake Esqr.
bil repeat	"	Princessa	{Rear Admiral Drake} {Captain Knatcbull}	70	577	Rear Admiral of the Blue &c. &c. &c.
ortunée	"	Alcide	" Thompson	74	600	
	"	Intrepid	" Molloy	64	500	
	"	Shrewsbury	" Robinson	74	600	

B.   If the Europe cannot keep up she is to fall into the Rear and the Adamant to take her station in the Line.

Given on board His Majestys ship London
at Sandy Hook 31t Augt. 1781
(Copy)   T Graves

Note by Editor.—As the fleet stood in for the Capes, with the wind from the northward, the Alfred was leading with the starboard tacks aboard; the signal to "wear together" brought the Shrewsbury in the lead, with the larboard (port) tacks aboard.   The action of September 5 was thus fought with the ships in the reverse order of the names above, Sir Samuel Hood's division forming the rear.

List of Men killed and wounded and guns dismounted on board His Majesty's Ships under the command of Rear Admiral Graves in an action with the French Fleet off Cape Henry the 5 Septr. 1781

	Killed	Wounded	Total	Guns Dismounted
Shrewsbury . . .	14	52	66	3
Intrepid	21	35	56	..
Alcide	2	18	20	..
Princessa	6	11	17	..
Ajax	7	16	23	3
Terrible	4	21	25	..
Europe	9	18	27	3
Montagu	8	22	30	4
Royal Oak . . .	4	5	9	..
London	4	18	22	3
Bedford	8	14	22	..
Resolution . . .	3	16	19	..
America	..	..	..	..
Centaur	..	..	..	..
Monarch	..	..	..	..
Barfleur	..	..	..	..
Invincible	..	..	..	..
Belliqueux	..	..	..	..
Alfred	..	..	..	..
Total . . .	90	246	336	16

Damages received on board His Majesty's ships under the command of Rear Admiral Graves in an action with the French Fleet off Cape Henry the 5th Septr. 1781.

Shrewsbury, Captain Mark Robinson.

5th Septr.—Captain Everitt of the Solebay reported, that at 5 minutes past 8 P.M., he spoke her, she having made the signal of distress—was informed that Captain Robinson had lost his leg, the first Lieutenant and 25 or 26 men killed, and 46 wounded, Mr. Retalick 2nd lieut. commanding officer—all her masts yards and sails so shattered, not able to keep the line—had on board at the beginning of the action 532 men.

Carpenter's damages—Foremast shot through in three different places, one of the trussel-trees shot through and the cross-tree wounded—the fore yard badly wounded in three places—fore top-sail-yard-arm shot away, and two shot thro the yard—spreet-sail yard wounded—three shot thro' the head of the main mast, and another above ten feet above the quarter deck which have much weakened the mast—main yard, wounded at both arms— Maintopmast shot thro' just above the cap, and the heel shot away main topsail yard, shot thro' in two places— mizzenmast almost cut off in two places—mizzen topmast shot thro' at the head mizzen yard wounded, six studding sail booms shot away—the spare topmasts, main topsail yard, fish for the mast, hand-mast, jib-boom, spars, and all the boats very much wounded.—Five shot under water, one of them gone thro'— One end of an upper deck beam much damaged—two upper deck standards, the spir-

ketting, clamps, etc., cut in several places— the plankshier, fife rails, blocks &c. on the quarter-deck, all shot
away—the outside much damaged by receiving so
many shot— When the larboard tacks are on board,
the ship makes 18 inches water in four hours.

Boatswain's damages — Twenty-eight lower and
eighteen topmt. shrouds and thirteen backstays & the
main and mizen stays all shot away; blocks, dead-eyes
and all the running rigging and sails cut to pieces.—

Gunners damages.—Two 18 prs. disabled and the
carriage of another.

Intrepid — Captain Anthony James Pye Molloy.

Carpenters damages.— Withoutboard, the head rails
shot thro—sixty-five shot holes in the starboard side,
and nineteen between wind and water—the rudder
much damaged — five side timbers, each of them cut
in two—the upper quarter-gallery shot to pieces, and
the stern-gallery much damaged. Gun Deck, the stan-
dard against the post shot away,—Upper Deck, three
port timbers and the quick-work greatly damaged, the
second shift of spirketting and the port cell, string and
quick-work, greatly damaged. Two shot through the
middle of the Bowspreet, and one thro' the spreet-sail-
yard, three shot in the foremast, and two very dangerous ones thro' the fore-topmast—foreyard much
wounded and the fore topsail-yard shot in two—two
shot in the main mast—the main topmast almost cut in
two, the heel of the main topmast shot to pieces. Sails
and rigging very much cut particularly the topsails—
All the boats damaged.

Alcide Captain Charles Thompson

Carpenters damages.—Jib-boom, Bowspreet fore yard and top gallant mast slightly wounded—three shot thro' the mainmast. Mizen topmast, topsail-yard, and gaff, shot away— Clamps standards, spirketting &c, on the Upper and Gun Decks, much wounded, the knee of the head & part of the figure,—spare main topsail yards & boats much hurt—many shot under water which makes the ship leaky.—

————

Princessa {Rear Admiral Drake
Captain Charles Knatchbull

Carpenters damages.—Main topmast shot thro' in three places Maintopsail Yard shot away 12 feet from the arm—a shot thro' the middle of the fore-mast 10 feet under the hounds—foretop gallant mast shot thro— Maintopgalltmast Driven and three studding-sail-booms, all shot away—fore yard arm shot almost off 12 feet away from the slings—long boat and cutter damaged two hanging knees and two port cells shot away—several shot in the side and under water.—

Boatswain damages,—Six Fore & eight main shrouds several topmast shrouds & great part of the running rigging and sails very much cut,—

[71]

Ajax Captain Nicholas Charrington.

Carpenters damages.—Upper Deck one shot thro the gangway and one thro the clamp—the plankshier blocks &c on the quarter deck torn to pieces—Mizzen topmast shot thro', one shot thro' the head of the mainmast, but not of much consequence—maintopsail yard wounded and the spare one shot through—main trusseltrees shiver'd by shot & require shifting—fore topsailyard wounded—fore topgallantmast shot away—a shot thro the cap and head of the foremast—the fore yard wounded in the slings—spare maintopmast and the boats wounded by shot.

Boatswains damages.—Ten lower and six topmast shrouds seven back stays, and all the stays shot away—running rigging and sails very much cut—

Gunners damages—Two Carriages, vizt. a 24 and a 9 Poundr. are wounded and a 9 pounder dismounted.

———

Terrible   Hoñble Captain Finch

Two large shot thro' the foremast, and two buried in it (the mast sprung before the action) main topsails and cross jack yards much damaged—several shot between wind and water. (the ship leaky before the action) The pumps blown, and only kept together by tarr'd canvas, lead, and wouldings—chains worn out, and but few links to repair them—pump leather all expended— makes two feet two inches water in 25 minutes.—

Europe. Captain Smith Child

Carpenters damages—Four shot in the mainmast, two of them gone thro'—the main yard wounded in two places—main top mast wounded mizen top mast and topsail-yard shot away—the spare topmasts boats &c much wounded—two standards and three hanging knees shot thro'—the fife rails plankshier and spirketting much wounded—twelve shot between wind and water and a great number in the upper works—the ship strains and makes water.

Boatswains damages.—Eleven lower shrouds, two topmast shrouds, two backstays, and all the mizen topmast rigging shot away, and the sails and running rigging much cut.

Gunners damages—a 24 Pr. and a 9 Pr. carriages damaged—and the carriage of an 18 Pr. render'd unserviceable—

———

Montagu Captain George Brown

Carpenters damages—Clamp spirketting and waterway on the Gun and upper decks shot thro in several places the hull much shatterd by shot—a shot thro' the main piece of the rudder, which has split it— The fore topgallantmast shot thro' Five shot in the main mast, one of which is gone thro'—the main yard shot half off —maintopmast shot thro' seven feet above the cap— mizen mast cut half off two feet under the hounds—

main top gallant yard shot to peices—studding sail booms shot away spare yards topmasts &c damaged by shot.

Boatswains damages—Nineteen lower shrouds, ten topmast shrouds, six backstays—the fore topmast stay and the main spring stay, all shot away—the running rigging and sails very much cut—

Gunners damages — four guns dismounted.—

––––––––

Royal Oak Captain John Plumer Ardesoif

Carpenters damages—Clamp spirketting and water way on the Quarter and upper decks, shot thro' in several places. Mizen mast and spare maintopsail yard wounded—five shot in the wales and twelve in the topsides.—

––––––––

London {Rear Admiral Graves
Captain David Graves

A large shot thro' the mainmast, and two in the foremast, fore top gallantmast shot away— Boats and booms much damaged — a number of shot in the side and several under water— The sails and rigging much cut.

Gunner's damages—Three guns (one 18 pr. and Two 12 prs.) dismounted — one of which being rendered unserviceable was thrown overboard.

[74]

Bedford — Captain Thomas Graves

Mizen topmast rendered unfit for service—a shot in the mainmast and two in the head of the foremast. The gammoning of the bowspreet and part of the knee of the head shot away — a shot thro' the jib-boom, fourteen in the side and several under water, but the ship not leaky.

Resolution — Captain Lord Robert Manners

The head rails shot away, mainmast and bowsprit wounded

Centaur — Captain John Inglefield

Two strakes of spirketting cut almost off, and the mainmast wounded.

Monarch — Captain Francis Reynolds

A large shot in the main mast about five feet below the cheeks, the bowsprit cut $\frac{1}{3}$d off just without the gammoning.

America
Barfleur
Invincible } Received no damage in the action.
Belliqueux
Alfred

T. GRAVES.

Endorsed 4 | The Line of Battle | the Numbers killed & wounded | & the Account of damages | sustained in the Action of the 5th of September 1781 | A | In R A. Graves Letter | Dated 14 Sepr. 1781.

Enclosure B

[Copy of the several Letters representing the State and Condition His Majestys Ship Terrible]

Sir   Terrible at Sea 9th Septemr. 1781.

Our Leaks since Yesterday have increased very much, to day we were alarmed when we came against a very trifling head Sea, with our Leaks gaining (over six hand Pumps kept briskly going) 2 feet 2 Inches in 25 Minutes, and we are all convinced that she will make much more in a gale of Wind, our Chain Pumps are very bad, should the least Accident happen, I am apprehensive the Ship cannot be saved, our Foremast is much wounded. It was sprung before we came into Action, and there are now two Shot thro' the Main Piece of the Foremast, two more lodged in it, we weighed one of the Shot which weighed thirty nine pounds, Should we be blown off the Coast we have but ten days Water on board.   WM. CLEMT. FINCH.

The Carpenter informs me that in smooth Water if the hand Pumps were kept still, the Ship would make six feet water in the hour.

Rear Admiral Graves
   Commander in Chief &c. &c. &c.

[76]

Memorandum enclosed in the preceding Letter.

The Pumps blown, and only kept together by Tar'd Canvas Lead & Wouldings; the Sprocket Wheels much decayed, and not one spare one in the Ship, the Chains by constant use worn out, we have however a few spare links to repair them, all the Winches Supplied the Ship from having been so often broke and repaired, are rendered useless, the Iron burnt out, so that we have for some time past been under the necessity to repair them with New Iron. The Pump Cisterns so much shaken by constantly Pumping that it gives employment to one Man to keep Caulking them and that without being able to do it effectually. The Pump Leather all expended.

———

Terrible at Sea 10th. Septr. 1781.

Sir

When I last sent you the state of the Terrible, I mentioned that the least Water she made was Six . . . feet an hour, the next four hours we pumped out 8 feet each hour, our Leaks increased during the Night; from 12 P. M. to noon this day We have had all our Pumps going, the Chain Pumps only Suck, and three times during those 12 Hours, and never stood still for more than ten Minutes each Time, our hand Pumps have never ceased; In this Situation I have thrown overboard 5 lower Deck Guns, not knowing how long I might have it in my Power to do so. If you do not forbid it

[77]

I shall be under the necessity of throwing over board
the Fore Castle and Quarter Deck Guns, for although
we do not make quite so much Water on this Tack, we
make too much to give us any great hopes of being able
to carry her into Port. Perhaps you may think Sir that
some of her Stores may be of Service to some other Ship,
and in our present Situation we should be as well without them.

I am Sir
Your most Obedt. humble Servt.
WM. CLEMT. FINCH.

To
 Rear Admiral Graves
 Commander in Chief &c. &c. &c.

———

Terrible at Sea the 11th. Septemr. 1781

Sir

I beg leave to send you the inclosed Certificates, and
to inform you that we find no Relief from the lower
Deck Guns being thrown over board, It is impossible
to keep Pumps workt better than ours have been all
Night, and they have barely prevented the Water gaining on us, I have all the Sick and wounded Men in the
Ward Room, I should be glad to begin by removing
them, I should be glad to receive your Orders where
they are to be sent, the Ships Company are divided into
six divisions about sixty each, with a Lieutenant and a
Proportional Number of Petty Officers, they are the

most equal division that can be made of them, as they consist of equal No. of Fore Castle Men, Topmen &ca. in each, the Marines are a very fine party of Men. I have ventured to hoist the Long Boat out in consequence of what you mentioned Yesterday.

I have the honor to be

Sir your most Obedt.

humble Servant

WM. CT. FINCH.—

Rear Adml. Graves
  Commander in Chief
      &ca. &ca. &ca.—

Copy of the Certificate given by the Officers of His Majestys Ship Terrible.

To the Hoñble. Wm. Clemt. Finch
Commander of H. M. S. Terrible

In Compliance with your directions to give in our opinions of the possibility of carrying the Ship into Port, we do hereby certify as follows, that during the last Night the Water gained at two different times on the Pumps, so that had any accident happen'd, to the Chains, which have seldom work'd two days without breaking, she must inevitably have founderd, and She still continuing not withstanding the fineness of the Weather, to keep all the Pumps constantly going (it is our opinions that it is absolutely impracticable to carry her into Port.

Given under our hands on board His Majestys
Ship Terrible at Sea the 10th. September 1781.

RICHD. NASH first Lieutt.
H. W. MILLER Second do
THOS. PROCTER Third do
CHAS. APTHORP Fourth do
JAS. JNO. COLVIL Fifth do
JOHN ROICE Master
JOHN MULES Boatsn.
WM. DYERS Gunner
JOHN KAINS Carpenter

And we do further certify that any assistance from
the Fleet would be ineffectual for the preservation of
the Ship, and that no additional number of Men could
keep her free, so as to enable us to carry Her into Port.
Given under our hands on board His Majestys
Ship Terrible at Sea the 11th. September 1781.

WM. CLEMT. FINCH .. Captain
RICHARD NASH ... first Lieutt.
H W MILLER ...... Second do
THOS. PROCTER ..... Third do
CHAS. APTHORP ... Fourth do
JAS. JNO. COLVIL .... Fifth do
JNO. ROICE .... Master
JOHN MULES .... Boatsn.
WM. DYERS .... Gunner
JOHN KAINS .... Carpenter

September 11th 1781. At a Council of War held this
day on board His Majestys Ship London upon the
Leaky and dangerous state of the Terrible, as repre-
sented by Captain Finchs two letters of the 9th and

10th Instant, and the little probability of her being able to get to New York or any other Port, we are of opinion to take out her People and sink her.

THOS. GRAVES
SAM HOOD
FRA: S: DRAKE

(Copy)

T. Graves

Endorsed (3) | Copy of the several letters | from Captn. Finch together | with the Certificate from the | Captain and all the other Officers | representing the state and | Condition of His Majestys Ship | Terrible with the Council of war on | the same | B | In R. A. Graves's Letter | Dated 14 Sepr: 1781.

[LETTER FROM REAR ADMIRAL GRAVES]

Sir

I have this moment put into my hands by the Pearl Capt Montagu the Packet brought by the Active Brig Captain Manley which arrived at New York the 10 instant, and was brought away the 11th. by the Pearl. The Zebra has arrived at [New] York from the West Indies as Capt. Montagu informs me. The Prudent had sailed from [New] York but has not joined me, and she may be to the Southward and had spoken I understand to the Pegasus, who had left me after the action with dispatches for [New] York.

I am Sir your most Obedt.

Humble Servant

THOS. GRAVES.

London off the
Cheasapeak C. Charles
14 Sepr. 1781.—

[81]

Endorsed 14 Sepr. 1781 | R A Graves | ℞ 13 Octor. at Night

Enclosure D

[INTELLIGENCE BY CAPTAIN DUNCAN OF HIS
MAJESTY'S SHIP MEDEA]

Thursday September 6th. 1781 in the Forenoon, made Sail for the Cheasepeak, that Evening got close to Cape Henry but too late to run in, spoke the Iris returning from chasing a Ship which she obliged to throw her Guns over board, and run her into Shoal Water, kept the Iris with me that Night, in the night spoke the Pegasus, she left the West Indies with Sir George Rodney and was bringing seven Victuallers all which She apprehended was taken by the French Fleet, the Pegasus was chased four days by them in the Lattde. 38. Longde. 72.

Friday 7th. Run into the Cheseapeak, observed that the French Fleet had left their Anchors behind them, I left the Iris at the Cape and directed Captain Dawson to cut away the Buoys after taking the bearings of them, We went up the Bay, two Ships were working down, one of which was a two Deck Ship, we could plainly discover her lower Deck Ports, Stern Gallery and a whole Mizen Yard, She hoisted English Colours and the Pendant she hoisted from the Quarter Deck, the other Ship was a Frigate; there were five Sails at Anchor higher up, one of which came down and joined them, she was not so large as the Line of Battle Ship, and considerably larger than the Frigate, no Poop, most probably a 40 Gun Ship; four that lay above were Small Vessels. when we had got pretty well up with those Ships, two large Ships made their appearance coming out of Elizabeth River, Captain Dawson took them to be Line of Battle Ships, they did not appear so large to us, they Anchord. The Line of Battle Ship, the 40 and Frigate seemed to be Anchord in a Line above the Horse Shoe, and near the entrance of the York River, got out of the Bay at Night, and next Morning saw the Fleet.

HENRY DUNCAN

Endorsed (5) | Copy of Intelligence from | the Chesa-peake, by Captn. | Duncan of the Medea, the | 7th of September, 1781. | D | In R. A. Graves's Letter | Dated 14 Sepr. 1781.

Enclosure E

[THE RESOLVE OF A COUNCIL OF WAR]

At a Council of War held on board His Majesty's ship London at Sea the 13 September, 1781, upon a report from Captain Duncan of his majesty's ship Medea, that they had seen the evening before, the French Fleet at anchor off the Horseshoe shoal in the Chesapeake, that the large ships appeared more numer-ous and to be in Divisions, but that it was too late to get near enough to form a close judgement.

Upon this state of the position of the Enemy the pres-ent condition of the British Fleet, the season of the year so near the Equinox, and the impracticability of giving any effectual succour to General Earl Cornwallis in the Chesapeake,

It was resolved, that the British Squadron under the command of Thomas Graves Esqr. Rear Admiral of the Red—Sr. Samuel Hood Bart. and Francis Samuel Drake Esqr. Rear Admirals of the Blue, should proceed with all dispatch to New York, and there use every possible means for putting the Squadron into the best state for service, provided that Captain Duncan who is gone again to reconnoitre shoud confirm his report of the position of the Enemy and that the Fleet should in the mean time facilitate the junction of the Medea.

THOMAS GRAVES

(Signed)   SAMUEL HOOD

Copy FRANCIS SAMUEL DRAKE
   T. Graves

Endorsed (6) | The Resolve of a Council of War | held on board H M S London | on the 13th September 1781. | E | In R A Graves's Letter | Dated 14 Sepr. 1781.

[REAR ADMIRAL GRAVES TO PHILIP STEPHENS]

London at Sandy Hook 22d Septr. 1781.

Sir:—

I beg you will be pleased to acquaint their Lordships with my having receiv'd their dispatches of the 24th July by ye Lively Sloop of War, directed to Vice Admiral Arbuthnot.—Also the several duplicates of their dispatches of the Third, fourth, Eighteenth and Twenty Second of May last—all of which I beg you will be pleased to assure their Lordships shall be paid every possible attention to.

I am

Sir your most Obedt.

humble Servant

Philip Stephens, Esqre: THOS. GRAVES.

Admiralty Office

London.

Endorsed 2 | Letter to Philip Stephens Esqr. | 22 Septr. 1781 | ℞ 3 Nov. 1781.

[REAR ADMIRAL GRAVES TO PHILIP STEPHENS]

London at New York 23d Septr. 1781.

Sir—

I beg leave through you to lay before the Lords Commissioners of the Admiralty the situation of Captain Mark Robinson, who in the action off Cape Henry Virginia on the 5 Septr: last, commanded His Majestys Shrewsbury.—

Captain Robinson led the British fleet consisting of nineteen sail of line of battle ships into action against the fleet of France, consisting of twenty four sail of the line; and when the Signal for close action was made, bore down and engaged the headmost Ship of the enemy in a very spirited and gallant manner; during the course of the action he had the misfortune to lose his left leg, his first lieutenant was killed and thirteen men, and

fifty one besides himself wounded. The urgent necessity for the fleet going to Sea so soon as possible made
it necessary for a man upwards of sixty years of age
after a recent amputation, to request to be superceded
in his command, though then at New York North
America, one of the most expensive places in the World.

These circumstances taken together call upon me in
a particular manner to recommend Captain Mark Robinson to their Lordships favor and protection.—

I am
Sir
Your most obedient
Humble Servant

Philip Stephens Esqr: THOS. GRAVES.

Endorsed Recd. 11 Febry | 1782

Minute 30 May | own rect. | let him know their | Ldps
recom̄datn. | to N Bd. for a | Pension of £300 a yr.

[REAR ADMIRAL HOOD TO GEORGE JACKSON[1] [2]]

Barfleur, off the Delaware, 16th of September, 1781.
Going to New York.

Private

My dear Jackson:—

On the 5th instant, about 10 A.M., one of the look-out
frigates made the signal for a fleet, and at eleven we
plainly discovered twenty-four sail of French ships of

[1] Assistant Secretary of the Admiralty.

[2] This and following letters of Hood to Jackson are from Letters
of Sir Samuel Hood (later Viscount Hood), edited by David Hannay, forming Vol. III, Publications of the British Navy Records
Society.

the line and two frigates at anchor about Cape Henry,
with their top sail yards hoisted aloft as a signal for
getting under sail. Soon after they began to come out
in a line of battle ahead, but by no means regular and
connected, which afforded the British fleet a most glorious opening for making a close attack to manifest advantage, but it was not embraced; and as the French
fleet was close hauled and the English line steered large,
the two vans got pretty near, at four, when the signal
for battle was hoisted — that part of the enemy's fleet
being to windward of their centre, and the centre to
windward of their rear. Our centre then upon a wind
began to engage at the same time, but at a most *improper* distance (and the London had the signal for
close action flying, as well as the signal for the line
ahead at *half a cable* was under her topsails, with the
main topsail to the mast, though the enemy's ships were
pushing on), and our rear being barely within random
shot did not fire while the signal for the line was flying.
No. 1 contains my sentiments upon the truly unfortunate day, as committed to writing the next morning, and
which I mentioned to Mr. Graves when I attended his
first summons on board the London. On the 6th it was
calm the whole day, and in the evening Mr. Drake and·
I were sent for, when Mr. Graves communicated to us
intelligence he had received from the captains of the
Medea and Iris, who had reconnoitred the Chesapeake,
which was as follows: That a ship of the line, a 40-gun
ship, and a frigate, were at anchor between the Horse
Shoe Shoal and York Rivers, and that they saw three
large ships coming down the bay, which they thought
were of the line. Mr. Graves also made known to us
a letter from Sir H. Clinton to General Earl Corn-

wallis, which he was desired to convey to his Lordship, if possible. The Richmond and Iris were detached upon that service, I fear to be cut off, and think the whole squadron should have gone; they might then not only most effectually have succoured Lord Cornwallis, but have destroyed the enemy's ships there. On the 7th and 8th, the enemy being to windward, had an opportunity of attacking us if they pleased, but showed no sort of inclination for it. On the 9th, the French fleet carried a press of sail, which proved to me beyond a doubt that De Grasse had other views than fighting, and I was distressed that Mr. Graves did not carry all the sail he could also, and endeavour to get off the Chesapeake before him; it appeared to me to be a measure of the utmost importance to keep the French out, and if they did get in they should first beat us. Instead of that, Mr. Graves put his Majesty's squadron on a contrary course just at dark, and at 8 o'clock made the signal and lay to. At daylight next morning nothing was to be seen of the French fleet from the Barfleur. This alarmed me exceedingly, and I debated with myself some little time whether I should venture to write Mr. Graves a few lines or not, as it is rather an awkward and unpleasant business to *send* advice to a senior officer. However, I at last took courage to do it, and having made the signal for my repeating frigate to come under the Barfleur's stern sent her with the letter of which No. 2 is a copy. This occasioned another summons to Mr. Drake and me on board the London, when I found, to my very great astonishment, Mr. Graves as ignorant as myself where the French fleet was, and that no frigates were particularly ordered (for we had several with us) to watch and bring an account of the enemy's motions. The question was put to me, what was most proper to be done? to which I replied that I thought the letter I had taken the liberty to send had fully and clearly explained what my sentiments were, but if it was wished I should say more, it could only be that we should get into the Chesapeake to the succour of Lord Cornwallis and his brave troops if possible, but that I was afraid the opportunity of doing it was passed by, as doubtless De Grasse had most effectually barred the entrance against us, which was what human prudence suggested we *ought* to have done against him. On the 13th, early in the morning, I received the note No. 3 from Mr. Graves, and No. 4 is my answer to it, which again called Mr. Drake and me on board the London. When the resolution contained in the paper No. 5 was taken, there was nothing else left to be done, irksome and much to be lamented as the alternative was. I unbosom myself to you in great confidence that you will not show what I write to a single soul. With every affectionate wish for health and happiness to you and yours,   I am, my dear Jackson,

Your most faithful and sincere

S. H.

Enclosure 1

[REAR ADMIRAL HOOD'S "SENTIMENTS UPON THE TRULY UNFORTUNATE DAY"]

Coast of Virginia, 6th of September, 1781.
Yesterday the British fleet had a rich and most plentiful harvest of glory in view, but the means to gather it were omitted in more instances than one.

I may begin with observing that the enemy's van was not very closely attacked as it came out of Lynn Haven Bay, which, I think, might have been done with clear advantage, as they came out by no means in a regular and connected way. When the enemy's van was out it was greatly extended beyond the centre and rear, and might *have* been attacked with the whole force of the British fleet. Had such an attack been made, several of the enemy's ships must have been inevitably demolished in half an hour's action, and there was a full hour and half to have engaged it before any of the rear could have come up.

Thirdly, when the van of the two fleets got into action, and the ships of the British line were hard pressed, one (the Shrewsbury) totally disabled very early from keeping her station by having her fore and main topsail yards shot away, which left her second (the Intrepid) exposed to two ships of superior force, which the noble and spirited behaviour of Captain Molloy[1] obliged to turn their sterns to him, that the signal was not thrown out for the van ships to make more sail to have enabled the centre to push on to the support of the van, instead of engaging at such an improper distance (the London having her main topsail to the mast the whole time she was firing with the signal for the line at half a cable flying), that the second ship astern of the London received but trifling damage, and the third astern of her (the London) received no damage at all, which most clearly proves how much too great the distance was the centre division engaged.

[1] This is the Captain Molloy who afterward, in a less "happy hour of command," incurred so much discredit on the 1st of June, 1794. (Navy Records Society, III, 32.)

Now, had the centre gone to the support of the van, and the signal for the line been hauled down, or the commander-in-chief had set the example of close action, even with the signal for the line flying, the van of the enemy must have been cut to pieces, and the rear division of the British fleet would have been opposed to those ships the centre division fired at, and at the proper distance for engaging, or the Rear-Admiral who commanded it would have a great deal to answer for. Instead of that, our centre division did the enemy but little damage, and our rear ships being barely within random shot, three only fired a few shot. So soon as the signal for the line was hauled down at twenty-five minutes after five the rear division bore up, above half a mile to leeward of the centre division, but the French ships bearing up also, it did not near them, and at twenty-five minutes after six the signal of the line ahead at half a cable being again hoisted, and the signal for battle hauled down, Rear-Admiral Sir S. Hood called to the Monarch (his leader) to keep her wind, as he dared not separate his division just at dark, the London not bearing up at all.

N.B. — This forenoon Captain Everett came on board the Barfleur with a message from Rear-Admiral Graves to Rear-Admiral Sir S. Hood, desiring his opinion whether the action should be renewed. Sir Samuel's answer was: 'I dare say Mr. Graves will do what is right; I can *send* no opinion, but whenever he, Mr. Graves, wishes to see me, I will wait upon him with great pleasure.'

[91]

Enclosure 2

[REAR ADMIRAL HOOD TO REAR ADMIRAL GRAVES]

Barfleur, at Sea, 10th of September, 1781.

Sir:—

I flatter myself you will forgive the liberty I take in asking whether you have any knowledge where the French fleet is, as we can see nothing of it from the Barfleur.

By the press of sail De Grasse carried yesterday (and he must even have done the same the preceding night, by being where [he] was at daylight), I am inclined to think his aim is the Chesapeake, in order to be strengthened by the ships there, either by adding them to his present force, or by exchanging his disabled ships for them. Admitting that to be his plan, will he not cut off the frigates you have sent to reconnoitre, as well as the ships you expect from New York? And if he should enter the Bay, which is by no means improbable, will he not succeed in giving most effectual succour to the rebels?

I trust you will pardon the offer of my humble sentiments, as they are occasioned by what passed between us, when I had the honour of attending your summons on board the London, on the 8th, in the evening.

I am, Sir,

Your most obedient, humble Servant,

(Signed)   SAM. HOOD.

Rear-Admiral Graves, &c., &c., &c.

Endorsed.—A copy of a letter from Rear-Admiral Sir S. Hood to Rear-Admiral Graves, 10th of September, 1781.

Enclosure 3

[REAR ADMIRAL GRAVES TO REAR ADMIRAL HOOD]

Admiral Graves presents his compliments to Sir Samuel Hood and begs leave to acquaint that the Medea has just made the signal to inform him that the French fleet are at anchor above the Horse Shoe in Chesapeake, and desires his opinion what to do with the fleet, and how to dispose of the Princesa.

London, Thursday Morning, 6 o'clock.

Endorsed.—Copy of a note from Rear-Admiral Graves to Rear-Admiral Sir S.Hood,with Sir Samuel's answer, 13th of September, 1781.

Enclosure 4

[REAR ADMIRAL HOOD TO REAR ADMIRAL GRAVES]

Rear Admiral Sir Samuel Hood presents his compliments to Rear-Admiral Graves. Is extremely concerned to find by his note just received that the French fleet is at anchor in the Chesapeake above the Horse Shoe, though it is no more than what he expected, as the press of sail the fleet carried on the 9th and in the night of the 8th made it very clear to him what De Grasse's intentions were. Sir Samuel would be very glad to send an opinion, but he really knows not what to say in the truly lamentable state we have brought ourselves.

Barfleur, Thursday Morning, 13th of September, 7 A.M.

Endorsed.—Copy of a note from Rear-Admiral Sir S. Hood to Rear-Admiral Graves, 13th of September, 1781.

[REAR ADMIRAL GRAVES TO PHILIP STEPHENS]

London at Sandy Hook the 26th Septr., 1781.
Sir:—

When my last dispatch was made up and sent away by the Medea I had not received the several accounts from the Chesapeake, which shew that the French fleet arrived off Cape Henry the same day that Rear Admiral Sir Samuel Hood with the Leeward Island Squadron arrived off Sandy Hook. The last advices from the Chesapeake dated the 8th & 16th Sept'r from Captain Symonds of His Majesty's ship Charon marked letter A shew the state of preparation on the Naval part there.

The letters marked B and C, from Earl Cornwallis, the Engineers, and the several Captains report of Old Point Comfort and Hampton road, were sent by the Pearl frigate into Boston Bay, and did not come to my hands until the 15. inst. and at this time only seems to show that the Cheasapeak was an early object of atten-

tion— The Prudent and several frigates of the West
India Squadron with dispatches for Rear Admiral Sr.
Samuel Hood, joined the fleet as it was returning to
the Hook.

The enclosed letter marked D from Captain Bazely
of the Amphion, will show the effect of the descent
upon New London.

The last letters from Captain Biggs of the Amphitrite in Boston bay dated the 10th Septr. mention his
having taken in company with the General Monk four
prizes, and of his having fallen in with on the 4th off
Cape Ann two French Ships, one a Ship of the line, the
other a large frigate, and was chaced by them. Captain
Biggs likewise acquaints me that the Magicienne
French frigate had been taken by the Chatham Captain
Douglas on the 2d inst. off Cape Ann and carried away
for Halifax, in the action the French lost sixty men
killed and forty wounded in the Chatham, one killed
one wounded.

Captain Mowatt in a letter from Penobscot dated the
7th inst. acquaints me with the arrival of the Charles-
town and Vulture Sloop on the 4th Septr. at that place,
with two victuallers for the garrison there, and that they
had proceeded with a third to St. Johns river, and were
to convoy the Young William mast Ship from thence
to Halifax, where she is to be taken up by the Warwick
or Chatham and brought to New York.

Captain Mowatt confirms an account we had seen in
the Rebel papers of the Astrea and Hermionne French
frigates having fallen in with the Charles-town, Alle-
giance and Vulture off Spanish River Cape Breton, as
they were convoying the coal Ships and some victuallers
for the St. Lawrence bound to Quebec. In the action

Captain Evans was killed, but gives no further particulars of our loss, nor have I received any later accounts though the Rebel papers mention their privateers having taken most of the convoy.

Captain Evans's zeal and ardour led him into this unfortunate dilemma, for the Warwick and Garland arrived at Halifax with the Quebec fleet after a passage of seven days, and the Assurance would have been remasted and ready to accompany him in eight days, and had he waited, would probably have turned the catastrophe; but he was anxious to give way to the pressing solicitations of General Haldimand, and joined the victuallers to his coal convoy.

Whilst the fleet was off the Cheasapeak I sent the Solebay to cruise off Charles-town[1] to acquaint the commanding officers there of the French fleet being in possession of the Cheasapeak and to warn any Ships or convoys, of the danger in approaching the Capes of Virginia; And I ordered the Iris to cruize off Cape Henry; and as I came to the Northward I added the Nymphe and Pearl to watch the motions of the enemys fleet, and to bring the earliest intelligence.

Upon my return to Sandy Hook with the fleet on the 20th I was agreeably surprized to find that three of the Pegasus's convoy of victuallers had arrived at New York but from the length of time the bread had been on board, very little of it is fit to eat. I must beg leave to mention the bad effects which attend the manner of stowing the Navy victuallers, the salt provisions and rum are constantly stowed in coals, which is always found to heat to such a degree, that the pickle is dried up and the meat stinks and is seldom fit to eat, the rum-

---

[1] Charleston, S. C., long called Charlestown.

casks damaged, and a very great waste of that expensive article, the great heat of the hold also injures the dry provisions and renders it generally bad. The army victuallers having no coals, their provisions are generally good, which is next to demonstration.

I beg leave earnestly to recommend that the method of stowing the provisions with coals may be forbidden, as a method wasteful to Government and injurious to the Seamen, and probably a cause of diseases raging so much amongst the seamen in this climate.

[[The critical situation of affairs in the Cheasapeak occasioned the consultation of flag and general officers —when it seemed to be the opinion of the army that no diversion which they cou'd make by land would afford relief to Lord Cornwallis, that unless the Navy Cou'd land them in York or James Rivers, they saw very little probability before them: The State of the Cheasapeak, the Strength and Situation of the enemy's fleet, and the condition of our own were consider'd, and it was concluded upon, that the Ships of war Shou'd take on board what provisions they could for the army, embark the General Sr. Henry Clinton and six thousand troops if possible, and so soon as it cou'd be got ready, to make an attempt to force its way, and that three fire-Ships shou'd be added to the one already here which are now preparing with every possible exertion, and it was hoped the whole might be ready in ten days]]

The arrival of Rear Admiral Digby on the same evening (the 21st) in the Prince George, with the Canada and Lion, whilst we were together gave the greatest Satisfaction.

[The whole fleet are as busy as they can be but I am very apprehensive that so much as is wanted to the fleet, such a poverty of every kind of Stores and provisions, and so much to do for the army afterwards, will consume more time than was foreseen. Every exertion of mine and of any other officer in the fleet I may venture to affirm will not be wanting—]

I am sorry to find too much reason to believe the account of the naval losses in Captain Symonds's letter of the 16th, and to add to it the capture of the Savage Captn. Stirling after a very gallant defence.

Enclosed you will receive a Rebel newspaper containing the best account of the French Fleet in the Chesapeake exclusive of the Rhode Island Squadron, of any I have been able to procure.

I am, Sir,

Your Most Obedient

Humble Servant

Philip Stephens, Esqr.   THOS. GRAVES.

Endorsed No. 1 | Letter to Philip Stephens, Esqr. | 26 Septr. 1781 | from | Rear Adml. Graves | ₧ 3 Nov. 1781 |

Enclosure A

[LORD CORNWALLIS TO REAR ADMIRAL GRAVES]

(A Copy)   Portsmouth, 26 July 1781

Sir:—

I was honored with your Letter of the 12th of July by the Solebay, in which you mention a Desire of having a Harbour secured in the Cheasapeake for Line of

Battle Ships. I immediately ordered the Engineers to examine Old Point Comfort, and went thither myself with the Captains of the Navy on this Station.

You will receive a Copy of the Engineer's Report, with a Sketch of the Peninsula, and the Opinion of the Officers of the Navy relative to the Occupying and fortifying of that Post:—The Commander in Chief having signified to me in his Letter of the 11th Inst. that he thought a secure Harbour for Line of Battle Ships of so much Importance in the Chesapeak that he wished me to possess one, even if it should occupy all the Force at present in Virginia; and as it is our Unanimous Opinions, that Point Comfort will not answer the Purpose; I shall immediately seize and fortify the Posts of York and Glocester, and shall be happy at all times to concur in any Measures which may promote the Convenience & Advantage of His Majesty's Navy.

I have the Honour to be

Sir

Your most Obedient &

most humble Servant

CORNWALLIS.

Rear Admiral Graves
&ca. &ca. &ca.

A Copy.

T. Graves

Endorsed 4 | Copy of Lord Cornwallis | Letter of the 26th of July 1781 | relative to Old Point Comfort | B | In Ad. Graves's Lre | 26 Septr. | ℞ 3d Novr. |

Enclosure B

[CAPTAINS HUDSON, SYMONDS AND EVERITT
TO LORD CORNWALLIS]

(A Copy)

My Lord. Richmond Hampton Road, 24 July 1781

I[n] Consequence of a Requisition that your Lordship received from the Commander in Chief of His Majesty's Troops and Ships, relative to a Post at Old Point Comfort, for the Protection and Security of the Kings Ships, that m[a]y Occasionally be sent to the Chesapeak,

We whose names are hereunto subscribed, have taken as Accurate a Survey of that Place as possible, and are unanimously of Opinion from the Width of the Channel and depth of Water close to it, that any Superior Enemys Force coming in, may pass any Work that can possibly be Established there, with little Damage, or destroy it, with the Ships that may be there under its Protection.

We have the Honor to be

My Lord | Your Lordships most Obedient

very humble Servants

CHARLES HUDSON.

THOMAS SYMONDS.

The Right Honble. C. H. EVERITT.

Lieut. General Earl Cornwallis

&ca. &ca. &ca. Portsmouth.

A Copy

T. Graves

[100]

The Barfleur

From "The King's Ships," by courtesy of T. H. Parker Bros.

Endorsed 5 | Copy of Captain Hudsons, | Symonds, and Everitts, | report of Old Point Comfort | B | In R. A. Graves's Letter | Dated 26 Sepr. 1781.

Enclosure C

[LIEUTENANT SUTHERLAND TO LORD CORNWALLIS]

A Copy

Billy Ordnance Transport
Hampton Road, 25 July 1781.

Agreeable to Your Orders, I have examined the Ground on Old Point Comfort with as much accuracy as I possibly could, and for Your Lordships' better information I have made a Survey of the Ground, upon which is laid down the Width and Soundings of the Channel.

I beg leave to offer what appears to me respecting the Situation of a Work on that Spot.

The Ground where the Ruins of Fort George lays, is the fittest for a Work, but at the same time must be attended with many Inconveniencies.

The Level of the Ground there, is not above two feet higher than the high Water Mark, which from a very short Distance to the Deep Water must be destroyed by a Naval Attack; — The Great Width and Depth of the Channel, gives Ships the Advantage of passing the Fort with very little risque; I apprehend, fifteen hundred Yards is too great a distance for Batteries to stop Ships,

[101]

which is the Distance here; Ships that wish to pass the Fire of the Fort, have no Occasion to approach near.

Nor do I imagine a Fort built there could afford any Great Protection to an inferior and weak Fleet, anchored near the Fort, against a Superior Fleet of the Enemy which must have it in their Power to make their Own Disposition and place our Fleet between them and the Fort, the Channel affording no Bay for the Security of Ships under cover of a Fort.

The Time and Expense to build a Fort there, must be very considerable, from the low Situation of the Ground, which must necessarily cause the Soil to be moved from a considerable Distance to form the Ramparts and Parapets, and every other Material must be carried there, as the Timber on the Peninsula is unfit for any Purpose.

These are the Remarks which have occurred to me on examining the Ground, a Situation of a Work on Old Point Comfort, for the Protection of the Harbour and Fleet, which I humbly submit to your Lordship.

I have the Honor to be with great Respect Your Lordships most Obedt. & very humble Servt.

ALEXR. SUTHERLAND
Lt. Engineer.

The Rt. Honble.
Lt. General Earl Cornwallis &ca. &ca. &ca.

The above is a copy
A Copy   Charles Hudson
       T. Graves.

Endorsed 6 | Copy of the Engineer's | Report of Old Point Comfort | C | In R. A. Graves's Letter | Dated 26 Sepr. 1781.

Enclosure D

[CAPTAIN SYMONDS TO REAR ADMIRAL GRAVES]

Sir:—

I did myself the Honor to acquaint you by the Whale Boat Resolution, with the number of the Enemys Ships that had arrived within the Capes and the force they were then supposed to be, and sent a Duplicate and Triplicate by the Mary Schooner and Guadaloupes Whale Boat, since which I am informed it is the Fleet from the West Indies, Commanded by Compte de Grasse, consisting of upwards of Twenty Ships of the Line, some say twenty five and four Frigates, with some armed Ships.

Their Troops are landed in James River, and the Boats supposed to be come down.

Since the first Blockade by the Triton and two Frigates, they were joined off the Rivers Mouth (but more advanced) by the Glorieux and Valiant.

On Thursday there was an appearance of an attack with the Ships but in the Afternoon one of the large ones weighd, and ran out of sight, and was followed yesterday by the remaining Ships, last Night I sent down two Schooner Boats to Reconnoitre them, who return'd this afternoon, and the Lieut. of the Charon informs me, that this Morning one Line of Battle Ship weighd from the East side of Towers Marsh, and ran down the Bay, and two Frigates which were in Company with her dropt down soon afterwards, and remain now at the Horse Shoe. A Large Schooner coming down from

Hampton prevented the Look out Boats from venturing too near Lynn haven Bay, but from the distance they were from it, tho' Cloudy, the Lieut. thinks, had there been a Fleet there, He should have seen it.

Most of the Cannon and Ammunition of the Charon are landed and great part of the Crew in Tents and employed in enlarging the Sea Battery, and assisting the Army, the Guadaloupe is moor'd head and stern, opposite a Creek above York Town to enfilade a Gulley should the Enemy attempt to cross it.

The Foweys Ammunition and Provisions are ashore, and She is hauled close in, and her Men assisting at the Batteries. The Bonetta at Gloucester side, Captain Dundas ashore with his Officers and Men to man the Batteries, assisted by thirty of the Foweys Men.

Captain Palmer of the Vulcan, lays prepared to Act should the Enemys Ships return, and come up, and has three Horse Vessels, fitted, to act on the same Service.

I have only to wish, whenever an opportunity offers, a Supply of Provisions may be sent for his Majestys Ships.

I send this by a Vessel belonging to the Quarter Master Generals Department and have the honor to be
Sir
Your most Obedient
and most humble Servant.
THOS. SYMONDS

Charon York River
Virga. 8 Septr. 1781
Rear Admiral Graves &ca. &ca.

Enclosure E

[INTELLIGENCE FROM HAMPTON ROADS]

A Person who was at Buckroe a little before Sun
down yesterday Evening, says he had a view of James
River, all Hampton Road, The Capes and Horse Shoe,
and he could only observe two Ships in Hampton Road,
two as low as the Cape, two Ships and a Brig, one of
which was working down, one Ship and a Brig at
Anchor by the Swash of the Horse Shoe, two small Vessels near them, and two Boats near Willoughby Point.
He adds in a Postscript, the night of the 4th, Morning
of the 5th, Night of the 5th, and Morning of the 6th,
a Firing was certainly heard far without the Capes.

Dated 7th. Septr: 1781.

Enclosure F

[CAPTAIN SYMONDS TO REAR ADMIRAL GRAVES]

A Copy.

A Letter from another Person, enclosed in the above
Intelligence says that the French Ships have left their
Station after some Fleet, some say it is a Fleet from the
SoWd, others report it is possible to be a Fleet from
New York, but no certainty of either, and adds that the
French Boats are come down James River, and are

gone to [New] York, and that it is reported Three thousand French Troops, will be landed in Gloucester or in its Neighborhood.

T. GRAVES.

Endorsed 7 | Copy of Capt Symonds Letter | from York River, dated the | 7th and 8th September 1781. | A | In R. A. Graves's Letter dated 26 Sepr. 1781.

Enclosure G

[CAPTAIN SYMONDS TO REAR ADMIRAL GRAVES]

Copy Charon York River Virginia, 16th Sepr. 1781.
Sir—

On the 8th instant I did myself the honor to acquaint you of the enemy's motions and the position of His Majesty's Ships to act for the protection of this post and sent a duplicate by another Vessel the same evening.

On the 12 I received certain information of an officer who was in the look-out-boat, that twenty large Ships were at anchor between the Horse Shoe and York Spit, and the next day I saw eleven or twelve Ships go up the Cheasapeak, four of which appeared to be frigates, and the same afternoon two Ships of the line and a frigate anchored at the mouth of this River and have continued ever since, and four line of battle Ships went up the Bay and anchored off the Patuxent.

This morning I learn that General Washington is

[106]

arrived at Williamsburg, that ten men of war are lying just below Egg Islands, and the body of the enemys fleet at the Horse shoe and that the Squadron from Rhode Island had joined the Compte de Grasse, and that their number consisted of thirty six Sail of the line besides frigates, that the ships that went up the bay were mostly transports and intended to bring down troops from Baltimore, and that as soon as they arrive at the enemys encampment, York will be attacked both by land and Sea.

I am happy to add that the Seamen work with the greatest Spirits and exertion in cutting down wood for redoubts or Co-operating in any piece of Service Lord Cornwallis is desirous of having them employed on.—

I have the honor to be | Sir
Your most Obedient and | most humble Servant
THOMAS SYMONDS.

Rear Admiral Graves
P.S. A flag of truce which I sent to the French Ships advanced at the requisition of Lord Cornwallis, is this morning returned and brought up Lieut. Conway of His Majesty's late Sloop Cormorant, which was captured by the French fleet, as were also the Sandwich armed Ship and South Carolina pacquet, the latter having Lord Rawdon on board, and I am Sorry to inform you that the Richmond and Iris are both taken and now in Lynne haven bay.

A Copy   T. Graves

Endorsed 6 | 16th Septr. 1781 | Copy of Captain Symonds letter | dated York river Virginia | A | In R. A. Graves's Letter | dated 26 Sepr. 1781.

Enclosure H

[CAPTAIN BAZELY TO REAR ADMIRAL GRAVES]

(Copy)

Amphion off New London, 8th Septr. 1781.

Sir—

I have the satisfaction to inform you that I arrived off this port at 2 A.M., on the 6th instant, at which time an unfortunate change of wind took place directly out of the harbour, which prevented my anchoring till ½ past 6. I then disposed of the armed vessels and Transports agreeable to Brigadier General Arnolds wishes, in order to effect a covering and landing of the troops, which was completed by nine oClock. The armed vessels and boats I immediately afterwards ordered to be put in preparation under the direction of Captain Shepherd of the Recovery, to proceed up the River and act in conjunction with the Army, at any moment their assistance was required to and in effecting the destruction of the port of New London &ca agreeable to your orders, which would have finally taken place, but for the alarm guns which were fired from the forts at day break, by this means I was deprived of getting hold of their shipping at anchor in the stream, which with most of those at the Wharfs, proceeded some miles up the river so far as to prevent by any possible means my taking or destroying of them. Those few remaining at the Wharfs were burned by the army with the towns on both sides, soon after they had got possession of them. The ardour and determined conduct shewn by the

Troops in storming of the ports deserve (in my opinion) the highest enccomiums.

I am now proceeding with all possible dispatch with the armed vessels and transports to New York. The Lurcher armed brig I have dispatched with General Arnold's Aid de Camp and Lieut. Burns of the Amphion, who will present you this letter, to whom I beg leave to refer you for any further particulars.

I have the honor to be

Sir

Your most Obedient Servant

JOHN BAZELY.

Commodore Affleck, &c &c,
New York.

A Copy. T. Graves.

Endorsed 9 | Copy of Captain Bazelys | Letter of the Destruction of New London | D | In R. A. Graves's Letter | Dated 26 Sepr. 1781.

Enclosure I

[SCHEDULE OF THE CONTENTS OF THIS PACKET]

No. 1—Letter to Philip Stephens, Esqr. 26 Sepr.
    2— do.   do.   acknowledging the receipt of their Lordships' dispatches, 22 Sepr.
    3—State and Condition of the Fleet on the 19th Septr. 1781.
    4—Copy of Lord Cornwallis's Letter of the 26th July, relative to Old Point Comfort.

[109]

5—Copy of Captain Symonds, Hudson's and Everitt's report of do.

6—Copy of the Engineer's report   do.

7—Copy of Captain Symond's Letter of the 8th Septemr.

8—Copy of   do.   do.   16th Septemr.

9—Copy of Captain Bazely's Letter of the destruction of New London.

10—Rebel Newspapers containing a List of the French Naval Force in the Chesapeake, exclusive of those under Monsr. de Barras from Rhode Island.[1]

11—Schedule.

Endorsed No. 11 | Schedule | In R. A. Graves's Letter | Dated 26th Sepr. 1781.

[REAR ADMIRAL GRAVES TO PHILIP STEPHENS]

London off New York the 26th Septr. 1781.

Sir

I have received by the Prince George Rear Admiral Digby, who arrived off the Bar in company with the Canada and Lion on the 24th inst., the Lords Commissioners of the Admiralty's order of the 19th July, to Vice Admiral Arbuthnot, to deliver up to Rear Admiral Digby appointed Commander in Chief in North America, attested copies of all orders relative to the said command, and also their Lordships order of the 9th

[1] Not available.

July, directing me to proceed in the London to Jamaica to reinforce the Squadron of His Majesty's Ships on that Station, and put myself under the command of Vice-Admiral Sr. Peter Parker or the Commanding Officer of the said Squadron &c &c. Also a letter directed on His Majesty's Service to Vice Admiral Sir Peter Parker or the Commanding Officer for the time being. All which I shall comply with so soon as the London can be spared from the Service of the Station, of which I shall not make myself the judge—their Lordships having been pleased to appoint me to serve where I must act in a Subordinate Situation.

By this conveyance I transmit for their Lordships information an account of the Ships purchased and armed, for His Majesty's Service the changes and promotions which have arisen from deaths and other accidents, of all which I hope their Lordships will be pleased to approve.

I must beg leave to state to their Lordships in my own behalf, that being superceded by a junior officer, and sent to another Station where I can only be second and possibly third in command, after having been nearly four years upon severe and very critical Services, imply's such a disapprobation of my conduct as will certainly discredit me in the opinion of mankind, who are generally inclined to construe mens real Sentiments from their actions. I dare hope their Lordships will not suffer me to remain long in so painful a situation.   I am
                    Sir
              Your most Obedient
              Humble Servant—
Philip Stephens Esqr.   THOS. GRAVES.

[111]

Endorsed Rear Adml. Graves | Letter to Philip Stephens Esqr. | 26th Septr. 1781 | ℞ 3 Nov 1781 | (5 Inclosures)[1]

[REAR ADMIRAL GRAVES TO THE LORDS COMMISSIONERS OF THE ADMIRALTY]

London off New York the 27th Septr. 1781

Sir—

I beg you will acquaint their Lordships that the Pearl frigate arrived of the Hook last night, being detached by Captain Ford of the Nymphe, left to watch the motions of the enemy in the Cheasapeak, with the enclosed intelligence, received from a Cartel bound to this port from the Cheasapeak, which he thought it prudent to send by a frigate to gain time.

I am
Sir
Your most Obedient
humble Servant
THOS. GRAVES.

P.S.

The Warwick from convoying the Quebec fleet, arrived at the Hook last Evening.

Philip Stephens Esqr.

Endorsed 27 Sepr. 1781 | Rear Adml. Graves | ℞ 3 Nov | (1 Inclosure)

[1] None available.

Enclosure

[INTELLIGENCE BY THE PEARL   CAPTN. MONTAGU]

Thursday the 20th Septr. 1781.   Sent the first lieutenant on board the Pensylvania Packet a Cartel from the
French fleet in the Cheasapeak bound to New York,
where he gained the following intelligence from a person who said he had been master of a brig that was
captured by the French.—

That the French fleet consisted of thirty six Sail of
the line mostly of 74 guns—that 28 sail of the line with
two frigates besides the Richmond and Iris, lay between the Capes of Virginia the day they parted,
(which was the 19th inst.) that two sail of the line and
some frigates were up the river and that a Squadron of
six sail of the line were at sea hed did not know where
they were gone but supposed cruizing and they were incomparable fast sailors.   That the French fleet had
received very little damage in the action in which they
had 23 Sail of the line and the Romulus he was on
board one of them during the action several of their
Ships of the line were up the rivers at the time our fleet
appeared off and coud not work down—   The Rhode
Island Fleet had not joined the day of action—   Genl.
Washington had joined the French army and had sur-
rounded Lord Cornwallis.
                                              GEO. MONTAGU.

(Copy) T. Graves.

Endorsed Intelligence from the | Cheseapeak by the |
Pearl | In R. A. Graves' | 27 Sepr. 1781.

[113]

[REAR ADMIRAL GRAVES TO PHILIP STEPHENS]

London in the North River New York
13th Octr. 1781.

Sir—

I am afraid that in the hurry of more important business, the account of captured Ships bought into the Service and commissioned, has not been so regular and full
as it ought to have been. I will therefore trouble you
with the detail though it may be a recapitulation.

In my letter of the 20th Augt. their Lordships were
acquainted with the distress'd State of the Swift brigantine Sloop of war, which has since been condemned
as totally unfit for Service. At the same time the
Avenger and Keppel both Sloops of war, were found
to be so much damaged as to be kept above water only
by doubling their bottoms. I therefore ordered to be
purchased, the Rattlesnake, American privateer Ship of
18 guns four pounders, prize to the Amphitrite, of 200
Tons burthen, a very complete vessel almost new and
requiring nothing more than to secure her magazine
and build Storerooms.

At this time the Belisarius privateer Ship of twenty
nine pounders and four small guns was brought in by
the Medea and Amphitrite. It was her first cruise she
was remarkably well constructed and quite new, of five
hundred tons and thought to be the most complete vessel ever taken from the Americans. I therefore purchased her and put her upon the establishment of a
twenty-four gun ship that she might not be bought by
American agents and act against us in a short time.

The Swallow Sloop of war being burned and the Rover Sloop of war wreck'd in the month of August, I order'd the Aurora-American Ship privateer of eighteen six pounders, prize to the Royal Oak to be purchased as she was a well built vessel, of exceeding good dimensions, large and esteem'd to sail remarkably fast, of three hundred tons burthen, and put her upon the Sloop established [establishment?] and called her the Mentor.

The 24h Septem: a Council of War of General and Flag Officers determining that three fireships should be added to the Fleet then refitting to go against the enemy, the Elizabeth, Empress of Russia, and Loyal Club, were chosen from amongst the transports for that Service and commission'd by the names of the Lucifer, Volcano, and Conflagration.

I flatter myself their Lordships will be satisfied with the propriety of my conduct in these several purchases, and that it was necessary to keep up the number of small active vessels for the protection of this very extensive coast.

The several promotions and appointments occasioned by those purchases, as well as those arising from deaths and other accidents will be brought together in one table, and I hope will meet with their Lordships approbation and be confirmed according to the dates of their Several appointments.

I am

Sir

Your most Obedient

Humble Servant

THOS. GRAVES.

Philip Stephens Esqr.

Endorsed No. 1 | Rear Adml. Graves | Letter to Philip
Stephens Esqr. | 13th Octr 1781 | ℞ 14 Nov.

[REAR ADMIRAL HOOD TO GEORGE JACKSON]

Barfleur, Sandy Hook, 14th of October, 1781.
Duplicate.
My dear Jackson:—
I wrote you by the last packet, a duplicate of which
you will have by another packet or the Lively. Both
have been said to sail day after day for several past.
Whichever this goes by you shall have a duplicate by
the other, from the desire I have of telling you what
really passes here—though, by-the-by, I am monstrous
angry with you for not writing me a line by the August
packet, as you must know she would find me upon this
coast.

On the 24th of last month I attended a consultation
of generals and admirals at Sir H. Clinton's, when it
was agreed to attempt by the united efforts of army and
navy to relieve Lord Cornwallis in the Chesapeake, and
I proposed to have three or four fireships immediately
prepared, with which the enemy's fleet may possibly be
deranged and thrown into some confusion, and thereby
give a favourable opening for pushing through it. This
was approved, and upwards of 5,000 troops are to be
embarked in the King's ships. While this business was
under deliberation, word was brought that Rear-Admiral Digby with the Canada and Lion were off the
Bar, and as the wind was against their entering the
port, I went out to the Prince George next morning

early, and had the happiness to find his Royal High-
ness,[1] and all on board, in most perfect health. I thank
God the disabled ships are now ready, and but for an
accident of the Alcides driving on board the Shrewsbury and carrying away her bowsprit and foreyard, I
imagine all the ships would have been here this day;
but I hope and trust they will be down tomorrow, and
that we shall be moving the day after if the wind will
permit. Every moment, my dear Jackson, is prescious;
and I flattered myself when we came in that we should
ere this have been in the Chesapeake, but the repairs of
the squadron have gone on unaccountably tedious,
which has filled me with apprehension that we shall be
too late to give relief to Lord Cornwallis. I pray God
grant my fears may prove abortive!

It would, in my humble opinion, have been a most
fortunate event had Mr. Graves gone off to Jamaica
upon Mr. Digby's arrival as commander-in-chief by
commission, and I am persuaded you will think so too,
when I relate one circumstance only. On the 7th I
received a letter from Mr. Graves, desiring I would
meet the flag officers and some captains, upon a consultation on board the London at ten o'clock the next
morning, and acquaint Captain Cornwallis and Captain Reynolds that their company was desired also.
Soon after we were assembled, Mr. Graves proposed,
and wished to reduce to writing, the following question,
"Whether it was practicable to relieve Lord Cornwallis
in the Chesapeake?" This astonished me exceedingly,
as it seemed plainly to indicate a design of having
difficulties started against attempting what the generals
and admirals had *most unanimously* agreed to, and

[1] Prince William, afterward King William IV.

given under their hands on the 24th of last month, and occasioned my replying immediately that it appeared to me a very unnecessary and improper question, as it had been already maturely discussed and determined upon to be attempted with all the expedition possible; that my opinion had been very strong and pointed (which I was ready to give in writing with my name to it), that an attempt under every risk should be made to force a junction with the troops the commander-in-chief embarks in his Majesty's fleet with the army under General Earl Cornwallis at York; and admitting that junction to be made without much loss, and the provisions landed, I was also of opinion the first favourable opportunity should be embraced of attacking the French fleet, though I own to you I think very meanly of the ability of the present commanding officer. I know he is a *cunning* man, he may be a good theoretical man, but he is certainly a bad practical one, and most clearly proved himself on the 5th of last month to be unequal to the conducting of a great squadron. If it shall please the Almighty to give success to the arms of his Majesty in the business we are going upon, I think we shall stand a tiptoe. The Torbay and Prince William arrived on the 13th, a noble acquisition, and makes my heart bound with joy. Why the Chatham is not with us also is matter of astonishment to me. With best affections to Mrs. Jackson,

Ever yours most sincerely,

S. H.

I trust you will bear in mind that I write to you most *confidentially*. *Desperate* cases require *bold* remedies.

[REAR ADMIRAL GRAVES TO PHILIP STEPHENS]

London at New York—the 16th Octr. 1781—
Sir—

Be pleased to acquaint their Lordships that the Santa Margarita arrived here the 7h inst. with her convoy from Cork, consisting of forty two sail for New York, three only had parted company. Their lordships orders by her dated the 11h June directed to Vice Admiral Arbuthnot I have left with Rear Admiral Digby to carry into execution, as well all other orders & regulations respecting the North American Station.

The Carysfort which I had sent to Halifax upon my returning with the Fleet, returned the 8h and in her way back had the good fortune to meet with a mast Ship bound to Cape Francois on the French king's account with a considerable quantity of masts for large Ships; she had only parted from her convoy a few hours before, and at this time of scarcity is a most valuable acquisition, there being hardly a spar left in the yard.

Captain Douglas acquaints me that the money for congress came in single men of war vizt. the Sybil, Magicienne, and Resolve. The enclosed letter from Sr. Andrew Hamond gives an idea of the strength of Halifax.

The Janus Captain O'Hara arrived here the 8h being part of the Jamaica convoy for Europe sent to this place by Captain Bowyer being leaky the 17h Septr. to refit, they parted company in the latitude 26° 26′ No. longitude 70° 0′ W. the builder reports to me that she must be lightend and taken upon the ways before she can go to Sea.

[119]

The Belisarius Sailed on the 8h with dispatches for Halifax, and carried the officers appointed to the Magicienne, which I had order'd to be purchased and was fitting at Halifax. The officers who have seen the Magicienne represent her as a very capital frigate, new, and equal to any of our six and thirtys. I have appointed Captain Thomas Graves of the Bedford to the command of her, and appointed Captain Scott from the Beaumont to take post in the Bedford but as Captain Graves who has distinguished himself in the action, desired to remain in the Bedford so long as there was a prospect of a general action I cou'd not resist so spirited an offer, and therefore sent Captain Scott with an order to fit the Magicienne out and bring her to this place.

The Torbay and Prince William arriv'd here the 11h having parted from the Jamaica convoy the 21t Septr. In a gale of wind and they went thro' the gulph tho' the convoy went thro' the windward passage.

The 13 inst. in a squall of wind the Alcide parted her cable and fell on board the Shrewsbury which carried away her fore yard and bowsprit This ugly accident threw us back just at the time the troops were embarked to fall down with the first division of the men of war from Staten Island to Sandy Hook. Two Ships parted their cables at Staten Island, & several drove in the North River.

The Nymphe return'd from cruizing off Cape Henry and brought in five prizes taken by her and the Amphion. The Nymphe was never able to look into the Cheasapeak the French cruisers constantly chacing off every thing which appeared.

The same day came in a dispatch from the Earl Cornwallis which gives us but little prospect of being able to effect a relief, I enclose a copy of as much as the General has communicated of the contents. Captain Symonds has not given me any account but by the boatmen we learn that a transport had taken fire from the Enemy's shot and burnt the Charon together with a second transport.

The Enemy having collected all their Naval strength between the Horse Shoe & York Spit plainly pointed out that they had little to apprehend from an attempt in James river. Lord Cornwallis letter confirms that opinion, and I am inclined to beleive that with the advantage of position and numbers, they think there is as little to apprehend from an attempt to force York River.

The excessive want of stores and provisions and the immense repairs wanted for a crazy and shatter'd Squadron, with many cross accidents which have interven'd, has thrown back the equipment of the Squadron to a great distance. They are not quite ready.—They are now very short of bread, and all the ovens will not keep up the daily consumption—Several Ships have parted their cables, others broke their anchors, and three been on shore; that I see no end to disappointments.

I am | Sir

Your most Obedient

Humble Servant

THOS. GRAVES.

Philip Stephens Esqr.

Endorsed No 2 | Rear Adml. Graves | Letter to P. Stephens Esqr. | 16h Octor. 1781   Recd. 14 Nov

Enclosure A

[LORD CORNWALLIS TO GENERAL CLINTON]

(Copy)

York Town Virginia, 12 M
11th October 1781.

Sir—

Cochran arrived yesterday, I have only to repeat what I said in my Letter of the 3d That nothing but a direct move to York River which includes a Successful Naval Action can save us.

The Enemy made their first Parallel on the Night of the 6th at the distance of Six Hundred Yards, and perfected it, & Constructed Places of Arms and Batteries with great regularity and Caution. On the Evening of the 9th their Batteries Opened and have since continued firing without intermission, with about Forty Pieces of Cannon, mostly heavy, and 16 Mortars from 8 to 16 Inches, We have lost about Seventy Men, and many of our Works are Considerably damaged.

With such Works on disadvantageous ground against so powerful an attack, we cannot hope to make a very long Resistance.

I have the honor to be | &ca.
Sign'd CORNWALLIS.

P.S. 5. P M
Since the above was written
we have lost Thirty Men.

Sir Henry Clinton K.B.

Endorsed No. 3 | Copy of a Letter from Lord | Cornwallis, dated York Town | Virginia 11th October 1781 | In R. A. Graves's Letter | Dated 16h Octr 1781. |

Enclosure B

[CAPTAIN DOUGLAS TO REAR ADMIRAL GRAVES]

Copy

Chatham at Halifax the 7th Septemr. 1781.

Sir—

I have the honor to acquaint you that I arrived here yesterday with the French Frigate La Magicienne, of thirty-two guns, twelve pounders, and two Hundred and eighty Men, commanded by the Seiur de la Bouchetiere which was taken by His Majesty's Ship under my Command on the 2d Instant, about three Miles from the Harbour of Boston. The French Officer behaved gallantly and engaged the Chatham (although close alongside) for half an hour, which gave time to a Store Ship which he had under his Convoy from Portsmouth in New Hampshire, to escape into Boston.

The Magicienne is a New Frigate and lately sheathed with Copper, She had Thirty two Men killed in the Action, and fifty five wounded. I have the satisfaction to inform you that only two Men were killed and four slightly wounded on board the Chatham.

I shall remain here only until I can get in a new

Main Mast, which will be ready in a few days, and I shall then proceed to execute your further Orders.

I have the honor to be | Sir
Your most Obedient | humble Servant
A. J. DOUGLAS.

Rear Admiral Graves &ca. &ca. &ca.

Endorsed No 4 | Copy Of Captain Douglases letter | upon the Capture of the French | Frigate La Magicienne, dated | Halifax 7th September 1781. | In R. A. Graves's Letter | Dated 16 Octr. 1781.

Enclosure C

[CAPTAIN HAMMOND TO REAR ADMIRAL GRAVES]

(Copy)

Halifax 10th September 1781.

Sir—

I have received by the Carysfort the Intelligence you have been pleased to send hither respecting the Sailing of the French Squadron.

I think it necessary to inform you Sir that although this Place is now renderd by its Fortifications extremely strong against an Attack from the Enemy, yet the Engineer has in planning the Defence always reckon'd upon a Number of Seamen to Work the Guns. There are in several Batteries upwards of 150 Peices of heavy Cannon mounted, and the Number of Artillery Men in the Garrison does not exceed eighty five Men.

As there are now in the Harbour more Prisoners than can conveniently be accomodated without having another Prison Ship, I shall send the Cartel which had been taken up by Sir Richard Hughes immediately to France, with one Hundred Prisoners on board, in which will go the French Captain and Lieutenants of the Magicienne whom I have exchanged for Captain Gayton, and his two Lieutenants.

I have the honor to be | Sir

Your most obedient

humble Servant

A S HAMMOND.

To

    Rear Admiral Graves

        &ca. &ca. &ca.

Endorsed No. 5 | Copy of Letter from Sir | Andw. Snape Hammond | dated 10th Septr. 1781. | respecting the state of the Fortifications | at Halifax. | In R. A. Graves's Letter | Dated 16 Octr. 1781.

Enclosure D

[LIST OF THE FRENCH FLEET IN THE CHEASAPEAK UNDER THE COMMAND OF LIEUT. GENERAL COUNT DE GRASSE 18H SEPTR. 1781]

	Guns			Guns
La Ville de Paris	104	*Flag Ships*	La Triton	64
La Duc de Bourgoyne	80		La Solitaire	64
La Languedoc	84		La Caton	64
L'Auguste	84		La Marseilles	64
La St. Esprit	84		St. Eveille	64
La Northumberland	74		La Provence	64
La Diademe	74		La Jason	64
La Souverain	74		La Refleche	64
La Glorieux	74		L'Ardent	64
La Citoyen	74		L'Experiment	50
La Victoire	74		La Romulus	44
La Desten	74			
La Palmier	74		FRIGATES	
La Neptune	74		St Andromaque	
La Sceptre	74		La Ralieuse	
La Hercules	74		La Surveillante	
La Zele	74		La Concorde	
La Bourgogne	74		La Gentille	
La Caesar	74		St Aigrette	
La Valiant	74		La Diligente	
La Scipion	74		La Serpente	
La Pluton	74		St Iris	
La Victor	74		La Richmond	
La Conquerant	74		SLOOPS	
La Magnanime	74		La Cormorant	14
			La Loyalist	16

Frigates bracket: From 40 to 32 Guns

ARMED SHIP

Sandurck   .   .   .   .

Endorsed List of the French fleet in | the Cheasapeak | No 6 in R. A. Graves's Letter | Dated 16 octr. 1781.

Enclosure E

A List of Ships Purchased into His Majestys Service, pr. order of Thomas Graves Esqr. Rear Admiral of the Red &ca. &ca. &ca. North America between the 27th of July 1781, and the 26th of September 1781.

me when urchased	Sort of Vessel	Name	Number of			
			Tons	Men	Guns	
1781						
ly 28th	Ship	Rattlesnake - - -	200	125	18	New. Bought in the Room of the Swift Sloop, Condemnd as unfit for Service.
gust 8th	Ship	Belisarius - - - -	500	160	24	Rebel Frigate. New.
ptr. 11	Ship	Aurora (now called the Mentor)	230	125	18	New. Bought in the room of the Rover wreck'd.—
' 22	Ship	La Magicienne - -	. .	280	32	French Frigate mounting 32 twelve pounders, allmost new, and Copperd.
' 25	Ship	Empress of Russia, now the Volcano Fire Ship				
' 25	Ship	Elizabeth, now the Lucifer Fire Ship.				
' 25	Ship	Loyal Club, now the Conflagration Fire Ship				

Thos. Graves.

Endorsed No. 7 | A List of Ships Purchased | pr. Order of Thos. Graves Esqre. | Rear Adml. of the Red &c &c &c | In R. A. Graves's Letter | Dated 16 Octr. 1781

[127]

Enclosure F

[CAPTAIN SYMONDS TO REAR ADMIRAL GRAVES]

(Copy)

Charon York River Virginia 29 Septr. 1781.

Sir

On the 16h Instant by a Vessel sent express from Lord Cornwallis, I did myself the Honor to inform you of the Situation of the Enemys Ships and their Numbers, as near as I could learn, the Experiment I find is one included in their Line.

The Enemy's movements from Cape Henry to York River since that time, has been different, some times twenty large Ships have layed for three or four Days between Cape Henry and Towes's Marsh, and in a Day or two after, four or five more have advanced higher up, at present the Body of the Fleet lay between the Horseshoe and York Spit, and two Sail of the Line and a Frigate below Towes's Marsh, about eight Miles from York Town.

On the 21t the Enemy's Ships advanced consisting of three Sail of the Line and a Frigate, from a Report from our Guard Boats, their not keeping that look out, which might be expected from advanced Ships I ordered four Vessels belonging to the Quarter Master Generals Department to be fitted as Fire Vessels, with the utmost expedition, and directed Captain Palmer of the Vulcan to proceed in the Night, whenever the Wind offered to endeavour to destroy the Enemy, or drive them from the Post they had taken as it prevented a

Communication from New York or the Eastern Shore, he took a favourable Opportunity of the Night of the 22d about twelve O.Clock to slip with the other Vessels, and ran down to the French Squadron, and though he did not meet with the Success which was to be wished, he obliged all the Enemys Ships to cut, and two Sail of the Line were run ashore, and on board each other, but afterwards got off, owing to very moderate Weather, one of which I am convinced met with considerable Damage as she ran down the next Day to join her Admiral. I cannot say too much in favor of Captn. Palmers behaviour on this Occasion, it was Spirited and well conducted, and had not the Enemy been alarmed at almost the Instant he was within hail of them, when they sliped, two Ships of the Line must have been destroyed.

In the small Vessels, I sent Lieuts. James and Symonds, of the Charm and Lieut. Conway of His Majestys late Sloop Cormorant, whose Conduct on this Business, I have every reason to approve of.

Since the Vulcan was burnt, I have fitted out two of the oldest Transports to act as Fire ships in Case the Enemys Ships should attempt to come up to attack the Sea Batteries.

Yesterday morning the Enemy appeared in great Numbers by Land, and this Evening have encamped within two Miles of the Town.

I have the Honor to be

Sir

Your most obedt. & very humbl. Sert.

THOMAS SYMONDS.

To
Thomas Graves Esqr.
&ca. &ca.

[129]

Endorsed No. 10 | Copy of Captn. Symonds | Letter, dated York River | 29th Septr. 1781. | In R. A. Graves's Letter | Dated 16 Octr. 1781.

Enclosure G

[SCHEDULE OF THIS PACQUET]

No 1 .... Letter to P. Stephens Esqr. 13 Octo
  2 .... Ditto   16 Octo
  3 .... Copy of a Letter from Earl Cornwallis dated 11h October 1781
  4 .... Copy of a letter from Captain **Douglas** of His Majesty's Ship Chatham dated 7h Sep. 1781.
  5 .... Copy of a letter from Sr. A. S. Hammond dated 10 Septr. 1781.—
  6 .... List of the French fleet in the Cheasapeak 18 Septr. 1781.—
  7 .... List of Ships purchased.—
  8 .... List of Promotions & Removals of Commission'd Officers.—[1]
  9 .... List of Promotions & Removals of Warrant Officers [1]
 10 .... Copy of Captain Symonds letter dated York River 29h Septr. 1781.—

Endorsed Schedule | In R. A. Graves's Letter | Dated 16 Octr. 1781

[1] Not available.

[REAR ADMIRAL GRAVES TO PHILIP STEPHENS]

London off Sandy Hook 19th Octor. 1781.—
Sir:—

My last letter cou'd not fix the time of my sailing,
The Ships were however moving down as they cou'd be
got ready, and on the 17th so soon as the tide serv'd, I
got under sail with the remainder of the squadron, except the Shrewsbury Montagu and Europe, and got
down with the help of the afternoon tide to Sandy
Hook.—

The next morning we embarked all the troops on
board the men of war from the transports, where they
had been in readiness for us some days, to the amount
of Seven thousand one hundred and forty nine (officers
included.) The Princessa went over the Bar with her
provisions and water in transports the same eveng.

The afternoon's tide all the Ships of easy draught of
water went over the bar, one of the ships left at York
joined us and this morning the whole fleet sailed and
got safe over the bar consisting of twenty five sail of the
line, two fifty's and eight frigates; and the whole are
now under sail for the Cheasapeak.

A numerous convoy appears off, which we judge to
be the English convoy as they are making for this place,
and the most advanced shew English colours; the Per-
severance that I sent out to speak with them not being
yet return'd, I cannot acknowledge the receipt of any
dispatches, and being willing to send the Generals and
my own letters immediately upon the movement of the
fleet, I wou'd not defer a moment to inform their Lord-

ships of so important a move— The Lively which car-
ries this letter will accompany the Packet to convoy
with greater certainty the counter part.

I am

Sir

Your most Obedient

Humble Servant

THOS. GRAVES.

P.S.

Enclosed you will receive the State & Condition of
the Fleet. T. G.

Philip Stephens Esqr.

Endorsed 19 Octr 1781 | Rear Adml. Graves | ℞ 14
Nov

[REAR ADMIRAL GRAVES TO PHILIP STEPHENS]

London at Sea 7 P.M. 19th Octr. 1781.

Sir—

I beg leave to acquaint you for their Lordships information, that the fleet mention'd in my letter of this
day, proves to be the Centurion and her convoy, which
are all arriv'd safe (except eight private traders) and
are now standing in for the Hook.

I am

Sir

Your most Obedient

Humble Servant

Philip Stephens Esqr.— THOS. GRAVES.

Endorsed 19 Octr. 1781 | R. A. Graves | ℞ 14 Nov

[132]

[ADMIRAL RODNEY TO GEORGE JACKSON[1]]

Bath, 19th of October, 1781.

My dear Sir:—

This morning I was favoured with yours of the 17th inst. and you may be assured that everything shall be done by me that can contribute towards settling the Eustatius affair, and that when the papers Mr. Crespigny intends reading are presented to me I will execute them as desired, and hope, on my arrival in town, every necessary paper for me to sign will be ready before I leave England, and all money affairs settled to the satisfaction of all parties; but at present I find myself very much out of order with a very violent pain in my stomach, which has continued these four days and reduced me much, which the news from America and Mr. Graves's letter has increased; for it is impossible for me not to feel most sensibly any news which appears to me of the most fatal consequences to my country, and more especially where the navy has been concerned. . .
In vain may plans be concerted to defeat the designs of the public enemy if inferior officers will take upon them to act in direct opposition to the orders and letters of their superiors, and lie idle in port when their duty ought to have obliged them to have been at sea to watch the motions of the public enemy, and prevent the junction of their squadrons. Had Mr. Graves attended to the intelligence I sent him six weeks before I left the West Indies, as likewise to two other expresses I sent

[1] Letters of Sir Samuel Hood, edited by David Hannay, Navy Records Society, Vol. III, 44.

him pressing his junction with his whole squadron with Sir Samuel Hood off the Capes of Virginia, he had been on that station long before De Grasse, and, of course, prevented the latter landing his troops in Virginia. The commanding officer, likewise, at Jamaica, had no right to detain the Torbay and Prince William, whose captains had my positive orders not to lose a moment's time (after seeing the Jamaica convoy safe at that island) in joining Sir Samuel Hood at or off the Chesapeake. . . . I likewise pressed Sir Peter Parker to send some of his ships with them, as I was assured the French fleet were intended for that coast, and that, in all probability, the fate of the war depended upon his Majesty's fleet being in full force, and that the blow on which depended the sovereignty of the [oc]ean must be struck off the coast of Virginia. I advised Sir S. Hood by all means to guard the mouth of the Chesapeake, to anchor in Hampton Road if [there was] occasion, to keep his frigates cruizing off the coast to the southward, that he might have timely notice of the enemy's approach, and to despatch one of his frigates to Mr. Graves, acquainting [him] with his arrival, and pressing a speedy junction, no one thing of which has been regarded. The Commander at Jamaica has detained the Torbay and Prince William. Mr. Graves, so far from joining Sir Samuel Hood off the Capes, lay idle at Sandy Hook, and suffered the French squadron from Rhode Island to join De Grasse, which cruizing from ten to forty leagues from Sandy Hook or by joining Sir S. Hood he might have prevented, and even, when he afterwards joined him, four of his line-of-battle ships were wanting. Ought any man, after the notice he had received, to have separated his squadron of line-of-battle ships?

The whole should have been kept in a body, and always ready to act at a moment's warning, and suffered no repairs, but momentary ones, till the campaign was over.

His letter I cannot understand, and his terms, particularly his cut up, a term neither military or seamanlike; it must have been a mistake in printing; he meant cut off the vans from the centre. The other part of the letter contradicts itself, and his mode of fighting I will never follow. He tells me that his line did not extend so far as the enemy's rear. I should have been sorry if it had, and a general battle ensued; it would have given the advantage they could have wished, and brought their whole twenty-four ships of the line against the English nineteen, whereas by watching his opportunity, if the enemy had extended their line to any considerable distance, by contracting his own he might have brought his nineteen against the enemy's fourteen or fifteen, and by a close action totally disabled them before they could have received succour from the remainder, and in all probability have gained thereby a complete victory. Such would have been the battle of the 17th of April had I been obeyed, such would have been the late battle off the Capes, and more especially if all the line-of-battle ships *had* (as they ought) been joined. Our numbers then had been twenty-five, viz. four of Admiral Graves and my two from Jamaica. In my poor opinion the French have gained the most important victory, and nothing can save America but the instant return of the fleet from New York with 5,000 troops and Digby's squadron; but even then the French fleet will have done their business and gone. If not, block them up to eternity; suffer none to escape from the Chesapeake; they will soon be tired of their station, and wish they had never taken the part of America. I could say much more on this subject, but it is impossible for you to conceive the fatigue the writing this letter has occasioned. I must conclude with saying that if they intend the war should be concluded, *there must be* but one General and one Admiral commanding in chief in America and West Indies.

Adieu, my dear Sir,

Yours most sincerely,

G. B. RODNEY.

My best respects to Mrs. Jackson.

Endorsed.—The 19th of October, 1781. Sir George Rodney on Graves's action of the Chesapeake.[1]

[1] This letter, while its tactical criticisms are perfectly correct, is otherwise wholly unjust to Graves. Graves was not idle in port. It had been well for his cause had he been, for he would then have received Rodney's despatch at a much earlier date. He was instead off Boston, by direction of the Admiralty. Nor did Rodney press Graves's junction with Hood off the Chesapeake. No doubt, however, such would have been Graves's action had he received Rodney's despatch. There is no intimation whatever in his despatch of July 7, 1781, that he understood that De Grasse's fleet was specially directed to the Chesapeake; nor was there any intimation that "the blow on which depended the sovereignty of the ocean must be struck off the coast of Virginia." He did not advise Hood, in his written instructions at least, "by all means to guard the mouth of the Chesapeake, to anchor in Hampton Road if [there was] occasion, to keep his frigates cruizing off the coast to the southward, that he might have timely notice of the enemy's approach, and to despatch one of his frigates to Mr. Graves, acquainting [him] with his arrival, and pressing a speedy junction. No one thing of which," adds Rodney, "has been regarded." His remarks are but the imaginings of what ought to have been advised by himself but was not advised in any such terms. No doubt this letter, if shown to the Board, as was probably done, did much to delay Graves's promotion, which was due in the natural order of things in 1781 to 1787.

[REAR ADMIRAL GRAVES TO PHILIP STEPHENS]

London at Sea 29h Oct. 1781.

Sir:—

In my last letter by the Lively Captain Manly, I desired you to acquaint the Lords Commissioners of the Admiralty of my having pass'd the Bar of New York with the Bristol Fleet, with seven thousand of the army embark'd, to go to the relief of Earl Cornwallis at York in the Chesapeake.

The Fleet accordingly sailed the moment the troops were put on board the last ships out, vizt., the Montagu and Shrewsbury, and proceeded the same day (the 19th) for the Chesapeake. We carried several small craft and whale-boats to send off at different stages for intelligence.

The 24th we received intelligence from a black man who was pilot of His Majesty's ship Charon, a white man who belonged to the Quarter Master General's Department, and another black man who had made their escape together from New York,[1] that Lord Cornwallis had capitulated on the 18th instant, the day before the Fleet sailed from Sandy Hook, a copy of which intelligence is enclosed.

The 26h one of our boats brought off some people from the shore near Cape Charles, who gave the same report of the capitulation.

The 25th His Majesty's Ship La Nymphe joined us from New York and brought dispatches from Lord Cornwallis dated the 15th, a copy of which is enclosed

[1] An error, evidently, for York = Yorktown.

[137]

and leaves little room to question the truth of the other intelligence. The three people being still on board and questioned again, and known for what they reported themselves to be, by several persons helped still to corroborate. I therefore determined to detach the Rattlesnake for Europe, to give the earliest information to their Lordships, that Government may be prepared to receive the particulars of so sad a catastrophe.—My former letter to their Lordships did not abound in hopes of success.

The West India Squadron under Monsr. De Grasse being found so much more numerous than that of Britain, wou'd still maintain its superiority when joined to the three ships of the line of battle left in the Chesapeake, and reinforced by the Squadron under Mons: De Barras from Rhode Island, and further strengthened by the advantage of position. I shou'd however, been happy to have tried every possible means to effect a relief cou'd we have arrived in time, that prospect being at an end, no addition of troops intended for Charles-town, nor an attempt against Rhode Island thought advisable, under the present situation of things, there appeared nothing so proper as to return with the Fleet to New York, and by removing the troops from out of the men of war, to put the West India Squadron into a condition to quit this coast as soon as possible. I therefore determined to leave this Station and retire to New York.

Unsuccessful as the event has proved, I hope their Lordships will not find any part of it has proceeded from the want of attention or exertion on my particular part.

I have dispatched a frigate forward to New York to

direct the transports to be at Sandy Hook, in readiness to receive the troops and to provide bread and water for any ships which may be deficient.

Two successive days before my leaving the neighbourhood of the Chesapeak, I sent the Warwick and Nymphe to reconnoitre, whose report I send enclosed. Both these days we saw the Enemys Fleet from our mast heads, and most of the last day, our Fleet lay to close off the back of the Middle Ground.

In the Evening I dispatched the Carysfort and Blonde for Charles-town[1] with Lieut. General Leslie, and a small detachment of the Artillery, with directions, (if the General found it necessary to withdraw the post from Wilmington) to proceed there and effect it as quick as possible, and then to convoy any empty transports or victuallers to New York.

> I am,
> Sir,
> Your Most Obedient Humble Servant,
> THOS. GRAVES.

Philip Stephens, Esqr.

Endorsed Vice Adml.[2] Graves | Letter to P. Stephens, Esqr., | 29th Oct: 1781 | Rcd. 25 Nov. 1781 at | 11 P.M. | (3 Inclosures).

---

[1] South Carolina.

[2] The secretary probably took the promotion of Graves, when his turn came, for granted. He was, however, passed over and was not promoted until September 24, 1787. (See Clowes, III, 567.)

Enclosure A

[LORD CORNWALLIS TO GENERAL CLINTON]

Copy.

York Town Virginia
15th October 1781

Sir,

Last Evening the Enemy carried my two advanced Redoubts on the left by Storm, and during the Night have included them in their Second Parallel, which they are at present busy in perfecting. My Situation now becomes very critical, We dare not shew a Gun to their old Batteries, and I expect their new ones will be open to-Morrow Morning. Experience has shewn that our fresh earthen Works do not resist their powerful Artillery, so that we shall soon be exposed to an Assult in ruined Works, in a bad Position and with weakened Numbers.

The Safety of the Place is therefore so precarious that I cannot recommend that the Fleet and Army should run great Risque, in endeavouring to save us.

I have the Honor to be
with great Respect
Sir
Your most obedient &
most humble Servant
(Signed)   CORNWALLIS

His Excellency
Sir H. Clinton K.B.

Enclosure B

[EVIDENCE FROM YORK TOWN]

Memo.
London at Sea 24th October 1781.

About four O'clock this morning a Schooner Boat came alongside with three Men in it, who upon being taken on board and examined, gave the following Account.

Jonas Rider a Black Man, says he left York Town on Thursday the 18th in a four Oard Boat in Company with a Captain and People belonging to the Sloop Tarlton, the property of a Mr. Young of New York, to which Place they were going.

That they left York Town to make their Escape, as it was said the Troops were going to give it up; There had been no firing for a Day and a half before he left it, and it was reported that Lord Cornwallis was making Terms to be sent to England and also respecting private property.

He gives an Account of his being taken twice, and of his escaping to a Dispatch Boat that had been sent from the Fleet the Day before Yesterday.—

James Robinson (a Black) Pilot to the Charon Man of War, left York Town with Rider because he heard there was a treaty to surrender the Place—

On Wednesday the firing ceased and a Flag of truce was sent out, which returned and the firing began again; that it ceased a short time afterwards, and he has not heard any since, tho' he was near the Place for two Days.

The Soldiers were all standing on their Works during the time the Flags were out, That the Merchants were getting all their things on Shore, as the Shipping were to be given up to the French.

On Monday was sennight he heard all the Troops were to go to Gloucester and march through the Country, that a great part were over, but it blew so hard the rest could not go, and the next Day they brought back those that went.

About Eight or nine Days ago the Enemy made an attack on our left and carried two of our Redoubts and killed most of the People that were in them; after which they placed Cannon there, that the next Night our People made a Sally and spiked Eleven Pieces.—

On Wednesday night he said he saw a large Bonfire in the Enemy's Camp.— One of our Magazines had been blown up.—

He says the Place was not given up, but that there was no firing, nor has he heard any since.— This Man produces Certificates, from several People that prove he was one of our Pilots.—

Robert Moyse left York Town with the above, he was told the Army had surrendered Prisoners of War, according to the Terms granted at Pensacola.— That all the People that could were making their Escape.— He is very positive they have capitulated, and that the Place was to be given up on Friday at one O'Clock; there has been no firing since; He understood that our People wanted Ammunition.

A Boat going from Lord Cornwallis to New York was taken,—but the Letters were in Cyphers.— That

Captn. Carey in a large Boat with thirty Oars had sailed on Monday Morning.—

This Man originally belonged to the Lapwing Dispatch Boat, and knew the Schooner to be the Mary as soon as he saw her.

Endorsed London at Sea 24 Octr. 1781 | The Evidence of Jonas Rider | James Robinson and | Robert Moyse from York | Town. | Virginia. | 2. | In Vice Adml. Graves's | Letter of 29 Octr 1781.

Enclosure C

[OBSERVATIONS OF CAPTAIN ELPHINSTONE]

Warwick Saturday 27th October 1781.—

At Sun set Cape Henry S W b W. dist. 2 or 3 Miles, Willoughby's point W b S. saw a Ship under sail in Lynnhaven Bay with Signals out, also one of the Line, and a Frigate on the North side of the Horse shoe; 31 Sail anchored at the upper part of the Middle ground, I imagine below the Egg Islands, as I could see Back River point. From the top I could only see the Lower Yards of the Ships at Anchor, in all we could count 45 Sail; all of them had Signals flying.—

Signed   G K. ELPHINSTONE—

Sunday 28th October—

Sent the Warwick and Nymphe in again to Cape Henry. A Ship of two Decks was under sail to meet them, two more in Lynn haven and forty four above the Horse shoe, in the whole Forty seven sail. Two large Ships were under sail from above to come down, and the advanced Ship shewed her Colours and fired a Gun under them, at two different parts of the day.—

Endorsed Observations of Captain | Elphinstone October the 27th | & 28th 1781 | 3. | In Vice Adml. Graves's | Letter of 29 octr. 1781

[REAR ADMIRAL GRAVES TO CAPTAIN MELCOMB]

By Thomas Graves, Esqr. Rear Admiral of the Red Commander-in-Chief, &c, &c.

You are hereby required and directed to receive on board, mine and the General's dispatches for Government and proceed with them on His Majesty's Ship under your command, immediately to England.

You are to use the utmost precaution to avoid falling in with the enemy, and to keep the dispatches constantly prepared with a weight ready to be sunk at a moment's warning.

You are to endeavour to fetch as high up the Channell as possible, and to convey the dispatches yourself to the Admiralty, in the most expeditious manner; suffering nothing to detain you upon your passage, nor to cause a moment's delay until you have safely deliver'd them at the Admiralty.   And for so doing this shall be your order.

Given under my hand on board His Majesty's
Ship London at Sea the 29th October 1781.

THOS. GRAVES.

To
Captain John Melcomb,
of His Majesty's Sloop | Rattlesnake
By Command of the Admiral

George Graves.

Endorsed Rattlesnake.

[REAR ADMIRAL HOOD TO GEORGE JACKSON]

29th of October, 1781.

My dear Sir:—

The Ranger cutter joined the fleet yesterday with the August packet from Antigua, by which I had the pleasure of your very kind letter of the 2nd of August, and thank you for it very sincerely.   It is a most flattering circumstance to me that my conduct on the 29th of April is so generally approved.

Mr. Graves has just sent me word he is about to send a ship to England.   His messenger brings the most melancholy news Great Britain ever received.   Lord Cornwallis capitulated to the combined forces of France and America on the 18th—a most heartbreaking business, and the more so, to my mind, as I shall ever think his Lordship ought to have been succoured,

[145]

or brought off, previous to the return of the French fleet to the Chesapeake, and which Mr. Graves had in his power to effect at his pleasure, after losing the glorious opportunity of defeating its intentions on the 5th of last month; but I have fully expressed myself upon the management of that day in my last letters by the Lively and the packet. I now feel too much, and my mind is too greatly depressed with the sense I have of my country's calamities, to dwell longer upon the painful subject. We are now, I am told, going back to New York to disembark the troops. I do not mean to go within the Bar, and as soon as the troops are out of the ships of my squadron I shall push away to the protection of the West India Islands. I think Admiral Digby would not do amiss if he was to send the greatest part of his squadron with me till the month of March, as he can put them in no place of safety except the Oyster Bay, in the Sound, and they may as well be at Constantinople for any good they may do.

Adieu, my dear Sir. With best affections to Mrs. Jackson,

> I am ever and most faithfully yours,
>
> SAM. HOOD.

[REAR ADMIRAL HOOD TO PHILIP STEPHENS]

Barfleur, off Sandy Hook, 3rd of November, 1781.
Sir:—

I beg you will be pleased to acquaint the Lords Commissioners of the Admiralty that the King's fleet under Rear-Admiral Graves returned here yesterday evening, and as the Rear-Admiral has this day put the ships I brought with me from the West Indies under my orders again, I propose returning to my station for the protection of his Majesty's islands committed to my care, so soon as the troops, army, provisions, ammunition, &c., are disembarked.

Herewith I transmit for their Lordships' information an account of the state and condition of his Majesty's ships under my command,

And have the honour to be, Sir,

     Your most obedient, humble Servant,

Philip Stephens, Esq.   SAM. HOOD.

Endorsed.—The 3rd of November, 1781. Sir Samuel Hood, off Sandy Hook. Received the 16th of December. Answered the 3rd of January, 1782. (1 enclosure).

CONSULTATION OF FLAG OFFICERS, HELD ON BOARD HIS MAJESTY'S SHIP LONDON OFF SANDY HOOK BAR THE 3D NOVEMR. 1781[1]

Question The French fleet remaining in the Cheseapeke, after the reduction of the British Forces in York River— Whether at this Season of the Year the British Fleet should separate,— or Whether so much danger is to be apprehended to the Posts upon the Coasts of No.

[1] The despatch of November 6, 1781, which contained this enclosure, is not available.

America as will make it necessary at the risque of the Leeward Islands, to keep the fleet longer assembled.

Resolved   That the British Fleet shall (in consideration of the situation of the two fleets) be equipped for Sea as expeditiously as possible, and separate when ready.

THOMAS GRAVES
ROBT. DIGBY
SAML. HOOD
FRAS. SAML. DRAKE
EDMD. AFFLECK

A Copy | T Graves.

Endorsed Copy of the Consultation | of Flag Officers | held on board his Majesty's | Ship London 3d Novr. 1781 | No. 7 | In R. A. Graves's Letter | Dated 6 Novr. 1781.

STATE OF THE TRANSPORTS & VICTUALLERS IN YORK RIVER, VIRGINIA[1]

Ships Names	Master's Names	State & Condition
Bellona	John Wardell	Taken
Shipwright	Thomas Kay	Burnt
Andrew	Francis Todiridge	Taken
Houston	Robert McLash	Sunk
Lord Mulgrave	Andw. Casterby	Do.
Harmony	John Duffield	Do.
Providence	Benjn. Huntley	Do.
Favorite	John Wilson	Do.
Emerald	Robert Tindall	Do.
Selina	John Crosskill	Do.
Sally	Arthur Elliott	Do.
Horsington	Chrisr. Jolson	Do.
Robert	Jonathan Moore	Do.
Race Horse	Chrisr. Chesman	Do.
Neptune	John Atkinson	Do.
Oldborough	Lionel Bradstreet	Do.
Present Succession	William Chapman	Do.
Two Brothers	Magnus Mariners	Do.
Success Increase	John Saunderson	Do.
Concord	Andrew Monk	Do.
Lord Howe	Thomas Woodhouse	Do.
Fidelity	Robert Pilmour	Sunk
Mackrell	William Fraser	Do.

VICTUALLERS.

Diana	John Perkin	Sunk
Mercury	Arthur Ryburn	Do.
Ocean	John Walker	Do.
Providence Increase	Thomas Berriman	Do.
Betsey	Jno. Younghusband	Do.
Nancy	Robert Hoakesly	Do.
Rover	John Beveon	Do.
Harlequin	Thomas Skinner	Do.
Elizabeth	Naval Victualler	Do.

(Copy)   G. Robertson Agent.

T. Graves

[1] Admiral Graves's despatch of November 9, 1781, which forwarded this document, is not available.

[149]

Endorsed State and Condition | of the Transports & Victuallers | in York River | Virginia. | No. 6 | In R. A. Graves's Letter | Dated 9 Novr. 1781.

THE FRENCH LINE OF BATTLE[1]

Chesapeak Bay off York River 22nd Octr. 1781.

	Guns		Guns
Le Neptune	78	Le Burgone	74
Le Provence	64	Le Valliant	64
L'Auguste	84	Le Ceazar	74
Le Magnanime	74	Le Citoyen	74
L'Hercule	74	Le Languidoc	84
Le Conquerant	74	Le Experiment	50
Le Duc de Burgone	84	Le Refleshé	64
Le Hector	74	Le Diadem	74
L'Septre	74	Le Scipion	74
Le Northumberland	74	Le Victor	74
L'Evillie	64	Le Triton	54
L'Gloryeaux	74	Le Pluton	74
L'Esprit	60		
Le Sollitaire	64	**Frigates**	
Le Marsellie	74	Romulus Occasion-	
Le Palmie	74	ally for the Line	44
Le Ville De Paris	110	L'Andromaque	36
Le Sovereign	74	La Railleure	36
Le Caton	64	La Concorde	36
L Lile	74	La Surveillante	36
Le Destaing	74	L'Harmione	36
Le Ardent	64	La Diligente	30
Le Jason	64	La Genteele	38

[1] Admiral Graves's despatch of November 9, 1781, which forwarded this document, is not available.

Admiral Lord Viscount Hood

From an original picture by F. Abbot

Endorsed A List of the French fleet | in the Cheasapeak
22d Octr. 1781. | No. 3 | In R. A. Graves's Letter |
Dated 9 Novr. 1781

[CAPTAIN SYMONDS TO REAR ADMIRAL GRAVES[1]]

York Town Virginia 20th Octr. 1781.

Sir:—

I am very Sorry to inform you, that the Garrison of
York, and the Vessels that remained in the River, sur-
renderd to the Enemy by Capitulation yesterday afternoon, after a seige of seventeen days.

On the 10th instant the Charon was set on fire by red
hot Shot and entirely consumed, the Guadaloupe was
Scuttled, and Sunk the 17th to prevent her from sharing
the same fate, or falling into the Enemys possession and
the Fowey was hauld into Shoal Water and bored.

It being agreed by the capitulation, that the Bonetta
should proceed to New York, to carry Earl Cornwallis's dispatches, and any People his Lordship thought
proper to send, Captain Dundas proceeds with his
Officers and Thirty Men with a Flag of Truce for that
purpose

The Number of Sick and wounded Seamen in the
Naval Tents, amounts to eighty five, which cannot be
removed for some time, but their own Surgeons will be
left to take care of them, during the siege Ten Seamen
were killed and Thirty two wounded. Enclosed I have

[1] Admiral Graves's despatch of November 9, 1781, which forwarded this letter, is not available.

[151]

the honor to send you the Articles of capitulation, and the state of the Transports and Victuallers.

And have the honor to be.

Sir your most Obedient

Humble Servant.

Rear Admiral Graves　　Sign'd　　THOS. SYMONDS.

&c &c &c

An Attested Copy

T. Graves.

Endorsed Copy of Captn. Symonds | Letter dated York Town | Virginia 20th Octr. 1781. | No. 5 | In R. A. Graves's Letter | Dated 9 Novr. 1781

LIGNE DE COMBAT DE L'ARMÉE FRANÇAISE AUX ORDRES DU COMTE DE GRACE LE 5—7BRE. 1781 FORMÉE PAR RANG DE VITESSE[1]

Scavoir

Le Pluton . . .	74	Canons——		MM.	Dalbert de Rious[1]
Le Marsellois . .	74	"	——	"	Castellanne[2]
La Bourgogne . .	74	"	——	"	Charitte[3]
Le Diadème . . .	74	"	——	"	Monteder[4]
Le Refleche . .	64	"	——	"	De Boades[5]
L'Auguste . . .	80	"	84	"	Bouganville Chef d'Escadre[6]
				"	Castellan Capitaine[7]
Le St. Esprit . .	80	"	84	"	Chabert[8]
La Caton . . .	64	"	——	"	Framont[9]
Le Cezar . . .	74	"	——	"	Despinouse[10]
Le Destin . . .	74	"	——	"	Gonnpy[11]
La Ville de Paris .	98	"	104	"	De Grace—General[12]
				"	Vaugiraud Major[13]

[1] Admiral Graves's despatch of November 9, 1781, which forwarded this document, is not available.

La Victoire	. .	74 Canons —— MM.	D'Albert [14]
Le Sceptre . . .	74	" —— "	Vandreuil [15]
Le Northumberland	74	" —— "	Brigueville [16]
Le Palmier . .	74	" —— "	Darros [17]
Le Solitaire . .	64	" —— "	Cice [18]
Le Citoyen . .	74	" —— "	D'Ethy [19]
Le Scipion . . .	74	" —— "	Clarel [20]
Le Magnanime .	74	" —— "	Le Begne [21]
L'Hercule . . .	74	" —— "	Turpin [22]
Le Languedoc . .	80	" 84 { "	Monteil Chef d'Escadre Comdr. Capitaine [23]
Le Zele . . .	74	" —— "	De Preville [24]
L'Hector . . .	74	" —— "	Daleiur [25]
Le Souverain . .	74	" —— "	De Glandever [26]
La Railleuse . .	32	" —— "	St. Corme [27]
L'Aigrette . . .	26	" —— "	Traversair [28]

Endorsed The French Line of Battle | in the Action off the Cheasapeak | the 5th. September 1781. | No. 2. | In R. A. Graves's Letter | Dated 9 Novr. 1781.[1]

[1]NOTE BY EDITOR.—The following is the revised list of names of commanding officers:

[1] D'Albert de Rions
[2] Castellane Majastres
[3] Charitte (Comte de)
[4] Montecler
[5] De Boades
[6] Bougainville
[7] Castellan (Chevalier de)
[8] Chabert Cogolin
[9] Framond (Comte de)
[10] Coriolis d'Espinouse
[11] Du Maitz de Goimpy Feuquières (Comte de)
[12] Grasse (Comte de), Vice-Admiral
[13] Vaugiraud de Rosnay, Chief of Staff
[14] D'Albert Saint-Hippolyte (Chevalier)
[15] Vaudreuil (Comte de)
[16] Briqueville (Marquis de)
[17] D'Arros Argelos
[18] Cicé Champion (Chevalier de)
[19] Thy (Comte de)
[20] Clavel Ainé
[21] Le Bègue (Chevalier de, later Comte de)
[22] Turpin Du Breuil (Chevalier de)
[23] Monteil (Baron de)
[24] Gras Preville (Chevalier)
[25] Renaud d'Allen
[26] Glandevez (Chevalier de)
[27] St. Cosme (Chevalier de)
[28] Traversais

By whom taken	Where taken	Name	Tons	Men	Guns	To whom belonging
Chatham		Magicienne	800	280	36	France
Do.		Polly	450	21	10	Rebels
Do.		Genl. Mark Privr.	250	94	22	. Do. .
Do.		Defence	180	65	18	. Do. .
Do.		Admiral Durell	180	7		England
Do.		Friendship	150	8		Rebels
Do.		Eagle	140	9		. Do. .
Do.		Isabella	60	4		. Do. .
Do.		Two Friends	45	5		. Do. .
Do.		Dove	30	6		. Do. .
General Monk	In Boston bay	Salem Packet	100	23	12	. Do. .
Amphitrite	and	Experiment priv.	300	20	22	Bristol
Do.	on the S W	Endeavour	70	8		England
Do.	Coast of	Union	100	9		. Do. .
Do.	Nova Scotia	St. John	90	10		Rebels
Do.		Minerva	95	10		. Do. .
Do.		Dolphin	100	11		. Do. .
Do.		Nero				England
Do.		Revenge priv.	40	30	8	Rebels
Belisarius		....				Portug
Garland & Warwick .		Greyhound priv.				Rebels
Pearl		Longsplice	30	5		. Do. .
Do.		Eleanor	70	8		. Do. .
Do.		Friendship	100	10		. Do. .
Do.		Senegal priv.	50	29	8	. Do. .
Carysfort	Off Nantucket		500	60	6	France
Pegasus & Rattlesnake	off Long Island	Deane priv.	160	110	16	Rebels
Solebay		Dan	300	18	8	England
Nymphe & Amphion .		Royl. Louis Priv.	450	188	22	Rebels
Do.		Molly	100	18		. Do. .
Do.		Lexington	85	10		. Do. .
Do.		Rambler priv.	90	48	10	. Do. .
Do.		Raccoon	50	10		. Do. .
Do.	On the	Lively Buckskin	70	11		. Do. .
now	Coast of	Juno	120	40	8	. Do. .
ea	Virginia	Favorite priv.	150	100	18	. Do. .
Fortunee		Felicity Do.	80	20	6	. Do. .
Iris		Jolly Tar Lre Marque	125	30	10	. Do. .
Do.		Samuel	200	11	4	England
Solebay	off Charles town	Savage	300	30	16	. Do. .
		late Eng Sloop War ..				
		Total		1366	260	

Kind of Vessel	From whence	Where bound	Lading	Capture or recapture
Frigate ...	Piscataqua	Boston	....	Capture ....
Ship	Boston	Sanco for Masts...	Ballast	.. Do. ....
. Do.	... Do.	On a Cruize		.. Do. ....
. Do.	Bilboa	Newbury	Brandy &c........	.. Do. ....
Brig	Jersey	Quebec	Wine	Re-capture .....
. Do.	Turks Island	Boston	Indian Corn......	Capture ....
. Do.	Salem	Guadaloupe	Fish & lumber....	.. Do. ....
Sloop	Old York	Boston	Deals	.. Do. ....
. Do.	Newfoundland ...	... Do.	Fish	.. Do. ....
. Do.	Virginia	... Do.	Tobacco	.. Do. ....
Ship	Bilboa	Salem	Silks	.. Do. ....
. Do.				Re-capture .....
Brig	Cork	....	Beef Pork &c.....	.. Do. ....
. Do.	... Do.		.... Do.	.. Do. ....
. Do.	Salem	Santa Cruz	Plank	Capture ....
. Do.	Virginia	Newbury	Tobacco	.. Do. ....
. Do.	Newbury	Guadaloupe	Plank	.. Do. ....
. Do.	Virginia	Glasgow	Tobacco	Re-Capture ....
Schooner .	Salem	On a Cruise......		Capture ....
. Do.	Lisbon	Limerick	500 bls beef .... 400 Cask butter.......	Re-Capture ....
. Do.	Salem	Cruising		Capture ....
. Do.	Boston	Salem	Wine	.. Do. ....
Sloop	... Do.	... Do.	Indigo	.. Do. ....
Brig	... Do.	... Do.	Cordage	.. Do. ....
Schooner .	... Do.	On a Cruize		.. Do. ....
Ship	... Do.	C. Francois.......	Masts &c.........	.. Do. ....
Brig	... Do.	On a Cruize		.. Do. ....
. Do.	Madeira	New York.......	Wine	Re-Capture ....
Ship	Philidelphia	Cruizing		Capture ....
Brig	... Do.	St. Thomas's.....	Tobacco	.. Do. ....
Do.	Salem	Baltimore	Wine	.. Do. ....
Do.	Philidelphia	On a Cruise......		.. Do. ....
Schooner .	... Do.	Havannah	Flour	.. Do. ....
Do.	C. Francois	Baltimore	Salt	.. Do. ....
Brig	Havannah	Philidelph	Sugar & Rum	.. Do. ....
Do.	New London	On a Cruize......		.. Do. ....
Schooner .	Philidelph	... Do.		.. Do. ....
Brig	... Do.	Havannah	Flour	.. Do. ....
Galley ...	Jamaica	Bristol	Rum & Sugar.....	Re-Capt ....
....	....	....	....	.. Do. ....
				T Graves.

[REAR ADMIRAL HOOD TO PHILIP STEPHENS]

Barfleur, in Carlisle Bay, Barbadoes, 10th of
December, 1781.

Sir:—

I sailed from off Sandy Hook on the 11th of last
month, with his Majesty's ships named in the margin,[1]
and having previously despatched the Nymphe and
Belliqueux to reconnoitre the Chesapeake, the latter
joined me on my given rendezvous on the 16th, and informed me that not a French ship was in the Chesapeake on the 10th. I immediately pushed away for my
station, not caring to wait a moment for the Nynphe,
and without meeting with any occurrence in my passage
deserving notice, I arrived here on the 5th, with all the
line-of-battle ships except the Royal Oak and Monarch,
which parted company in a gale of wind and thick
weather on the 17th. The Intrepid's, Alcide's and
Shrewsbury's lower masts ought to be shifted; they
were wounded in the action of the Chesapeake, very
badly fished at New York for want of proper materials,
and were in so crippled a state in the passage that I
was compelled to carry a very moderate sail to preserve
the masts from tumbling over the side, and there not
being a single lower mast for a 74-gun ship in this country, I am securing those of the Shrewsbury and Alcide
in the best manner I can, and shall give new ones to the
Intrepid. . . .

[1] Barfleur, Princesa, Royal Oak, Alfred, America, Invincible,
Monarch, Canada, Torbay, Alcide, Intrepid, Montagu, Resolution,
Centaur, Prince George, Ajax, Shrewsbury, Pegasus, Sybille, Sala-
mander.

I endeavoured all I could to prevail upon Admiral Digby to send the whole of his line-of-battle ships with me, as the letters I wrote him, of which I herewith send you copies, will show, but I could only obtain four.

With all his ships, which can be of no use upon the coast of America before the 1st of April, together with a few that may probably be soon here from England, I should have been equal, if not superior to the Count De Grasse. . . .

As a packet was sent away the day before I arrived, with an account of De Grasse's fleet being at Martinique, though it might be reasonably expected I should make my appearance every hour, as the captain of the Ranger brig had delivered the letters I had written to the Governor and senior captain, I thought it right to make known to their Lordships my arrival here as soon as possible. I therefore propose to despatch the Ranger as soon as she comes back from St. Lucia, to which place I sent her to make known my return to this island the moment I anchored.

I have the honour to be, with great truth and regard, Sir,

Your most obedient and most humble Servant,

SAM. HOOD.

P. S.—I was obliged to leave the Prince William at New York, as her rudder required to be unhung, which occasioned me to write the letter you will herewith receive to Rear-Admiral Digby.

P. S.—I have, since writing the above, received a letter from Rear-Admiral Drake, to acquaint me that the

bread sent on board the Princesa was so very bad it
could not be received, and that the contractor has no
other.

S. H.

Endorsed.—10th of December, 1781, Barbadoes, Sir
Samuel Hood. Received 7th of January, 1782, at midnight.

[REAR ADMIRAL GRAVES TO PHILIP STEPHENS]

London, Port Royal Harbour 20h Decr. 1781.

Sir.—
Be pleased to acquaint the Lords Commissioners of
the Admiralty that I sailed from the Bar of New York
in the London the 10h November, and arrived at Antigua the 6h Decr. to put on shore my prisoners, having
taken on the passage a French ship called the Imperi-
eux of 800 tons, 38 guns and 319 Men, from Cadiz for
Philidelphia; laden with Salt, some arms, cannon, and
mixed goods, besides medicine. The 9th I sailed from
Antigua, and arrived at Jamaica the 17th. and delivered their lordships pacquet to Sr. Peter Parker, according to their orders of the 9h July, receiv'd by Rear
Admiral Digby.

I hope their lordships have found the request I submitted to their considerable, not unreasonable. The two
Admirals so lately under my command being both of
them Commanders in Chief upon separate stations,

makes me become so much the object of observation, that I hope there is nothing blamable in my conduct, as to deserve the present painful humiliating situation. I have obeyed with readiness their Lordships commands, and I flatter myself they will not suffer me to remain long under so much anxiety of mind.—

I am

Sir

Your most Obedient

Humble Servant,

THOS. GRAVES.

PS.

Enclosed you will receive a list of the Prizes taken by the cruisers on the North American Station between the 20h Augt. and 31 Octo. being the most correct account I have been able to obtain.—

T. Graves

Philip Stephens Esqr.

Endorsed ℞ 5 Febry 1782 | ansd.

[REAR ADMIRAL GRAVES TO PHILIP STEPHENS]

London Port Royal Harbour 4th May 1782.

Sir:—

I beg you will remind the Lords Commissioners of the Admiralty, that in my letters of the 27th of September and the 20th of December 1781, I entreated their Lordships would be pleased to consider my particular situation and recall me; instead of requiring me to serve in an inferior situation at Jamaica, whilst a Junior Officer who relieved me at York, continued in the supreme Command.

The Island of Jamaica being at this time out of danger, from the success of Sr. Geo. Rodney against his Majesty's Enemy's, gives me a fair occasion to renew my request, and to pray that I may be recalled.

If that should be inconvenient—that I may have leave to quit my Command, and return to my native country a passenger.

The many calumnies in the News-papers, and the injurious representations of my conduct, which pretend to derive their authority from the debates in the houses of Parliament, make it necessary for me to clear up this matter;— And to require the liberty to do so, from their Lordships hands.

If the representation made of me, be credited, it is a reflection upon Government that I am permitted to serve. If not, I hope their Lordships will signify their opinion of my conduct and allow me the opportunity of stating many things which may not be so proper in a letter.

I feel myself particularly aggrieved by a publication in the Morning Post of the 8th November, 1781, under a pretence of its being spoken by Lord Denbigh in the House of Lords, where much vigilance and attention is insinuated on the part of Sr. Samuel Hood—and much implied censure let fall upon me.

Sr. Saml. Hood's letter to me, is dated at Sea, off

Cape Henry the 25th of August, 1781,—wherein he says, "I am now steering for Cape Henry in order to examine the Cheseapeake, from thence I shall proceed to the Capes of the Delaware, and not seeing or hearing any thing of De Grasse, or any detachment of Ships he might have sent upon the Coast, shall then make the best of my way off Sandy Hook."—

Except in the time of his continuance at the entrance of the Cheseapeke, it runs so much in the tenor of the speech attributed to my Lord Denbigh that the reader can hardly doubt of its being the authority.

The fact is, that Sr. Saml. Hood changed his opinion before the Nymph left him.— That it was the South part of Virginia, somewhere about Curratuck that he was off on the 25th of August, and he arrived on the 28th following at Sandy Hook, not two hours later than the Nymph; That he never saw the Capes of the Cheseapeke, nor any other land until he made the Neversink.

Their Lordships will pardon me for saying that credulity itself can hardly admit, that between the 25th and the 28th of August Sr. Saml. Hood could continue for nine days before the Cheseapeke.

I would not venture to confirm the conclusion drawn from the dates, if their Lordships did not know it officially, from my letter as well as from Sr. Saml. Hood's, (if he sent any officially upon his arrival at the Hook;) and the letter alluded to could not have been sent home until after the arrival of Sr. Saml. Hood, and the event made known.

I am confident their Lordships will see my uneasy

situation in its full extent, and grant me the liberty and indulgence I sue for.—

I am Sir

Your most Obedient

And most Humble Servant

THOS. GRAVES.

Philip Stephens Esqr., Secretary to the Admiralty.

Endorsed 4 May 1782 | Rear Adml. Graves | ℞, 12 July by the | Vigilant Packet.

Minute 9 Augt. | Refer him | to Mr. Stephens | Lre of the 14 | of March last (of | which inclose him | a Triplicate) acquaintg. | him that R. A. Rowley | was directed to give him | permission to return to | England. | Send Triplicate of Mr. | Stephens's Lrē of the same date to | R. A. Rowley.

[PHILIP STEPHENS TO REAR ADMIRAL GRAVES[1]]

14th March 1782.

Sir:

I have received and communicated to My Lords Commis'rs of the Adm'ty your Letter of the 20th of December giving an account of your proceedings in the

[1] Admiralty 2, 575, p. 68.

[162]

London from the time of your leaving New York to your arrival at Jamaica, and inclosing a List of the Prizes taken by the Cruizers on the North American Station between the 20th of August and 31st of October last.

In return to the observations you have made upon being superceeded in the Command in North America by a Junior Officer and sent to the Jamaica Station where you can only serve in the Second Post their Lordships are pleased to direct me to acquaint you that you are much mistaken if you apprehend that they thereby meant to convey any disapprobation of your Conduct; for nothing could be more distant from their thoughts. They conceived that the sending you to Jamaica, as it continued you in active Service, would be received as a mark of their Attention, to you, and that the recalling you to England upon Rear Admiral Digby's arrival at New York might have created a suspicion that your Conduct was not approved.

The Commanders-in-Chief at the Leeward Islands, and Jamaica were both Senior Officers to you; For their Lordships, at the time they made that Arrangement, did not know that Sir George Rodney would come to England; So that there was no alternative, but to recall, or send you to serve under a Senior Officer. But as their Lordships find by your Letter abovementioned that you feel yourself uneasy in your present situation, And as they conclude that the mode in which you wish to be relieved in the anxiety of your mind, tho' not directly expressed, is the having permission to return to England, they have given direction to Rear Admiral Rowley to allow you to come home with the first Con-

[163]

voy he sends to England, or in any other manner that may be more agreeable to your inclination.[1] I am, &c.

P. S.

Rear Admiral Graves, Jamaica.
    By the Preston
    23'd Apr. 82.

Duplicate sent under Cover to Mr. Bell
at Falmouth, to go by the May Pacquet.
Triplicate by the Pacquet 10th August 1782.

THE LONDON'S JOURNAL

From the 1st to the 12th day of September, 1781. S. Hemmans, Master.[2]

Saturday, September 1, 1781.

Sandy Hook N 24 W Dist. 24 Leagues. Modt Breezs throughout Anchd. here ye Solebay & Huzssare ½ past 3 PM Weighed with y Rist of our Squad & ran out over y Bar & Jond. Adml. Hood Fleet who Saluted us with 15 Guns which we Returnd. hoistd. in ye. Long Boat & Md. ye Sigl. for all, Lieut at 7 Bore away & M Sail Standing to y Suthwrd in all 19 Sail of y Line

---

[1] Graves did not start from the West Indies until July 25, when he sailed from Bluefields, Jamaica, in charge of a great convoy of merchantmen and met the disastrous gale mentioned in the Introduction. He reached Plymouth October 17, 1782, and on the 21st was ordered to strike his flag.

[2] Admiralty Logs, 2383.

a fity Gun Ship & Some Frigts with a Fier Ship. Saw Strang Sails in Diferant Points of y Compass which we Chaced. But Did Not Com up with Sound. 24 Fath fine clear sand

Wednesday, September 5, 1781.

Cape Henry W. ½ South Dist. 4 or 5 Leagues. Fresh Breezs. & Cloudy y Middle & Latter Mod & Clear at 6 AM Made ye Richmond & Soelbay Sigl. to Com within Hail Sent them to Look Into Chesepeek for y Enmiens Fleet ½ past 9 ye. Solebay Md ye. Sigl. for a Fleet in ye. S W ½ Past 10. Md y. Preparative Sigl. for Action at 10 ms. after to Call In all Cruzeres at 11 Discoverd. a fleet of Large Ships at Anchor in Lynn haven Bay Md y Sigl for a Line a Head at 2 Cables Dist. formd. ye. Line & Standing for Lynn haven Bay at ye. Same time Clearing Ship & Geting Ready for Action

Thursday, September 6, 1781.

Cape Henry W. b S. Dist 3 Leagues. Modt. & fair throughout ½ past 12 Discovered ye Enmieny Geting Under Sail ¾ past 12 Md. y Sigl. for the Line a head at 1 Cables Lenght Asunder at 1 Hauld Down y Sigl. for y' Line & Md. y Sigl. to form an East & West Line at 1 Cable Lenght at 8 Min past Md. ye. Sigl. for y Rear Division Adl. Drake to make Moor Sail y ware Inclinable to Be Squaly took a Reef in the Topsails 20 Min past 1 Md y Sigl. for ye. Leading Ship Lead more

[165]

to Starboard 25 Min past 1 Repd. ye. Sigl for ye. Rear
of ye. Fleet to Make More Sail ½ past 1 Md. ye Center
[Centaur] Sigl. to keep in her Station 35 Min past 1
md y Sigl. for ye. Leading Ships to Lead more Larg
39 Min past 1 md. y Resolution, America & Bedford
Sigl. to Get in their Station at 2 found ye Enmeyes to
Consist of 24 Sail of y Line And 2 Frigats thire Van
Bore S′ 3 Miles Standing to ye. Eastward with their
Larboard Tacks On Board in a Line a Head at 4 Min
past 2 finding our Van Approaching to Nere a Shole
Calld. y Middle Ground Md. ye. Preparative Sigl. to
Veer 15 Min After Md. y Sigl. & Woor together
Brought too In Order to let y Centure of y Emneys
Ships Com a Brest of us 21 Min after Made ye. Bed-
ford Sigl. to gett in her Station ½ past md. ye. Sigl.
for ye. Leading Ships to Lead More to Starboard 40
Min After Made ye. Salamander Fire Ship Sigl. to
Prime 52 Min After made ye. Royal Oak Sigl. to keep
ye. Line 55 Min after md. y′ Terrible Sigl. to gett into
her Station 56 Min After md. y Princessa Sigl. also at
3 md. y Alcide Sigl. Likwise at 17 Min Starboard 27
After Md. y′ Sigl. for y Rear of y fleet to fill ½ past 3
Md. y Sigl. for ye. Ships a Stern to make more Sail
34 Min After Md. ye. Sigl. for ye. Ships of y Van to
keep More to Starboad. 46 Min After Md. ye. Sigl.
for a Line a head at 1 Cable Lenght ye Enmemy Ship
Advancing Very Slow & Even Approaching y′ Adml.
Judging this to be Momant of Attack Md. ye. Sigl. for
ye Ships to Bear Down & Engage filld. ye. Main Topsail & Bore Down to y Enmemy 3 Min After Repd.
[repeated] it 11 Min after hauld Down ye. Sigl. for y
Line a Head that it it Might not interfear with y Sigl.
to Engage Close ¾ past 4 y Van & Center of our fleet

Cummencd. ye. Action 22 Min After Hoistd. y Sigl. again for y Line a Head y Ships not Sufficiantly Extendd. 27½ hauld it Down again & Md. ye. Sigl. for a Close Action. 40 Min After Md. y Royl. Oak Sigl. to keep her Station. 11 After 5 md. y Montagu Sigl. to keep her Station 26 Min After Repd. y Sigl. for a Closer Action ½ past our Rear Bore away 35 Min After Md. ye. Solebay & Fortunens Sigl. to Come within hail 15 Min past 6 y Adml. Sent y Solebay to ye. Ships in y Rear & ye Fortunee to y Ships in y Van with Orders for y Ships to keep in a Parallel with y Emnemy and Well a Breast of them. During ye. Night & in ye. Morning when he md. y Sigl. for a Close Action that evry Ship would be as nere ye. Enmey as Posable 23 Min After Md. ye. Sigl. for a Line a Head at 1 Cables Lenght aSunder & Hauld Down ye. Sigl. for a Close Action ½ past 6 ye fier ceasd. on Bout Sides ½ past 7 Md. y Night Sigl. for ye. Line a head at 2 Cables Length Asunder at y Montagua hail us and Said She Could not keep y Line Being so Much Damage at 10 y Fortunee Informd. ye. Adml. that ye. Shrewsbury had ye. Capt. and Many Men Woundd. & ye. first Lieutanent Killed. Bouth her topsail yards Shot away & was than Impld. getting outhers up & that ye Intrepd. was Much Disabld. in Every Respect ye. Princessa Main Topmast So Much Damagd as to Expect evry Moment to fall at 7 Cape Henry N W Dist 3 Leagues. at 8 found our Four & Main Mast Dangerous by Wounds Standing & Runing Rigging Much Cut ye. Iner Gammoning of ye. Bowsprite Shot a Through Sails much Damegd. 3 Guns Dismountd. one of which was thrown over Board we had 2 Men Kill'd & 18 Woundd. at Midnight ye. Enemy to Leeward.

Friday, September 7, 1781.

Modt. & Clear y Van of y Enmey fleet South & y
Rair W S W & y. Appeared in a Line a Head on y
Larboard Tack ye. Kings Ships in a Parallel Line with
them & a Breast at 6 Md. ye. Orpheus Sigl. for her
Capt ye. Nymph Repd. ye. Shrewsbury Sigl. to Speak
ye. Adml. Md. y– Solebay & Medea Sigl. for their
Capts. Adml. Drake Hoistd. his Flag on Board ye.
Alcide Sailmakers Employd. Repairing ye. Sails.

Saturday, September 8, 1781.

Mod & Cloudy W. at 11 A M Saw y land Bearing
W B S Dis 6 or 7 Miles at 50 Min past md. y Sigl. for
ye. Van of y fleet to Make More Sail at Noon y Emeny
Tackd their Centure S B E aBaut 8 Miles Md. ye.
Preparative Sigl. for ye. fleet to tack md. y Sigl. &
Tackd. together md. y to form a Quarter Line

Sunday, September 9, 1781.

D W ye Enemys fleet S S E Dist 4 or 5 Leags. ½ past
7 AM Md. y Sigl. to make More Sail at 10 AM Partd.
Compy. ye. Richmond & Iris ½ past 11 y Terrible Md.
y Sigl. of Distress Ansd. Do. & Sent ye. Orpheus & Fortunie to her Assistance.

Tuesday, September 11, 1781.

Light Breezs. & fair Wr. at 7 PM Md. y Sigl. for all
Lieut. hoisted out y Long boat Recd. from H M S

Terrible 12 Marines & 30 Barrels of Powder and Som Gunners Stores.

Wednesday, September 12, 1781.

Light Airs & Fogy PM Recd. from His M S Intrepd. 13 Seaman Md. ye. Sigl. for all Officers to Repair on Boad. ½ past 8 H M S Terrible was Set on Fire ½ past 9 Md. y Night Sigl. to make More Sail at 10 Sent ye. Fortunie ahead to ye. fleet md. y Fortunie & Orpheus Sigl. to within Hail.

H	K	F	Courses	Winds	Soundings	Colour of the Ground
1	- -	- -	- - - -	W N W		
2						
3						
4						
5						
6	- -	- -	- - - -	N W b N		
7						
8						
9	I	I	South	N b W		
10	2	2	"	"	16	fine brown Sand
11	I	3	"	"	17	fine White do.
12	I	4	"	"		
I	4	3	"	N b E	13	
2	4	4	S E b E $\frac{1}{2}$ E	N N E	15	"
3	5	"	S E	N E	16	"
4	5	2	"	"	21 21	"
5	5	"	"	"	22	"
6	5	"	"	"	21	"
7	2 "	4 "	"	"	21	
8	3	4	S S E	"	21	
9	6	"	So.	"	23	
10	6	"	"	"	24	
11	3 2	" 3	S W b W	"	22	
12	5		"	"	24	

Remarks &c Saturday Sepr. 1st 1781

Modte. Breezes & Cloudy Wr. Anchd. here H M. Ship

Hussar & Solebay from New York Discharged 43 Men

into the Hussar

Made the Sigl. & Got under Weigh & run Over the Barr

Joind. the Squadn. under the Command of Adml. Hood

returned Adml. Hood's Salute with 13 Guns hoisted in

the Longboat Made the Sigl. for all Lts.

Bore away as did the Fleet.

the Never sunk N W b N 5 Leags.

the Fortunee made the Sigl. for a Strange Sail

made the Solebays Sigl. to Chace & the Fortunee.

Made the Richmond's & Solebay's Sigl. to join the Fleet

Latd. Obsd. 39° 19′ N
in Company with the Ships.

Vizt. Barfleur Rear Adml. Hood, Princessa Rear Adml. Drake Alfred Shrewsbury America, Invincible, Monarch Richmond Alcide Adamant Le Nymphe Orpheus, Belliqueux, Terrible Santa Monica Solebay, Intrepid La Fortunee Resolution Europe Sybile Centaur Royal Oak Bedford Montagu Ajax Jane Sloop, Salamander Fire Ship

---

1 Admiralty Logs, No. 2383.

H	K	F	Courses	Winds	Sound-ings	Collour of the Ground
1	4	6	S W b W	N E	23	fine Gray Sand
2				"	23	Do.
3	Up	N N	W of N W		24	
4	3	"	S W b W	"	23	
5	3	6	"	"	18	
6	3	4	"	"		
7	1	6	S S W	E b S	20	
	1	6				
8	3	6	"	"	19	fine White Sand
9	3	"	"	"	20	
10	3	4	"	"	21	
11	2	4	"	"	24	
12	2	"	"	"	24	
1	3	"	"	"	25	
2	3	"	"	"	25	
3	3	"	"	"	23	
4	2	4	"	"	24	
5	2	"	"	N N E	24	
6	1	4	"	"	24	
7	1	"	S W	"	24	
	"	6				
8	2	6	"	"	25	
9	1	4	"	"	24	
10	1	"	"	"	24	Dark brown Sand
11	"	6	"	"	24	
12	"	4	"	"	24	

Modte. & Clear Sent the Princessa & Barfleur fresh Beef

the Nymph made the Sigl. for seeing the Land Opened

4 barrels of Pork Contents 416 Short 5 ps.

Made the Fortunee's Sigl. to Chace and also the Nymph

& Sybil

several Strange Sails in Sight.

he America to Chace

Performed Divine Service Light Airs & Variable
   Latd. Osbd. 38° 33′ N

H	K	F	Courses	Winds		Collour of the Ground
1	1		W S W	So.		
2	1		W b S	S b W		
3	1				26	
4	1				26	
5	2				20	Coarse brown Sand
6	2	3			19	
7	3	3	W b S		14	
8	3				15½ 16	Large Gravel
9	3	2			17	
10	3	6			17	White Sand
11	3	3	S D½ E		17	
12	3		S E	S S W	19	
1	2	4			19	
2	1	6			18	
3	2				21	
4	2				19	
5	1				20	
6	1				21	
7	1				21	
8	2	4	S E b E	S W b W	24	
9	2	4	W b S	S b W	23	
10	2				23	
11	2	4			19	
12	3	4	Wt.	S S W	19	

Light Airs

2 Strange Sail in the S W

Call'd in all Cruizers

Modte. & Hazey

Made the Sigl & Tkd.

he Medea joind the Fleet with a Prize Brig

Made the Nymph's Sigl. to Chace

Made the Sigl. & Tkd.

arted Compy. with the Medea & her Prize & the Iris

Modte. Breezes & Cloudy
  Latd. Obsd. 38° 20′ N

H	K	F	Courses	Winds	Soundings	Collour of the Ground
1	3	1	W b S	S b W	17	fine Wt. Sand
2	3	4			15	
3	3				12	
4	2	6	S E ½ E		12	
5	3				12	
6	3	4	S E	S S W	19	
7	3	4			21	
8	3				22	
9	3	4	S E b S	S W b S	23	
10	3		S S E	S W	25	
11	2	5			30	
12	2	4	S E b S	S W b S	34	
1	1		N W b N			
		4				
2	2	4	W b N	S W b S	37	
3	3	3			32	
4	3	2			24	
5	3				25	
6	3	4	W b N ½ N		24	
7	6				25	
8	3	4	W b N		17	
9	3	6			15	
10	3	3	S S E	S W	16	
11	2	7			16	
12	2	6			16	

Modte. & Cloudy Answd. the Nymph's Sigl. for Seeing

the Land.

Saw the Land Made the Sigl & Tkd.   Opened a Cask
of Beef, Contts 208 pieces.

Answd the Nymph's Sigl. for 3 Sail in the NE

Made the Sigl. for the Ships to Windward to bear

down on the Admls. Wake

Fresh Breezes & Cloudy

Made the Sigl. & Tkd

Fresh Gales & Cloudy

Made the Nymph's Sigl. to keep 2 Points on the

Larbd. Bow & the Sana. Monica to look out in the S E

Saw the Land Made the Sigl. & Tkd.

Fresh Breezes & Cloudy
   Latd. Obsd. 38° 15′ N

H	K	F	Courses	Winds	Soundings	Collour of the Ground
1	2	6	S b E ½ E	S W b W	19	
2	2	4	S S E	S W	17	
3	3	6	W ½ N	S S W	17	
4	2	6			18	
5	3	4		N W b N	16	
6	1	6		N W	16	
	1		South			
7	1	4	S W ½ W	W N W	16	
8	1	4	South		16	
9	2	5	S W		16	
10	3	4		N W	18	
11	5	6			16	
12	4	4	S S W	N N W	16	
1	4	4			17	
2	5	2		N N E	17	
3	6				18	
4	6				23	
5	6	4			15	
6	6	3	S W		16	
7	5	4			16	
8	5	3			13 / 10	
9	4	4	S W b W		16 / 15	
10						
11						
12						

Fresh Breezes & Hazey Saw 2 Sail in the S E

Made the Sigl. & Tack'd

Answd. Sana. Monica's Sigl. for Seeing the Land

Made the Sigl. to Call in all Cruizers

Made the Sigl. & Tkd.

Modt. & Cloudy

Fresh Gales & Cloudy People Empd. Scrubing their Hammocks

Made the Fortunee's Sigl. to Chase to the S E

Made the Nymph's Sigl. to keep 2 points on the Larbd. Bow

The Solebay made the Sigl. for a Fleet in the S W. Cape
Henry Wt. 6 Leags.   Made the Sigl. to prepare for Action
& to Call in all Cruizers Discovered a Fleet of Large Ships
at Anchor near Cape Henry Made the Sigl for the Line
of Battle ahead at 2 Cables Length.
At Noon Cape Henry W ½ S 4 or 5 Leages.

H	K	F	Courses	Winds	Remarks &c.
1	4	3	W b S	N N E	Modte. & fair ½ past 12 dis-
					the Sigl. for the Line ahead
					the Line ahead, and Made
					At 8 Min. after 1 Made the Sigl.
					the Weather inclining to be
					1 made the Sigl. for the leading
					the Sigl. for the Rear of the
					to keep her Station. 35 M. past
					39 Minutes past 1 Made the
2	2	0	"	"	their Station. At 2 found the
					and 2 frigates their Van bearing
					board Tacks on board. in a
					approaching too near a Shoal
					to Wear 11 M. Afterwards made
					to let the Center of the Enemy's
					Bedford's Sigl. to Get into
					-ing Ship to lead more to
					to Prime 52 M. Made the
					the Terribles Sigl. to Get into
3					and at 3 made the Alcide's
					for the Van Ship to keep
					the Fleet to fill ½ past 3
					more Sail. 34 M. made
					Starbd. 46 Min. Made the Sigl.
					Ships advancing very Slow

covered the Enemy's Fleet getting under Sail Made
1 Cable length distant At 1 hauld down the Sigl. for
the Sigl to form an Et. & Wt. Line at 1 Cable length
for the Rear Division (Adml. Drake) to make more Sail.
Squally took a Reef in the T. Sails 20 Minutes past
Ship to lead more to Starbd. 25 Min. past 1 Rept.
Fleet to make more Sail ½ past 1 the Centaur's Sigl.
1 the Sigl. for the leading Ship to lead more Large.
Resolution's America & Bedford's Sigl. to Get into
Enemy's fleet to Consist of 24 Ships of the Line
So. 3 Miles standing to the Eastward with their Lar-
Line ahead. At 4 Minutes past 2 finding our Van
(called the Middle Ground) made the preparitive Sigl.
the Sigl. and Wore together. brought to in Order
Ships come abreast of us 21 M. past 12. Made the
her Station ½ past 2 made the Sigl. for the lead-
Starbd. 40 M. Past 2 Made the Salamander's Sigl.
Royal Oak's Sigl. to keep the Line 55 Min: Made
her Station 56 M. Made the Princessa's Sigl. also
Sigl. likewise At 17 Minutes past 3 Repd. the Sigl.
to Starbd. 27 M. Made the Sigl. for the Rear of
made the Sigl. for the Ships A Stern to Make
the Sigl. for the Ships in the Van to keep more to
for a Line ahead at 1 Cable length the Enemys
and evening approaching the Adml. judging this to

H	K	F	Courses	Winds	Remarks, &c.
4					be the Moment of attack made
					their Opponents, filld. the Main
					repeated it. 11 M. hauld down
					interfere with the Sigl. to Engage
					-menced the Action 22 M.
					not being Sufficiently extended.
5					for close Action, 40 Min. the Royal
					her Station. 20 Min. Repd. the
					Min. Made the Solebay's &
6					6 the Adml. Sent the Solebay
					those in the Van with Orders
					the Enemy and well abreast
					Line 1 Cable length and haul'd
7					ceased on both Sides ¼ past
9	2	6	S E b E	N E b E	Cables length assunder. at 9
					the Line being so much
10	2	6			The Fortunee inform'd the
					and many Men wounded
					and was then Empd. getting
					in every Respect. The
					as to Expect it every
					3 Leagues. Found our
					-ing and Running Rigging
					Shot through Sails Much
					thrown over board, 2 Men

Ships head to the Eastward

the Sigl. for the Ships to bear down and Engage

Topsail & bore down to the Enemy.   3 Min. past 4

the Sigl. for the Line ahead that it might not

close ¼ past 4 the Van & Center of our Fleet com-

hoisted the Sigl. again for the Line ahead the Ships

27 M. haul'd down the Sigl. for the Line ahead and made the Sigl.

Oaks Sigl. to keep her Station 1 M past 5 the Montagu's to get into

Sigl. for Close action ½ past our Rear bore up 35

Fortunee's Sigl. to come within Hail.   15 Min past

to the Ships in the Rear and the Fortunee to

for the Ships to keep in a parallel Line with

of them during the Night 23 Min. Sigl. for the

down the Sigl for Close Action ½ past the fire

7 made the Night Sigl. for the Line ahead 2

the Montagu Hail'd Said She could not keep

Damaged.

Adml. that the Shrewsbury had the Captain

& first Lt. Killed both his Topsail Yds shot away,

One up the Intrepid was much disabled

Princessa's Main Topmast so much   Wounded

Moment to fall.   At 7 Cape Henry N W

Main & Fore Mast Dangerously Wounded Stand-

much Cutt.   Inner Gammoning of the Bowsprit

Damaged 3 Guns Dismounted One of Which was

Killed & 18 Wounded at 9 Modte. & Clear the

H	K	F	Courses	Winds	Remarks, &c
					Van of the Enemy's
11	3	1	S E ½ E	E N E	in a Line ahead
					them and abreast
12	2	4	S E	"	Do. Wr. the French
1	1	2	"	"	
2	2	4	"	"	
3	2	2	S E ½ S	"	
4	2	3	"	"	Do. Wr. the French
5	2	3	"	"	Made the Sigl.
6	1	4	S E	"	Made the Orpheus's
7	1	6	"	"	the Nymph Repd.
					the French Fleet
8	1	6	"	"	Made the Adamant's
9	1	4	"	"	Made the Solebay's
10	1	4	"	"	of our Van much
					-ing the Main-
11	1	6	"	"	Made the Alcide
					Line
12	1	4	"	"	The French Fleet

Fleet South & the Rear W S W and Appear'd
on the Larboard Tk our Ships parallel with

Fleet to Leeward about 3 Miles

Fleet as above
for forming a Line a Battle ahead
Sigl. for her Captain
the Shrewsburys Sigl. to Speak the Adml.
extending in a Line to Leeward
Sigl. to Come within Hail
& Medea's Sigl. for their Captains Observed some
Disabled Empd. Reeving & Splicing the Rigging fish-
mast, &c.
& Princessa's Sigl. to change Stations in the

to Leeward about 5 Miles parrallel with Ours

H	K	F	Courses	Winds	Soundings	Remarks, &c
1	2		E S E	N E	15	Modt. Breezs. & Clear Wr.
2	2	3	"	"	15	Empd. Repairg ye. Rigging
3	2	2	"	"	15	Unbent ye. fore topsail &
4	2	"	"	"	16	Do. Wr. Sett T Gt. Sails &
5	1	4	S E b S	E b N	"	ye. Signl. for ye. Line ahead
6	2	"				
7	2	"	S E	E N E	"	Do. Wr. in T. Gt. Sails
8	1	6	"	"	17	
9	1	3	"	"	18	Light Airs & Cloudy. ye. Van
10	1	2	"	"	18	
11	1	3	"	"	19	Hd. Ship & Sett top Gallt.
12	1	"	E N E	S E	21	Do. W
1	1	4	E b W	S E b S	18	
2	1	4	"	"	17	hauld. Down ye. Sigl. for ye.
3	Ships head from East to North			Calm	"	at ye french fleet in Sight
4	"	"	"	"	"	Light Airs & Cloudy Wr. with
5	Ships head from N E to S E				"	at 5 made ye. Day Sigl. for
6	"	"	"	"	"	
7	"	"	"	"	"	
8	Ships head S to S W				"	Do. Wr. ye. Center of ye.
9	Do. from W S W to E b S					S b W Dist 4 Leagues
10					22	Made Severl. Ships Sigl. for
11	Up	S S E off E S E				Md. ye Sigl. to Veer Do.
12	Up	W N W off S W b S N W			22	Do. Wr. empd. Repairing ye.

Carpenters Empd. fishing the Main mast Seaman

ye. french fleet in sight

Bent Anouther

out first Reef Mizen Sail at Sun Sett haul'd Down

made ye. Night Sigl. for ye. Line ahead

J Melcomb.

Ship Kd. & ye Line tacking in succession

Sails

C. P.

Line ahead

Bearing S b W 2 Leags.   J. Luck

lighting in ye S E Qr. ye. Enemy's fleet Still in Sight

ye Line ahead.

J. Melcomb

Enemys fleet

Sail Maker Empd. Repairing ye Sails

Officers ye. Carpenters Empd. fishing ye foremast

Veerd. Ship to ye Wtd.

Riging   J. Luck

   Lattd. Obsd. 36 08 No.   C P

H	K	F	Courses	Winds	Soundings	Remarks, &c.
1			Up W b	S S W		Modt. Breezs. & fair mad ye.
2			Off W N	W		to get into her Station Rould-
3	2		West		19	ye. Line of Battle ahead & Md.
4	3				18	8 to 1 at a Quarter past 3 hauld
5	2		J. Melcomb		15	ahead at 2 Md. ye. Sigl. for ye.
6	2					for ye. Leading Ships to keep
7	2	3			16	West 4 or 5 Leags. Made ye.
8	1	4	S E	S S W	17	of ye Land from W b N to
9	1	4			16	of Battle ahead
10	1	4			17	C P.
11	1	4	S E b S	S W b S	18	
12	1	4			20	Modt. Breezs. and fine
1	2		S S E	S W	23	
2	2	2	S b E	S W b W		at ½ past 2 ye. Solebay hauld
3	2	4				Van of Them Bore South &
4	2	4	S ½ E			Do and. Wr. Saw ye. flash of
5	2	2				
6	2		South	W S W		Saw 3 Strang Sail in ye
7	2					
8	2	4			19	Do. wear. Made ye Sigl. and wore
9	3		No.		19	Opend. 4 Barrels of Beef Con-
10	3		N W		17	to Bear Down into ye Adml.
11	2		W N W	S W	17	Saw ye Land from ye. Mast ye fleet to Make more Sail at
12	2				17	Private Sigl. for ye fleet together and Quarter Line.

Sigl. for ye. Line of Battle 10 Min After Made ye Oarspus Sigl.

ing ye. fore Mast at 18 Mints. before one hauld. Down ye. Sigl. for

ye. Sigl. for ye. Division on ye. Starb tack to lead on ye. Larboard

Down ye. Sigl. for Veering ye. Line & ans. Sigl. for ye. Line of Battle

Van to fill Upon ye. Wind at 20 Min past 2 Made ye. Sigl.

ye Wind 10 Min after hauld it Down Saw ye. Land Bear

Sigl. for ye. Van to tack at 7 Modt. & Hazy Tkd. Ship ye. Extremes

S b E Dist at 4 Lea at 7 Made ye Night Sigl. to keep ye Line

wear.   J. Luck

us to acquaint ye. Adl. ye. french fleet had Just tackd. & ye.

they Appeard. to be Stearing from ye. wind

a Gun Bearing East   J. Melcombe

N.E.

Ship ye. Van of ye. Enemy South ye Rear E S E Dis. 6 or 7 Miles

-tents 208 pieces ½ past 8 Made ye. Sigl. for ye. to Windward

Wake

head bearing W b S 6 Leags. Dist 50 M pt 11 Made ye Sigl. for ye Van of
Noon ye Enemy Tackd. their Center S b E Dist at 8 Mile Md ye
10 After made ye Sigl. and Tackd. and Md. ye Sigl. to form ye Bow
                                    J Luck

  Latt Obsd. 36° 4 North

H	K	F	Sound-ings	Courses	Winds	Remarks &c.
1	1	4		So.	W S W	Mod & Cloudy Wr.
2	1	4		S E	Vble	Squally with Thunder &
3	"	Up		N W off	W D	H M S Iris Medea Pegasus
4	"	"	21			Do. Wr. Made ye Singl to
5		Up	E b S	off S E	N E b N	Contents 336 pieces Short
6		"	19			Do. Wr. Enemys fleet S S E
8	1	4		East N	N E	Do. Md. Sail got Down top
9	3	2				
10	3	4	23			partd. Company ye Richmond
11	3					handed ye Mizen Top
12	2	6	30			Fresh Breezs. & Cloudy
1	2	6				
2	2	6				
3	2	6		E b S ½ S	N E b N	
4	2	6				Fresh Breezs. & Cloudy
5	2	5				Do. W at daylight ye
6	2	6		E S E	N E	ye fleet H M S Richmond
7	3					½ past 7 Made ye Sigl
8	½	11		N W b N		Fresh Breezs & Clear Wr.
9	3			N N W		
10	2	4				Split ye Mizen T Sail
11	3			N b W	N E b E	Md. ye Pegasus Sigl.
12	2	4	40			Handd. ye fore & Main top And sent ye Fortunee & Orpheus & Cloudy

Lighting & Rain Close Reefd. ye topsails Joind. ye fleet

ye. Center of ye french fleet S S E Dist 4 Leagus.

Veerd. Do. Wore Ship I Send a Cask of Port No. 6 C C

8 pieces.

Dist 4 or 5 Leags. ½ past 7 Md. ye Sigl. to Make Sail

Gt. Yards   J Luck

& Iris

Sail

Weather with rain

Enemys Fleet bore South Dist 4 Leags Missing from

& Iris

& Ship

ye Center of ye Enemys fleet S b E Dist 4 Leag

Unbent it and Bent a Nouther

for ye Captain

Sails at Noon ye Terrible Md. ye Sigl. of Dist. Ansd. Do.
to her Asistance. French Fleet S S E 4 or 5 Leas. Fresh Gails
   Latt Obs 35-48 N

H	K	F	Sound-ings	W.	Courses	Remarks &c.
1			Up off	N b W N W	N E b E	Fresh Breezs. & Cloudy
2			6	N b W	½ W	Made ye Sig'l to Make
3	1	4	25			ahead at too Cables
4	1	5	24			Do. Wear ye Rear of ye
5	1	4	19	N b W	.	-penters Empd. a Occasionally
6	1	5	15			Do. Wear. ye Center of y
7	1	6		North	E N E	Md. ye Sigl. & Wore Ship
8	2	4	18	S E		The Terrible md. ye Sigl.
9			19	Up S E b E	off S S E	Night Sigl. to Lay By
10						
11			20			
12			21			Modt. Breezs. & Cloudy md.
1	2	4	20	S E b E	N E b E	
2	2	4	21			
3	2	4	21			
4	2	2	21			Fresh Breezs & Cloudy
5	2	5				found Missing from ye
6	2	6				ye Mizen Topsail Md. ye
7	2	4				
8	2	6	25	S E	E N E	Do. Wear.
9	2	3	68			
10	2	5		S E b S		
11	2	6				Got Down ye fore T G
12	1	3		N N E		Do. Wear. Made ye Sigl.
	1	3				

More Sail After Lying By an to form ye Line of Battle

Length asunder

Enemy's fleet S E ye Van E b N Dist 9 or 10 Miles ye Car-

Enemy fleet East too or 3 Leags.

Sett ye fore Top Sail ye french fleet E N E Dist 5 or 6 Ms.

to speak ye Adml. Bore Down to Speak her Md. y

on ye Larb tack

ye Sigl. to make Sail After Lying By

fleet ye Pegasus & Solebay french fleet out or Sight Sett

Montague Sigl. to into her Station

mat and Got up a Nouther

and Tackd.

Latt Obsd. 35 15 C R

H	K	F	Soundings	Courses	Winds	Remarks, &c.
1	2		no Ground	N N E	East	Modt. Breezs. and Cloudy
2	1	6	75			
3	1	5				½ pt. 3 Made y Sigl for
4		6				
5	Up	N	N E off	off N N W		Do. Wear. Opend. a Cask of
6	Up	No.	off	N W	E N E	Making After Lying by
7		Up	No. off	N N W		
8	2		23	N ½ W		
9	2		23			
10	2	1	22	North		
11	1	4	22	N b E	E b N	
12	1	6	22			Light. Breezs. & fine Weather
1	1	6	22			
2	2		22			
3	1	6	22			
4	1	"	22			Light. Airs Do. Wear.
5	1	"	25			Out 3d. reef Topsails
6	1			Up N b W	off N N W	Brot. too Maintop sail to ye Mast
7						
8			24			
9				Up N b E	off N W	Empd. Supplying Difft. Ships
10						The Terrible leakd. so much
11			23		East	at 11 Saw ye Land Bearing
12				Up N N E	off N N W	Do. Wear. Receivd. from H M S

Weekly Accounts

J Luck

Beef Contents 208 pieces 8 Short at● md. ye Sigl. for
C. P.   J Melcombe

J Luck

J Melcombe

at 7 Md. ye Sigl. for all Lieuts. hoistd. out ye Long Boat

with Water Supplyd ye Alcide with 20 tun of Water
that ye fleet was Impd. in getting her Stores out of her
W N W Dist 7 Leags.
Terrible 12 Merines 30 Barralls of Powder & some Guners Stores. J. Luck.
  Latt Obs 35-30 North

H	K	F	Sound-ings	W.	Courses	Remarks &c.
1		Up		N E off E b E	E S E	Light Airs & Clear Wr
2		Up		E b N off N E	b E S E b S	
3		Up		E off N E b E	S S E	
4		Up		E S E off E b E	S	Do. Wr. Sett ye Lowr. and
5						
6						Md. ye Sigl. for all Officers
7		Up		S E off E b S	S S W	
8						Do. Wr. ½ past 8 H M Ship
9			20			to make Sail at 10 Sent
10	1	4	21	No	S S W	
11	4	4	21	"	"	
12	4	5	21	"	"	Modt. & Clear Wr.
1	4	3	22			
2	4	4	22			
3	4	6	21			
4	4	4	21	"	"	Do. W. C. P.
5	6		21		S W	
6	5	6	20	N N W ½ W	"	Squally with Rain Md. ye
7	4	4	18	N W b N	W S W	Got up T. Gt. Yards
8	4	"	16	N W		Modt. & Cloudy Wr. Md. ye
9	3	4	16	N N W	Wt.	lett ye Reefs out of the
10	2	4	16			Sett T Gt Sails
11	2	2	19	N b E	N W b W	
12	1	"	20	N E	N N W	

Recvd from H M S Intrepid'13 Seaman

Topmast Shouds

to Repair on Board their Respective Ships. C P

Terrible was Sett on fier at ½ past 9 Md. ye Night Sigl.
ye Fortunie a head to Lead ye fleet

J Melcombe

Midias Sig to Com within Hail

Orphues & Fortunee Sigl. to Come within hail
Topsails

J. Melcombe

Latt Obsd. 36-44 N The Fleet in Company

A LOG BOOK OF HIS MAJESTY'S SHIP BARFLEUR BETWEEN
THE 1ST AND THE 11TH OF SEPTEMBER, 1781,
BY SAML. BLYTH MASR.[1]

September 1st, 1781

Moderate Breezes and Cloudy ½ past 2 the La
Nymph came out of the Hook. at 3 Adml. Graves got
under Way. Hove into ⅓ of a Cable. ¼ past 4. Saluted
Admiral Graves with 13 Guns and Weighd. Join'd. Company the London, (Adml. Graves) Europa, Royal Oak,
Bedford, America, Adamant, Richmond, and Solebay.
at 8. pm Sandy Hook Lighthouse West 5 or 6 Miles.
¾ past 8 Wore pr. Sigl. ½ past 9 Set T:Gt: sails—
at 10. Out 2d. Reefs T:Sails Sandy Hook Light house
W N W ½ W & Never Sunk W S W—Set M:Sail.
at 12 the Adml. E B S, and the High land of Never
Sunk W ½ N 3 Leagues— In T:Gt: sails and down
Stay sails— ½ past 1 AM the Admll. bearing 4 pt. before the Beam—at 2 Haul'd up & Made Sail to get in
Our Station. at 3 Admiral South—Shortned Sail. ½
past 8 Set Top Gt: Sails. In Company—London, Prin-
cessca, Alfred, Belliqueax, Invincible, Monarch, Centaur, America, Resolution, Bedford, Royal Oak, Montague, Europe, Terrible, Ajax, Alcide, Intrepid,
Shrewsbury, Adamant, Santamonica, La Fortunee, La
Nymph, Sybil, Richmond, Solebay, Jane & Salamander.

---

[1] Admiralty Logs, No. 2160.

Signals Made

At ½ past 1 Made the St. Amonica's Sigls. for her Captain. ¾ past 2, For the Masters of the Invincible, Monarch, Resolution & Montaqua. ½ past 3. The Sigl. to Weigh—at 5 Admiral Graves Made the Sigl. for all Lieutenants—½ past 8. Admirals made the Sigl. to Make Sail, after laying by. ½ past 8 to Alter the Course, repeated both the Sigls.

AM—at 2. Adml. Made the Sigl. to Alter the Course 4 points. at 5 Adml. Made the La Fortunee's to look out ahead, and the St. Amonica's to look out 2 pts. on the Larboard Bow—And at 7. the Solebay's to Chace to Windwd., ½ past 7 the Richmond's to Look out 2 points on the Starboard Bow—at 8 the La Fortunee's to look out in the N.E. Qr. at 25 Minutes past 8. The Richmonds to Make More Sail—¾ past 9 to recall the Richmond 5: Minutes past 10: the Admiral fir'd a Gun to inforce the Signal—We repeated the Signal, at the Same time the La Fortunee fir'd a Gun & Hoisted her Colours—½ past 10. Admiral made the La Nymph's to look out 2 points on the Larboard bow.

September 4th, 1781

Light Breezes and Hazey weather Tack'd Fresh Breezes and Hazey Adml E B S in 2d. Reefs Top sails Set the Main Sail.

AM.—Do. Wr. Admiral E S E ½ past 12 Hauld down the tacking Signal ¼ past 1 AM Tack'd to keep our

Station. Fresh Breezes and Cloudy weather Adml.
N B W. ¼ past 4 up M:Sail at 6. Down Top Gallant
Yards ¾ past 8. Up T:Gt: yards Set T:Gt: Sails ¼
past 9. Tack'd & Out 2d. Reefs of the Topsails ¾ past
10. In T:Gt: Sails Fresh Breezes and Clear weather
In Company as before

Signals Made

P.M.—20 Minutes past 1 La Nymph Made the Signal
for Seeing the Land. at 3. Repeated the Sigls. to Tack.
¼ past 5 Shrewsbury Made the Sigl. for a Sail in the
N E Qr. ¼ past 6 Repeated the Sigl. for the Weather-
most Ships to bear down. at 12 Repeated the Sigl. to
Tack.

AM—at ½ past Repeated the Sigl. Wear at ½ past 7.
Repeated the Sata Monica's Sigl. to Chace in the S E.
¾ past 8 The Adml. Made the Sigl, for Seeing the
Land. at 9 Repeated the Sigl. to Tack ¼ past 9 Repeated the La Nymph's Sigl. to look out 2 points on the
Larboard bow. ¾ past 8 La Fortunee Made the Sigl.
for Seeing a Sail in ye N. W. Qr.

September 5th, 1781.

Fresh Breezes and Hazey weather ½ past 2 Tack'd
Join'd Company H. M. S. Richmond. ½ past 3 Set T.
Gt. Sails. Tack'd. Squaly weather. Close Reef'd the
Topsails & Down T. Gt. Yards Thunder Lightening &
rain. at 7. fair weather & Moderate Set the Fore Sail &

Close Reef'd Topsails—at 8 Admiral S. E. B. S. ½ S. AM. Fresh Breezes and fair weather. Admiral S E B S ½ S Do. Wr. Latd. 37° 02' No. Out 3d. Reefs of the Topsails. Let Out the 2d. & 1st. Reefs of Topsails. Saw the Land bearing N W Saw a Strange Sail. in the N E Qr. standing into the fleet. Saw a Fleet bearing W B S at Anchor within Cape Henry. at 11 Set Studding sails at Noon all our Fleet in Company. Cape Henry W B S 2 Leagues.

Signals Made.

½ past 1 pm Adml. Hood made the Sigl. to a Ship joining the Fleet—after parting Company. at 2 Repeated the Signal to Tack. ¼ past 5 Repeated the Sigl. for all Cruizers. 20 Minutes past 5. Repeated the Signal to Tack. ½ past 11 Repeated the Signal to Alter the Course One pt. to port, AM. ¼ past 6. Adml. Hood Made the Solebay and Richmonds Signl. to come within hail. ½ past 6. Adm'l. made the La Fortunee's Sigl. to Look out in the S E Qr. at 7 for the Nymph to look out 2 points on the Larboard bow at Do. the Alfred Made the Sigl. for Seeing the Land. at ¾ past 9 the Solebay made the Sigl. for a Fleet in the SW Qr. at 10. the Bedford Made the Sigl. for 16 Sail in the SW Qr. at 5 Minutes past 10. the Admiral Made the Signal to prepare for Action. The Barfleur repeated the Sigl. for preparing for Action. and Clear'd Ship for Action, at Do. the Admiral made the Sigl. Call the Cruizers from the SW Qr. and fifety Minutes past 10 he made the La Nymph's to come with Hail. Repeated the Sigl. for the Line ahead at two Cables length asunder.

[201]

September 6th, 1781

Moderate and fair weather. Took in the Studding sails & first Reefs of the Topsails. at the same time Bunted the Main Sail. at 2 The Enemy's fleet coming out in a line ahead standing to the Eastward—at ¼ past 2, Wore per Signal as did all the fleet together—Cape Henry WBS 2 Leagues. at ½ past 3 the Admiral Hoisted his Colours as did the Fleet—at 4 the Admiral haul'd down the Signal for Altering the Course as did the Barfleur. Cape Henry West 2 or 3 Leagues—at ½ past 4 the Vane [van] Ship began to Engage at the Same time the Signal was made for Engaging—¾ past 5 the Enemies Shot went over Us—about 50 Minutes past 5, the Barfleur & Monarch, Open'd their fire on the Enemy—35 Minutes past 6 Haul'd the wind and Tack'd to gain Our Station. at 7 retack'd for Do. at ½ past 7 the Solebay past and Ask'd Us where the Alfred was—45 Minutes past 7 Observed the Admiral's Night Signal for the line of Battle, haul'd down the Day Sigl. The Orpheus join'd the fleet in the time of the Action— at 10 Shortn'd Sail & ½ past brought too. at 12 fill'd. The Admiral bearing SE about ½ Miles Dist. the Enemies Rear Ships, S ½ W 3 Miles—½ past 12 Set T:Gt: Sails and Staysails—at 4. the Admiral bore SEBE Dist. 3 Miles. The Enemy's fleet from SBE to ESE ½ past 6 in T: Gt: Sails & Back'd the Main T: sail, at 7. fill'd the Main Topsail—Light Breezes and Clear—at 9 the Medea Join'd Company. at 11. Admiral Drake Shiffted his Flag to the Alcide, and the Princessa and Alcide Change Stations in the Line. Captain Everet came on board the Barfleur. at Noon Light Airs and fair Weather.

Signals.

P.M. at ½ past the Admiral made the Sigl. for the line ahead. at one Cables length aSunder, which we repeated. at 1 the Admiral Made the Sigl. for the line of bearings East & West a Cables length aSunder. Which we repeated—¼ past 1 the Admiral made the Sigl. for the Rear Admiral, and his Division to Make More Sail—25 Minutes past 1 Adml. made the Sigl. to Alter the Course to port. 29 past 1 the Admiral made the Sigl. for the Rear Admiral & his Division to make more Sail—32 Minutes past 1 Adml. made the Centaur's Sigl. to keep a more regular line—36 Minutes past 1. Adml. made the Sigl. to Alter the Course to Starboard. 40 Minutes past 1, Adml. made the America's Sigl. for being out of her Station. 45 Minutes past 1. We made the Alfred's Sigl. to make More Sail—48 Minutes past 1. Adml. Drake Made the Intrepid's Sigl. for being out of her Station. 51 Minutes past 1, Repeated the Sigl. for the line ahead to Cables length a Sunder. at 6. Minutes past 2 We repeated the Sigl. for the Fleet to Wear together & came to Sail on the Other Tack—at 15. past 2 Adml. fir'd a Gun & put his helm a weather—52 Minutes past 2 the Adml. made the Sigl. for the Leading ship to Alter her Course to Starboard— at 9 Minutes past 3 the Admiral made the Princessa's, Alcide's and Intrepid's Sigl. to Alter their Course More to Starboard. at 19 Minutes past 3, the Admiral fir'd a gun to Enforce the Alcides Sigl. at 29 Minutes past 3 the Admiral made the Sigl. for the Admiral commanding in the 2d. part and his Division to make more Sail. Which we Answer'd and repeated—31 Minutes past 3 Admiral made the Sigl. for the Fleet to

Alter the Course to Starboard, Which we repeated—
40 Minutes past 3, the Adml. made the Bedford's Sigl.
to Close. 54 Minutes past 3. the Admiral made the Sigl.
for the line ahead one Cables length a Sunder. at 4 the
Admiral Made a Sigl. with a Blue & Yellow
Checquer'd flag with a White pandant over it. at 11
Minutes after 4. the Admiral fir'd a gun to Enforce the
Last made Sigl. ¼ past 4. We repeated the Signal.
at 17 past 4. We repeated the Sigl. to Engage the Enemy. 55 Minutes past 4. the Admiral Made the Signals for the Alcide to keep her Stations in the Line
More regularly. 20 Minutes past 4. haul'd down the
White pendant & keept the Blue & Yellow Checquer'd
flag flying under the Red flag—25. Minutes past 5
haul'd down the Sigl. for the Line. at the Same time
the Sigl. for Closer Action was flying. ½ past 6. the
Admiral Haul'd down the Signal for Closer Action,
and Made the Sigl. for the Line a head at One Cables
length a Sunder which we Answer'd. half past 6. the
Admiral Haul'd down the Signal for Engaging, as did
the Barfleur. 48 Minutes past 6. the Barfleur Made the
Centaur's Sigl. to come to Closer Action. at ¾ past 7.
repeated the Night Signal for the line of Battle.

AM—45. Minutes after 5 Adml. made the Sigl. for the
line of Battle ahead ½ a Cables Length a Sunder—at
6 Adml. made the Sigl. for the Solebay to come
with[in] hail—½ past 6. Adml. made the Richmond's
Sigl. to come within hail—½ past 6 Saw the Shrewsbury & Intrepid with Sigls. out to Speak the Admiral.
at 7 Adml. Made the Sigl. for the Orepheus's Captain,
and at 9, for the Medea's Captain. ¾ past 11, Adml.

made the Princessa and Alcide's Sigl. to Change Stations in the Line

September 7th, 1781

Moderate and fair weather Made and Shortned Sail Occasionally to preserve Our Station. ½ past 2, Set T:Gt: Sails—at 3 set Main Sail. ½ past Do. Tack'd to get in Our Station & at ¾ past Do. Tack to gain our Station Set the Jib & Middle Stay sail. at 5 Saw the Land bearing from W B N to S S W 5 or 6 Leags. Do Wr. Set Top Gallant sails. ½ past 9 in T:Gt: Sails. at 10, up Fore Sail—at 11. the Enemy fir'd Several Guns. Made false fires & Rockets—½ past 11 Set T:Gt: Sails. Light Airs at 12, the Body of the Enemy's fleet bore S S E— ½ past 12, Tack'd Ship Close in the Monarch's Wake —The Adml. E N E Dist. 5 or 6 Miles Set the Main Sail & Mid-Stay sail in Stays—at 3, set T:Gt: Studding sails—at 4, the Admiral E N E. 3 or 4 Miles—The Body of the Enemy fleet S E Light Airs and Variable ½ past 4, Haul'd T:Gt: Studding sails—at 5, Saw the Land—at 8 the Extreems of the Land from S W B W to N W off Shore about 6 Leagues—The Enemies fleet from E S E to S B E 7 or 8 Miles at 11 Set Studding sails and Royals—at Noon the Highland & Roanoak W S W. 5 or 6 Leagues Adml. E N E 4 Miles. The Enemy's fleet from S E ½ E to E ½ S 5 Miles Latd. 36° 07'

Signals Made

PM—at 40 Minutes past 3, the Admiral Made the Sigl. for the Admiral in the port and his Division to

Make More Sail, which the Barfleur repeated—by [but] could make no More Sail but the Middle Staysail. R Grindall at 18 Minutes past 8, Repeated the Sigl. for the Line a head.

AM—at ½ past 5, Repeated the Signal for the Line of Battle a head ½ a Cables length a Sunder. ½ past 8 Admiral Hood made the Sigl. for the Invincible and Alfred's Captains. At 11, The Adml. Made the Sigl. to Veer. Repeated Do.

September 8th, 1781

Light Breezes and fair Weather. the Enemy's fleet Close on the wind with their Starbooard tacks on board. ¼ past 1, In Studding Sails. ¾ past 1, brought too by the wind. at 4, the Enemy's fleet bore from S E B S to S E ½ E 3 or 4 Leagues off their heads to the Westward —The Body of Roanoak S W B W 5 Leagues. Made & Shortned Sail Occasionally—¾ past 5, Tack'd—at Sun Set the Extreems of the Land of Roan:oak, from S W B S to W S W ½ W 4 or 5 Leagues at 8, Saw lights bearing S E ½ E. The Adml. N W B N. and the Body of the Enemies fleet S E B S. at ¾ past 9, the Alfred & Belliqueax bore up. ¼ past 10 Shortned Sail the Alfred, Belliqueax, & Invincible being 4 points to Leeward of their Station—at 12, the Admiral bore N N W ½ W and the Alfred S E ½ E Made Sail Occassionally. ½ past 1, Saw a light bearing S E B S Which we take to be one of the Enemies Rear Ships— at 33, past 2, the Solebay hail'd us, and Sail the Enemy's fleet was Tack'd—at 3 Down F:T:Staysail at ½ pt. 3.

Up Mizon & down T :G.Stay sail. at 4, the Adml. bore
N B W. at Daybreak Saw Twenty one of the Enemies
Ships bearing from S E B E ½ E to S E ½ S. at 7 The
Vane [van] of the Enemy began to Tack—at 8, Wore
Ship—the Admiral No. 1½ Miles at Noon Roanoak
West 5 or 6 Leagues In Company 19 Sail of the Line 7
Frigates, one Sloop & a fire ship Latd. 36° 04′ N

Signals Made

PM—¼ past One the Admiral Sigl. for the Ships that
Leads on the Starboard Tack to lead on the Larboard.
after 1, Admiral Haul'd down the Sigl. for the Line,
as did we. at 28 Minutes after 1, Admiral Hoisted the
Sigl. for the line—as Did we. 55 Minutes after 1,
Adml. made the Sigl. for the Vane to fill. We repeated
Do. ½ past 2, Adml. Made the Sigl. for the Fleet to
Haul Close to the wind—at 5 Repeated the Sigl. to
Tack.—at 8, Repeated the Sigl. for the Line of Battle
a head—

AM—35 Minutes past 7, the Princessa Made the Private Sigl. to three Ships in the N E Qr. at 43 Minutes
past 7 Repeated the Sigl. to Tack—at 8 Repeated the
Signal for the fleet to Wear together. at 10 Minutes
past 8, the Admiral Haul'd down the Signal for the Line
as did we—at 14′ past 8, the Admiral Hoisted the Signal for the line—as did we—23 Minutes past 8, Adml.
Made the Signal for the Leading Ship to Haul the
Wind. 40 Minutes past 8, for the Ships to Windward
to bear down in the Admls. Wake—Which we repeated—20 Minutes, past 10, Barfleur made the Santa

Monica Signal for being out of her Station. ¾ past 11, The Enemy's fleet Tack'd. The Admiral Made the Sigl. for the Vane of the fleet to make More Sail—at Noon the Admiral Made the Sigl. for the fleet to Tack together. Which we repeated—

September 9th, 1781

Light Airs & fine weather. ½ past 3 Close Reef'd the T:Sls. & brought too M.T.S. to the Mast—Light Breezes with Lightning, Thunder & rain. Join'd Company three Frigates ¼ past 4 Wore Ship. ½ past 4 a boat came on bd. from the London. at Do. Admiral Hood went on bd. the London, at 7. He returned again from the London. ½ past 7 fill'd & Made Sail at 8 Saw some flashes of Guns bearing S B E. Adml. E.B.S. Fresh Breezes and Cloudy. at 9 the Adml. E ½ S. at 10 Squally with rain. Bent the Mn. Staysail. Adml. E ½ S. at 11 Squally with rain. Adml. E ½ S at 12 Do. Wr. Adml. E ½ S at Squaly & Cloudy. ½ past 5 A M the Body of the Enemies fleet S ½ E 8 or 9 Miles. Down T.Gt. yards. at 7 Wore Ship. at 8 Do. Wr. ¾ past 9 Set the Jib & Main T.Staysail ¼ past 11. Down Jib & M.T.staysail. ½ past 11. In Mizon & F.T. Sails. at Noon Back'd the M. T. sail.

Signals Made

PM—at 10 Minutes past Noon Repeated the Sigl. to Tack. 21 Minutes past Noon the Adml. Haul'd down the Sigl. for the Line of Battle ahead. at 28 Minutes past Noon Repeated the Sigl. for the Bow & Quarter

line. at 10 Minutes past 2 the Admiral Haul'd down
the Sigl. for the Line Bow & Quarter as did we. at 4
Repeated the Signal for the fleet to Wear together.
40 Minutes past 5, the Admiral Made the Princessa
Sigl. to come within hail. at 50 Minutes past 5, Admiral
made the Signal for a Boat from the Montague,
Shrewsbury, Bedford, Fortunee, & Sybil. At 6 The
Admiral S W B S & the Enemis Fleet S B E 3 or 4
Leagues. ½ past 7 Repeated the Admiral's Signal for
Making Sail after lying by.

AM—at 7. Repeated the Admirals Signal for the Fleet
to Veer together. At Noon the Terrible Made the Signal of Distress, Which the Admiral Answerd.

September 10th, 1781

Fresh Breezes and Hazey Wr. at 20 Minutes past 1 a
boat came on board from the Pegasus. ½ past 1 fill'd.
The Enemy's fleet from S E to E B S at 4. the Admiral
S ½ E 2 or 3 Miles. Twenty five of the Enemy's fleet in
Sight, Extending from S E ½ E to E B N. at 6, the
Vane of Our fleet N B W ½ W. the Adml. S B E. The
Body of the Enemy's fleet E B N 7 or 8 Miles. Set the
M.T.Staysail ¼ past 6 Wore. The Body of the Enemy's
fleet E B N. 7 or 8 Miles. at 8 hove too M.T. Sail to the
Mast. Fresh Breezes and Cloudy. at 9 Saw Several
Rockets. and flashes of Guns bearing N E B N. at
12, the Adml. S.B.W. ½ past 12. fill'd and bore up to
gain Our Station. at 4, the Admll. S E ½ E Made &
Shortned Sail Occasionally to keep Our Station. at Do.
Wr. at ¾ 10 Spoke the Santamonica, and Order her to

send her boat on board. at Noon Set the Main Sail at Noon the Admiral S E B E ½ E. In Company 19 Sail of the Line. a 50 Gun Ship, 7 Frigates, 1 Sloop of War & a fire ship

Signals Made

PM—at ¼ past 1 Repeated the Signal for the line of Battle 2 Cables length aSunder. ½ past 1 Repeated the Signal for the to fill. at 6. Repeated the Signal to prepare to Veer. ¼ past 6. Repeated the Signal to Veer. at 8 Repeated the Signal to Brace too and lye by. at 12. Repeated the Signal for Making Sail after lying by.

AM—at 10. We made the Santamonica's Signal to come with hail. ½ past 11, Repeated the Signal to Tack.

September 11th, 1781

Fresh Breezes & Squaly. ¾ past Noon Tackd. at 3 Spoke the Terrible. at 4 Shortned Sail & brought too, and Sent a Boat on Board the Admiral. at ½ past 4 Hoisted out a Barge Sir Samuel Hood Went on board of the London at 6. in Cutter. at 50 Minutes past 6, Sir Samuel Hood return'd In Barge ½ past 7 fill'd and Set the Fore Sail. at 8 the Adml. E B N at 12 Set Jib & Staysails The Adml. N W ½ N 1 Mile. ½ past 12 down Jib & Staysails Light Airs and fine Weather the Adml. N W at 6 Out 3d. & 2d. Reefs of the Topsails. Hoisted out the Boats to Assist the Terrible Employ'd Stowing the Booms Light Breezes and fair Weather,

The Boats Attending the Terrible the Land bearing N W In Company with 19 Sail of the Line, a fifty Gun Ship, 6 Frigates, a Sloop and a Fire Ship. Latd. 35° 37 Longde. Made 0.28 Et.

Signals Made

PM—¾ past 3 the Adml. Made the Sigl. for Weekly Accounts. Answerd it. at 20 Minutes past 5, the Admiral Made the Sigl. for the Captain of the Intrepid at 25 Minutes Made the Signal for the Captain of the Terrible. at 25 Minutes past 7 Repeated the Signal for Making More Sail after lying by.

AM—at 7 the Admiral made the Signal for all Lieutenants. Answerd. Do. at 8. Made the Sigl. for the Boats of Our Division.

JOURNAL DE NAVIGATION DE L'ARMÉE AUX ORDRES DE
MONSIEUR LE COMTE DE GRASSE, LIEUTENANT
GÉNÉRAL, PARTIE DE BREST LE VINGT DEUX
MARS DIX SEPT CENT QUATRE VINGT UN[1]

Du trois Septembre au quatre. Vents du Sud-Ouest,
joli frais, beau temps. Midy et quart, signal au Saint
Esprit, à la Bourgogne, au Réfléchy et au Scipion.
Trois heures et demie, l'Aigrette signale une voile. Signal à l'Aigrette et à la Railleuse d'appareiller. Quatre
heures et demie, ces deux frégates sortirent. Cinq
heures et demie, le mot de l'ordre. Dix heures matin,
l'Aigrette signale une voile dans l'Est Sud Est. Le
général est attentif.

Du quatre Septembre au cinq. Deux heures et demie,
signal d'un bâtiment à rame en dérive sans espoir de la
sauver. Six heures et quart, une corvette fit route dans
la baye. Idem, on découvrit deux voiles. Aussitôt
l'armée mit pavillon et l'amenèrent de suite. Trois
heures et quart, matin, l'Aigrette sortit et la Railleuse.
Sept heures et demie, matin, l'Aigrette échone et demande ancre et grélins. Idem, signal d'envoyer des
ancres et grélins à l'Aigrette. Sept heures trois quarts,
l'Aigrette annulle le signal fait précédemment. Dix
heures, le Marseillais signale six voiles dans l'Ouest;
ensuite, il en signale vingt cinq. Idem, signal de faire
branle-bas, et celui de faire revenir promptement les
canots et chaloupes qui étoient à terre. Dix heures et
demie, signal de se tenir prêt a appareiller. Onze

[1] Archives de la Marine, B⁴, 184.

heures et demie, une frégate de l'ennemi tira un coup de canon. Idem, l'Aigrette signale vingt trois vaisseaux. Le général est attentif. Onze heures trois quarts, signal à virer à pic.

Du cinq Septembre au six. Vent du Nord Est à l'Est Nord Est, joli frais, beau temps. Route estimée du moment du départ à midy. Sud Est 1° Sud. Chemin estimé, dix huit lieues et demie, latitude arrivée estimée Nord, 36° 20′. Longitude arrivée occidentale: 77° 50′. Mouvement. Midy et quart faire appareiller sans autre signal. Midy et demie, l'Auguste fit une signe à la troisieme division. Le général quitte la section à l'ancre. Idem, signe de former un signe de vitesse sans ordre, m'observer de posts. Midy trois quarts, l'armée mit pavillon et flamme. Une heure, ordre aux vaisseaux de tête de tenir le vent. Deux heures et quart, l'ennemy prit les amures à babord. Idem, signal aux vaisseaux de tête d'augmenter de voiles. Deux heures trois quarts, même signal. Trois heures, le Languedoc fut prendre son poste. L'Auguste signale la Bourgogne de forcer de voiles. Trois heures trois quarts, les ennemis mirent leur pavillon. Idem, ordre à tous les vaisseaux de suivre les mouvements des vaisseaux de tête en serrant la ligne. Quatre heures, ordre aux vaisseaux de courir deux quarts largue. Quatre heures et quart, faire tenir le plus près. Combat. Quatre heures et quart, le combat commença. Cinq heures trois quarts, signal aux vaisseaux de tête de courir deux quarts largue. Six heures, ordre aux vaisseaux de tenir le plus près. Etant hors de portée de l'ennemi, le feu cessa. Six heures et demie, signal de ralliement. Sept heures, la queue de l'ennemy cesse le feu et le rôtre, ensuite. Huit heures trois quarts.

L'Aigrette vint nous dire de la part du général de gouverner à sept quarts, largue. Cinq heures et demie, matin, le Diadème signale qu'il est hors d'état de combattre. Cinq heures et quart, signal de reconnoissance. Cinq heures et demie, ordre aux vaisseaux de tête d'augmenter de voiles. Sept heures, une frégate demande si notre mature étoit fort endommagée; on lui repondit qu'oui. Elle alloit se désarmer pour donner du monde au Diadème. Sept heures et demie, le Caton demande du secours. Le général est attentif. Dix heures et demie, ordre aux vaisseaux de tête de forcer de voiles. Onze heures trois quarts, signal detenir le plus près. Idem, le Pluton demande à parler au général.

Du six Septembre au sept. Vents du Nort Est au Sud, petit frais. Route estimée à midy: Sud Sud Est 4° 45′ Est. Chemin estimé: cinq lieues un tiers. Latitude arrivée estimée Nord 36° 06′. Latitude observée, Nord: 35° 54′. Longitude arrivée, occidentale: 77° 41′. Variation o caze observée Nord Ouest 1° 20′. Hauteur méridienne 59° 42′. Une heure trois quart, la Railleuse signale le Pluton. Quatre heures trois quarts, ordre aux vaisseaux de tête de tenir le plus près babord amures. Onze heures du soir, faire virer l'armée lof pour lof. Cinq heures et demie, matin: signal de reconnoisance. Dix heures et quart, le Réfléchy demande la permission d'envoyer à bord du general. Onze heures et quart, signal de ralliement.

Du sept septembre au huit. Vents du Sud Sud Est à l'Ouest Nord Ouest. Route corrigée à midy Est Nord 30′ Sud. Chemin corrigé, neuf lieues et demie. Latitude observée Nord 35° 53′. Longitude arrivée occidentale 77° 05′. (Variations ocaze observée Nord Ouest 1° 15′. Hauteur meridienne 59° 20′. Difference sud, trois minutes.) Une heure trois quarts, faire virer l'armée lof pour lof tout à la fois. Deux heures, le Souverain demande à parler au Général. Le général lui accorde. Idem, signal de ralliement. Deux heures et quart, pris les amures à babord. Le général répéta le signal de ralliement. Deux heures et demie, signal au Souverain de se mettre à la tête de l'armée. Quatre heures et quart, signal d'augmenter de voiles. Le commandans sont chargés de la police de leur escadre. Cinq heures et quart, la Railleuse nous dit que quand le général signaleroit de tenir le vent, il faudroit gouverner à sept quarts et, à la répétition de ce signal, gouverner à six quarts. Idem, le mot le l'ordre. Cinq heures et demie vire par la contre marche l'armée ennemie. Cinq heures et demie, signal de virer vent devant et faire augmenter de voiles. Six heures et quart, rallier l'armée en échiquier sur la ligne du plus près, tribord amures. Six heures et demie, faire tenir le vent à l'armée. Cinq heures et quart, matin, signal de reconnoisance. Cinq heures trois quarts, ralliement en échiquier. Six heures trois quart faire virer l'armée vent devant tout à la fois. Sept heures et demie, signal de serrer la ligne. Huit heures, ordre au vaisseau de tête de gouverner pour passer de l'avant de l'ennemy. Huit heures et quart, faire serrer la ligne. Huit heures trois quarts, le Caton signale trois voiles sous le vent. Neuf heures et demie, ordre aux vaisseaux de tête de tenir le plus près. Onze heures et quart, le Pluton signale la terre au vent. Onze heures et demie, faire virer l'armée vent devant, tot à la fois. Onze heures trois quarts, rallier l'armée en échiquier sur la ligne du plus près, babord, tribord amures.

Du huit septembre au neuf. Vents variable, temps

orageux, pluye, vent. A midy, la route estimée avalu
les Sud Est quart Sud 2° 15′. Chemin estimé, six lieues
et quart. Route corrigée selon la hauteur, Sud Est
quart Sud 3° 15′. Chemin corrigé, neuf lieues. Latitude arrivée, estimée nord 35° 28′. Latitude observée,
nord : 35° 31′. Longitude arrivée occidentale de Paris :
76° 45′. (Hauteur meridienne 59° 17′. Difference
nord, trois minutes.) Mouvement du huit septembre
au neuf midy et quart. Le Languedoc signale le numero sept et mit ensuite pavillon bleu. Une heure, le
Languedoc fait tenir le vent à la deuxième escadre toute
à la fois. Une heure et quart, signal de raliement à
l'Echiquier sur la ligne du plus près babord, tribord
amures, au plus près du vent. Deux heures et demie,
le général et partie de l'armée mit en panne Trois
heures et demie, le Languedoc fait signal de raliement
au Sceptre. Quatre heures et quart, faire virer l'armée
lof pour lof tout à la fois. Six heures et quart, rallier
l'armée en échiquier sur la ligne du plus près, tribord,
les amures à babord, la route au plus près du vent. Sept
heures trois quarts, faire prendre des ris. Quatre heures
et quart matin, mis en panne, le grand hunier sur le mât.
Cinq heures et quart, fait voir que nous sommes de
l'armée. Six heures, rallier l'armée à l'ordre de bataille, l'amure à babord, dans l'ordre naturel. Sept
heures et demie, faire tenir le vent à toute l'armée. Huit
heures, même signal. Huit heures et quart, faire virer
l'armée lof pour lof tout à la fois. Huit heures et demie,
l'armée vire lof pour lof. Idem, raliement à l'Echiquier
sur la ligne du plus près babord, les amures à tribord
au plus près du vent.

Du dimanche neuf septembre au dix. Depuis hier,
midy, à ce jour, même heure, les vents régnèrent de

l'Est Nord Est à l'Est Sud Est, jusques sur les huit
heures du matin qu'ils remontèrent à l'Est Nord Est,
joli frais, beau temps, la mer belle, sous différentes
voilures, les amures à tribord. A six heures et demie
du soir, relevé au compas, la tête de l'armée ennemie au
Ouest Nord Ouest, 3° Nord et la queue au Ouest quart
Sud Ouest, 4° Sud, à toute vue de dessus le gaillard. A
midy, la route estimée à voillu le Nord Ouest quatre
Nord 3° 15′ ouest. Chemin estimé, vingt une lieues
trois quarts. Route corrigée selon la hauteur: Nord
Ouest quart Nord 30′ Ouest. Chemin corrigé, vingt
trois lieues. Latitude arrivée estimée Nord 36° 24′.
Latitude observée, nord: 36° 28′. Longitude arrivée
occidentale de Paris: 77° 33′. Nous changeâmes, dans
la nuit, notre vergue de petit hunier et racomodâmes
nos voiles. Le matin, on ne vit plus l'ennemy. (hauteur
meridienne 58 00′. Difference nord 4′.) Mouvement,
midy et quart, l'Aigrette signal d'ordre aux vaisseaux
qui ont signalé l'ennemi, de faire les signaux de correspondance entre le général et les frégates de découverte
qui s'éxécuteront par le moyen des voiles dont messiurs
les capitaines ont seuls connaisance. Le général est
attentif aux signaux. Une heure et quart, l'Aigrette
signale que l'ennemi vire de bord. Le général est attentif. Deux heures et quart: Le Palmier signale que
l'ennemi tient le plus près, tribord amures. Le général
a distingué les signaux. Deux heures trois quart le
Caton avertit qu'il a une voye d'eau. Le général distingué les signaux. Idem, signal que les premiers signaux qui seront faits seront pris dans la table numéro
trois. Idem, le Caton fait signal numéro un pris dans
la table numéro trois. Idem, avertir que les signaux
fait par un seul pavillon seront pris dans la table nu-

mero un. Trois heures, le Caton fait un signal connu des capitaines. Le général a distingué les signaux. Trois heures trois quarts, signal que les signaux qui seront faits seront pris dans la feuille trois. Le général est attentif aux signaux. Idem, signal connu des capitaines. Trois heures trois quarts, avertir un vaisseau incommodé que l'armée se réglera sur sa voilure et qu'il se mettra à la tête ou au vent. Cinq heures et quart, une frégate signale le fond à cinquante brasses. Le général distingué. Huit heures trois quarts du soir, signal que l'on a connaissance de l'ennemy et qu'il est essentiel que chaque vaisseau prenne son poste. Cinq heures et quart, matin, signal de reconnaissance. Cinq heures trois quarts, on découvre une escadre dans l'ouest nord ouest. Le général a distingué. Six heures, signale ralliement en ordre de bataille. Six heures et demie, faire passer à poupe du général l'Aigrette et le Pluton. Idem, le Souverain demande à chasser. Accordé. Six heures trois quarts, annuller la permission de chasser. Sept heures, signal de ralliement. Sept heures et quart, faire forcer de voiles à toute l'armée. Sept heures et demie, signal de ralliement. Sept heures trois quarts, faire chasser toute l'armée dans le Nord. Neuf heures trois quarts, faire passer à poupe du général l'Aigrette et la Railleuse.

Du dix septembre au onze. Vents de l'Est à l'Est Nord Est, petit frais, presque calme. A midy, la route estimée Nord Ouest quart Ouest 2° 15′ Ouest. Chemin estimé: onze lieues et quart. Route corrigé: Nord Ouest quart Ouest 3° 1′. Chemin corrigé. Onze lieues et quart. Latitude arrivée estimée Nord: 36° 45′. Latitude observée Nord 36° 48′. Longitude arrivée occidentale de Paris 78° 06′. A midy, relevé le cap Henry: 34 Nord à deux lieues et demie. (Hauteur meridienne 50° 17′. Difference nord 3′. Variation estimée Nord Ouest 1° 15′.) Mouvement, midy et demie signal de gouverner au Nord Nord Ouest. Une heure et quart, un vaisseau découvre deux voiles sous le vent. Le général est attentif. Deux heures et quart, le Glorieux qui rallioit tira un coup de canon. Deux heures trois quarts, signal à tous les vaisseaux de mettre leur numero. Le général a distingué. Quatre heures, ordre aux vaisseaux de tête de tête de diminuer de voiles. Six heures et demie, le général fait une signal que nous ne pumes distinguer. Cinq heures et quart du matin, signal de reconnoissance. Six heures et quart, le général mit en panne, tira un coup de canon et mit pavillon rouge à la vague d'artimon. Idem, nous avons sondé à quatorze brasses, sable gris. Six heures et demie, signal que les vaisseaux les plus à portée des chasseurs répéteront les signaux. Sept heures, faire passer à poupe du général le Souverain. Idem, la Railleuse decouvre une voile de l'avant. Le général distingué. Sept heures trois quart, faire rallier les vaisseaux et fregate de l'armee. Huit heures, le Citoyen découvre cinq voiles de l'avant. Le général a distingué.

Idem, le Citoyen signale la terre au vent. Idem, l'ennemi court largue, babord amures. Le général est attentif. Huit heures et demie, faire tenir le vent à toute l'armée. Neuf heures et quart même signal avec un coup de canon. Idem, le général fit des signaux de reconnoissant et signal à la Concorde qui rallioit. Neuf heures et demie, le Glorieux signale que les bâtiments que l'on voit sont ennemis. Idem, l'Auguste signale que les bâtiments qui restent ouest nord ouest sont francais. Neuf heures trois quart, faire chasser toute l'armée sans observer d'ordre. Onze heures, signal au Destin de virer vent devant. Onze heures et demie, faire chasser toute l'armée au vent. Idem, la Railleuse tira un coup de canon. Signal de reconnoissance à l'armée de Monsieur de Barras. Idem, le Glorieux demande à chasser. Le général lui accorde.

Du onze septembre au douze. Vents du sud, petit frais, beau temps. Route estimée, depuis midy, au mouillage : Nord nord ouest 5° ouest. Chemin estimée : quatre lieues. Latitude arrivée estimée nord, 36° 59′. Longitude arrivée occidentale de Paris 78° 13′. Relevé le cap Henry : Sud 10° Est, deux tiers lieue. Le cap Charles : Nord 13° 4′ Est. La pointe formant l'entrée d'Hampton : 1° Nord. . . . (Mouille's au Cap Henry le onze.) Mouvement : une heure trois quarts, le Glorieux signale que l'ennemi court vent arrière. Deux heures et quart, le Glorieux tira plusieurs vollée sur deux fregates angloises dont une des deux amena. Deux heures et demie, faire virer vent devant la Railleuse. Deux heures trois quarts, faire virer l'armée vent devant, lof pour lof. Trois heures et demie, le Languedoc donne ordre aux vaisseaux de répéter les signaux des chasseurs et ceux du Général. Quatre heures, signal d'envoyer du secours au Glorieux et de mettre les canots à la mer. Quatre heures trois quarts, faire, préparer l'armée au mouillage. Cinq heures et demie, la seconde frégate angloise amena. Cinq heures trois quarta, l'Expériment et l'Andromaque rallièrent venant de la riviere de Chesapeak. Six heures, l'armée mouilla. Sept heures et demie, matin, faire venir à bord du général le second capitaine du Languedoc. Idem, faire aller à bord du général le major de l'Escadre bleue et blanche. Dix heures et demie, signal à la Railleuse.

Du douze septembre au treize. Vents du Nord Ouest

au Sud Ouest, joli frais. A midy l'escadre de monsieur de Barras appareilla et vint mouiller parmi nous. Midy et demie, faire venir à bord du général les officiers chargés du detail. Idem, signal au Saint Esprit, une heure et quart, signal au Zélé. Deux heures et demie, le Diadème découvre des voiles et demande à chasser. Le général lui accorde. Trois heures trois quarts, l'Hercule signale des voiles dans le Nord Nord Est. Quatre heures et quart, le Pluton mouilla avec la frégate angloise le Richmond. Cinq heures et demie, Signal, le mot de l'ordre et au Caton de faire la ronde. Six heures et demie, signal à l'Andromaque. Six heures, matin, signal à l'Expériment et à la Bourgogne. Sept heures et demie, le Languedoc signale des vaisseaux de guerre dans le Nord Nord Est. Sept heures trois quarts, signal à la Concorde et à la Surveillante. Neuf heures et quart, flamme d'ordre. Dix heures trois quarts, la Concorde appareilla.

LIVRE DE BORD DU VAISSEAU LE CITOYEN
29 AOUT—11 SEPTBRE. 1781[1]

Mecredy vingt neuvième. (Suite du journal de monsieur le chevalier Déthy capitaine du Citoyen.) Les
vents toujours variables de l'ouest sud ouest au sud ouest
petit fraix clair, l'armée a continué tenir le vent babord
amure; au lever du soleil la sonde a rapporté vingt six
brasses fond gris tirant sur le jaune, sable fin.—A neuf
heures, l'armée a mis pavillon au Souverain qui rallioit
avec la prise qu'il avoit fait de la corvette le Sandwihs.
Cette corvette ressembloit à une flutte sans figure, sans
aucune marque de batiment de guerre; elle portoit du
canon de dix huit. Elle avoit été construite précisé-
ment pour remonter les rivières. Elle avoit été fort
utile dans ces régions qui ne sont que rivières. On dit
même qu'elle avoit beaucoup contribué à la prise de
Charlestown. Deux de nos frégates ont chassé dans la
partie de l'Est. Le général leur a fait signal de ne pas
perdre l'armée de vue. A dix heures la sonde a rapporté dix sept brasses même qualité de fond. A midy
la latitude observée a été 36° 49 nord. La routte a valu
selon l'estime le Nord Ouest, chemin sept lieues un tiers
ainsi que la Corrigée. La longitude arrivée ouest 78°
49 ce qui nous met à terre au Sud du cap Henry. A
deux heures, j'ay arrivé sur l'armée pour m'y rallier.
J'étois trop en avant. Les vents étoient sud petit fraix;
à deux heures et demie, vu la terre dans l'Ouest quart
Sud Ouest. La sonde a rapporté quatorze brasses, sable

[1] Archives de la Marine, B⁴ 238, fol. 108v°–133v°.

d'un gris jaunâtre et fin avec des petits morceaux de coquillages. A cinq heures et demie, même profondeur. Le général a fait un signal que je ne pouvois discerner par le peu de vent qu'il y avoit et par ce que j'en étois éloigné. Je le luy ai marqué par un autre signal. C'étoit le renvoy de la section des mouvements généraux à celle de l'ancre. A dix heures et quart, le général, ayant fait signal l'armée de se préparer à mouiller avec une ancre à jet en ligne de bataille Est Sud Est et Ouest Nord Ouest; au coucher du soleil, le cap Henry restoit à l'Ouest; corrigé distance six lieues. C'est un terrain de sable blanc très bas et boisé. L'armée a continué singler au Ouest Nord Ouest jusqu'à sept heures qu'elle a mouillé. J'étois, par les onze brasses, sable fin et jaune; à deux heures du matin, les vents étoient toujours au sud faibles. La frégate, qui étoit à croiser aux environs de l'armée, a passé parcourant touts les vaisseaux de l'armée pour avertir que l'intention du général étoit d'appareiller sans signal à quatre heures du matin; à trois heures trois quarts, j'ay été sous voile; mais, il etoit presque calme. (En marge: Le Souverain rallie à l'armée avec une prise. Mouillé à l'Est Sud Est du général.)

Jeudi trentième. Au point du jour, le calme m'empêchant par les courants de faire mettre le cap à la routte du général qui avoit un peu d'air, toujours dans la partie du Sud et me trouvant embarrassée entre plusieurs navires qui portoient comme luy, j'ay mis mes quatre canots à la mer pour revenir sur babord; et, y étant venu, j'ai singlé avec un peu d'air au Sud à l'ouest nord ouest pour m'élever un peu et me tirer du milieu des vaisseaux. A neuf heures, les vents ont été Est Sud Est petit fraix. L'armée a singlé à l'Ouest sur le cap

Henry. A dix heures, le général a fait signal à l'armée depasser à la section de l'ancre. J'ay diminué de voile, attendant les ordres qu'il avoua donner. A dix heures et demie, il a fait signal de mouillage sur trois colonnes avec une grosse ancre. Les commandants des escadres chacun à la tete des leurs. J'ay alors mis en pane pour attendre l'Auguste qui forçoit de voiles. J'ay fait servir à onze heures au moment qu'un canot parti de la côte du sud du cap Henry venoit à moy. Il a été abordée le Diadème, croyant, malgré que nous avions notre pavillon et flammes de distinction, que nous étions anglois. A onze heures et quart, le signal a été fait pour faire branle-bras général, ensuite de passer à la section des mouvements généraux. A midy et demie, l'armée a mouillé à l'entrée de la riviere de Chesapeak. J'étois par les onze brasses, vase sableux et noir. Le cap Henry restoit au Sud Est quart Sud à deux lieues de lieue, le cap Charles au Nord Nord Est 3° Est, la terre la plus au fond de la baye à l'ouest 5° sud ouest. (En marge. Variation observée: on tire: 2° 41, nord ouest. À six heures et demie le général a fait signal aux vaisseaux qui étoient en avant de réppéter les signaux des chasseurs. Un canot a été à bord du Diamède, persuadé que nous étions anglois. Celui qui le menoit étoit un royaliste qui a été reconnu et consigné à bord du général. Il est trois hommes dans le courant de la journée.

Vendredy trente unième. A sept heures du matin, les vents au sud ouest petit frais et clair, la partie du nord ouest un peu obscure, le général a mis flamme d'ordre. J'y ai été a bord. Les ordres portoient de préparer les troupes pour la descente; à deux heures après midi, le signal a été fait pour les embarquer; partie des vaisseaux de l'armée ont porté les leurs à bord des frégates

et autres batiments destinés pour monter dans les rivières; les orages, les tonnerres et les vent variables y joint
la pluye à verse qui tomboit ont duré jusqu'à quatre
heures et quart du soir auquel temps le général a fait
le signal d'embarquer les troupes dans les chaloupes à
ceux comme le Citoyen dont la chaloupe devoit être
armée avec les soldats de Barrois passager incorporés
dans un des régiments destinés à la descente. La chaloupe étoit à bord de l'Andromaque; y débarquer les
effets et le détachment des hussards qui le Scipion avoit
à son bord et dont la Sienne qui étoit avariée ne pouvoit
les porter; j'ai fait tirer plusieurs coups de canon avec
le pavillon en berne pour la faire revenir; mais, les
orages ayant derechef commencé, le général, voyant que
bien des vaisseaux ne pouvoient avoir pu remplir leurs
objets par le mauvais temps qu'il faisoit, a annullé le
signal et laissé écouler cette marée qui a commencé a
quatre heures. L'Experiment, les frégates la Diligente
et l'Andromaque ainsi que les corvettes ont appareillé
avant la nuit pour monter dans la rivière James. (Le
marge: Le flot à quatre heures du soir).

Samedy, premier Septembre. A quatre heures du
matin, le général a fait signal d'embarquer les troupes
destinées aux chaloupes et canots. Je me suis hâté de
faire embarquer le détachment de Barrois dans ma
chaloupe armée avec deux officiers et je l'ai envoyée au
général portant avec elle les jours de vivres ordonné;
à cinq heures, toute cette flotte est partie du bord du
général. La frégate l'Andromaque, ainsi que le Sand-
wishs qui étoient restés à l'ancré, ont appareillé pour les
escorter et monter avec eux. A sept heures, le général
a signalé un bâtiment suspect, on luy a tiré dessus
comme il traversoit l'armée; c'étoit une des prises dont

celle du Glorieux qui, chargée de troupes, s'étoit élevée au large pour remonter en rivière. A dix heures, la frégate l'Aigrette est arrivée avec une corvette appellée la Loyaliste qu'elle avoit pris le jour de notre entrée dans cette baye en chassant avec le Glorieux en avant de l'armée, dans la rivière Chesapeak, dans le nord ouest de notre ancrage; elle avoit aussi une goalete chargée de planches. Cette corvette avoit vingt deux canons. A onze heures et demie, le vaisseau le Diadème a signalé un batiment dans la partie de l'Est. A deux heures, le général a hissé pavillon anglois qu'il a amené aussitôt; ce batiment a pris le large. A cinq heures du soir, le Triton a appareillé ainsi que le Vaillant pour monter la rivière d'York.—Flamme d'ordre à bord du général pour distribuer dans l'armée les prisonniers de guerre et les planches de la goalete aussi de manière que le Citoyen s'est libéré d'une centaine de prisoniers qu'il a donnés à divers vaisseaux. Les vents, dans la journée, ont régné de l'Est à l'Est fraix; grosse mer, beaucoup de pluye et de tonnerre; dans la nuit, vent de Nord Nord Est.

Dimanche deuxième. Le vent de Nord Nord Est, petit vent, beau temps clair. Le vaisseau le Vaillant qui n'avoit pu monter hier au soir a appareillé ce matin pour aller en rivière. Le flot a été, aujourd'hui, à la pleine lune à cinq heures et demie du soir. La frégate l'Aigrette a appareillé l'après midi pour aller en croisière au large; à trois heures, elle a signalé deux voiles au vent qu'elle pourroit attaquer avec avantage. A neuf heures du soir, elle a tiré sur ces bâtiments qu'elle a pris et conduit dans la baye sur les deux heures du matin. Nota que le général, dans la journée, avoit mis flamme d'ordre pour signifier à tous les vaisseaux de l'armée le traité fait pour les refraîchissements et provisions qu'on acheteroit sur le pays dans un imprimé qui avoit été remis à chaque vaisseau ; mais les gens du pays n'ont pas voulu y souscrire.

Lundy troisième. Les vents ont été dans la journée variable du Sud Sud Est au Sud Sud Ouest, fraix, le temps couvert. Le général a fait à partie des vaisseaux de l'armée leurs signaux particuliers ; nous avons été du nombre. Le Citoyen a eu pour sa part deux femmes, un capitaine, deux enfants et quelques autres prisonniers des aux bâtiments que l'Aigrette avoit pris. A trois heures après midy, l'Aigrette et la Railleuse ont appareillé pour aller reconnoitre une voile qui paroissoit au large et qui avoit été signalé. Les vents ont été variables du Sud Ouest à l'Ouest Sud Ouest petit fraix, le temps pluvieux et à l'orage. Dans la nuit, les frégates ont rentrés en tête de la baye ou elles ont mouillé.

Mardy quatrième. Les vents, dans la journée, ont été variables du Sud Sud Est au Ouest Sud Ouest petit vent. Le temps a été nuageux, clair au large. On a signalé des battiments en différentes fois. Mais, les frégates n'ont pas appareillé. Le Solitaire est rentré plus en dedans. Les vents, dans la nuit, ont sauté au Nord Est et Nord Nord Est fraix, avec orages.

Mercredy cinquième. Les vents de Nord Nord Est continuant fraix, la mer agitée, le temps nuageux, l'air froid ; à sept heures du matin, le frégate l'Aigrette qui étoit encore mouillié sous le cap Henry et s'y trouvoit engagée à ne pouvoir appareiller (la Railleuse ayant entré dans la nuit) a fait signal qu'on luy portât une ancre et un grelin. Le Général en a fait le signal à la Railleuse qui, au moment qu'elle travailloit pour l'embarquer dans sa chaloupe l'Aigrette a annulé son signal et a appareillé a huit heures courant le bord au large pour s'élever et profiter du flot pour entrer. Le flot étoit établi depuis sept heures environ à neuf heures et demie. Les vaisseaux qui étoient mouillés les plus en tête de la baye ont signalé vingt cinq voiles dans la partie de l'est. Le général a repondu aussitôt au signal. La vigie du haut de mâts en comptoit vingt quatre à dix heures et quart. Le général a ordonné de faire branle-bas et de faire revenir tous les bâtiments à rame qui étoient à terre à bord de leurs vaisseaux. J'avois mon petit canot à terre pour prendre de la viande pour les equipages. J'ai fait mettre aussitôt le pavillon en berne pour le faire retourner mais inutilement. A onze heures, la frégate l'Aigrette qui venoit de la bordée dans la baye a signalé au général trente une voiles. A onze heures et demie, le général a fait signal à l'armée de virer à pic et, à midy, d'appareiller sans autre signal. A midy et quart, signal à l'armée de passer à la section des mouvements généraux. A midy et demie, le général a fait signal à l'armée de se former en ordre de bataille de vitesse sans égard au poste que l'on doit occuper, et avertir l'armée que les signaux fair par un seul pavillon seroient pris dans la feuille numero deux. Le Citoyen a appareillé à midy et trois quarts après avoir filé son ancre d'affourche J'etois sous les huniers et voiles d'étay. Le flot étoit encore fort et portoit sur la côte du cap Henry. Je travaillois à mettre mon ancre en haut et y accrocher le capon quand le frégate l'Aigrette qui entroit dans la baye en ce moment m'a hellé et parlant à monsieur de Koeflod qui tient la place de lieutenant en pied en l'absence de monsieur de Saint Marc et qui étoit sur le gaillard d'avant à faire accélérer la manoeuvre que si je nevirois de bord je pourois risque d'échouer sur le cap Henry et que definitivement je revira que je n'avois pas du temps à perdre. Monsieur de Koefold à qui le capitaine de l'Aigrette s'étoit adressé en passant est venu de l'arrière pour me le communiquer. J'avoit de la peine à me decider à virer. Monsieur de Koefold m'a dit que je devois croire ce que tout le monde avoit entendu. Je demanday moy même à l'Aigrette ce qu'elle m'avoit crié. Elle me répondit que son pilote l'assuroit que si je continuois à courir je rencontrerois un banc de sable. J'ai reviré et couru la bordée au Nord Nord Ouest avec le vent de Nord Est et Nord Nord Est. J'ai été force, en courant cette bordée, de passer de l'arrière du général qui appareilloit et que je ne voulois pas déranger dans sa manoeuvre; enfin, à un heure et quart, me trouvant débarrassé de tous les vaisseaux qui étoient sous voile pour sortir de la baye, j'ay reviré aux amures babord et fait routte pour sortir aussi. Le général étoit un peu de l'avant à moy, il avoit appareillé à une heure en faisant signal à la partie des vaisseaux qui étoient sorti et qui se formoient, de tenir le vent. A une heure heure et demie, l'ancre de poste ayant été accrochée, j'ai forcé de voile pour sortir de la rade comme pour prendre un poste. Il étoit environ une heure trois quarts quand j'ay eu doublé le cap Henry. J'avois ordonné à Monsieur de Koefold de faire passer tout le monde à son poste et de remplacer ceux qui manquoient aux batteries. J'avois ordonné aussi qu'on y employât toute la troupe ainsi que messieurs les officiers pour remplacer les absents, mais, le nombre des soldats n'a pas été suffisant à remplir le vuide. Il a fallu désarmer les canons des gaillards et ne me garder, pour faire les manoeuvres nécessaires, que les officiers mariniers de la manoeuvre

quelques gabiers destinés à leurs mâts, le pilote et
quelques timoniers pour reppéter les signaux avec la
mistrance. Il manque à bord du Citoyen, entre les
absents, les morts, les malades, environ deux [cents]
hommes et cinq officiers. Après avoir armé mes deux
batteries aussi bien que je le pouvois j'ai fait carguer les
basses voiles pour me placer à l'arrière du vaisseau le
Northumberlan qui étoit un peu en avant et sous le vent.
J'étois occupé de ma manoeuvre quand le vaisseau le
Palmier m'a intimé que son intention etoit de prendre
ce poste. Le Solitaire, qui forçoit de voiles, égal en
marche au Palmier et le tenant de très proche, ne m'a
pas permis non plus de m'y placer sans risque d'avaries;
pour ne point entrer à disputer derechef j'ai arrivé et
pris mon poste de l'arrière du Solitaire; mais, voyant
que j'étois forcé à tout instant de mettre en pane; j'ai
tenu le Vent pour doubler ces deux vaisseaux et forcer
de voiles pour aller en avant. (En marge: le Scipion
forçoit de voile ainsi que ceux qui suivoient.) Le
Scipion, qui me suivoit, ayant fait la même manoeuvre
pour ne pas rompre l'ordre de bataille qui commençoit
à se former j'ai repris mon poste de l'arrière de ce vaisseau et je me suis occupé pour ne pas le gêner à être
toujours sur le qui vive ou en pane ou le perroquet de
fougue sur le mât. A deux heures, le vaisseau l'Auguste
qui commandoit les vaisseaux qui s'étoient formé en
tête de la ligne leur a fait signal de forcer de voile. A
deux heures et demie, l'armée ennemie qui étoit en
bataille à bord opposé à la nôtre a viré lof pour lof
toute à la fois, à une lieue et demie de distance et au
vent; ils étoient vingt et un vaisseaux de guerre dont
trois à trois ponts. Les vents étoient Nord Nord Est,
petit vent clair; à trois heures et quart, le vaisseau

l'Auguste à fait signal au vaisseau de tête d'augmenter
de voile. Le général a reppeté le même signal; à trois
heures et demie, le vaisseau le Languedoc a fait routte
pour venir prendre le commandement de la queue de
l'armée. Les ennemies, après avoir viré à nos amures,
étoient en partie en pane; ils ont fait servir au moment
que le Languedoc couroit à bord opposé, entre les deux
lignes de bataille, pour aller prendre son porte. Les
ennemies, ayant fait servir babord amure comme nous
ils ont mis leurs pavillons et flammes. Nous avions le
nôtre depuis notre départ de la baye. Les vents ont
commencé à varier au Nord Est, ensuite à l'Est Nord
Est, petit fraix. Le général a fait signal aux vaisseaux
de tête de serrer la ligne et à l'armée de suivre les
mouvements des vaisseaux de tête successivement en
serrant la ligne. A trois heures trois quart, le général
voyant le vent refuser toujours, a fait signal aux vaisseaux de tête qui se trouvoient par leurs positions à
portée de l'ennemi et au vent du corps de bataille de
porter deux quarts largues pour rétablir l'ordre de la
ligne les vents refusant aux vaisseaux de la tête de notre
armée et faisant portée deux quarts largues les ennemis
arrivoient aussi. Alors, le général a assuré sa mizaine
ainsi que beaucoup des vaisseaux de l'armée que se trou-
virent au corps de bataille. Les ennemis arrivoient
toujours lentement suivant obliquement nos vaisseaux
de tête quand, à quatre heures et quart, nos vaisseaux de
tête ont commencé à tirer sur les ennemis qui étoient
très à portée, ce que par leurs positions obliques autant
que je pouvoit en juger on pouvoit les combattre avec
avantage. Le feu est devenu vif au deux avant gardes.
Le général leur a fait signal de serrer la ligne et de tenir
le vent. L'on combattoit de fort proche jusqu'en avant

du centre de notre armée; mais les ennemis, au lieu
d'engager bien l'affaire, mettoient en pane au moment
qu'ils faisoient leurs décharges. L'amiral luy-même,
crainte de trop approcher, mettoit tous sur le mat à
quatre heures et demie; le feu a commencé au centre de
l'armée de l'avant et de l'arrière du général; les ennemis
maîtres du vent ne se livroient que de fort loin et simple-
ment pour qu'il soit dit qu'ils ont combattu. Il n'en
étoit pas de même à la tête des deux armées; ou ne voyoit
que feu et fumée de part et d'autre. A cinq heures et
quart, le général a reppeté aux vaisseaux de tête de
tenir le vent. Ils étoient très foibles et variables à l'Est
et Est Est Nord. Notre arrière garde se trouvoit en
échiquier par le refus et la faiblesse du vent; à cinq
heures trois quarts, le vaisseau à trois ponts commandant l'arrière garde ennemie a arrivé ainsi que deux
vaisseaux qui étoient à l'avant de luy sur le Palmier et
le Solitaire et, après avoir arrivé quelques minutes, il
a mis en pane esseyant si ses coups de canon parvien-
droient jusqu'à ces vaisseaux. Il a commencé par tirer
quelques coups ainsi que les deux autres vaisseaux qui
avoient mis en pane comme luy. Les vaisseaux de
l'arrière garde ennemie tenoient toujours le vent; le feu
est venu général jusqu'à nous; mais il n'a pas duré long-
temps, les ennemis restoient en pane. La tête de notre
armée tenoient le vent; de forcant de voile, nous serrions
autant qu'il étoit possible notre ligne. Ce vaisseau à
trois ponts, à six heures un quart environ, n'a plus tiré;
mais le feu a continué jusqu'à nuit clause du côté de
l'avant garde. Le Citoyen a en quelques coups de canon
dans les voiles aux au-bans et autres manoeuvres ainsi
qu'au corps de vaisseau; j'avois beaucoup plus d'avantage que ce vaisseau à trois pont, à ce qu'il m'a paru car

presque touts les boulets de ce vaisseau tomboient à la
mer avant de parvenir jusqu'à moy au lieu que je voyois
que le peu que j'ai fait tirer il ne s'en est guère perdu
ou, du moins, ils dépassoient. Au coucher du soleil, le
cap Henry restoit au ouest nord ouest 5° nord, distance
trois lieues, la terre la plus Sud au Sud Sud Ouest 5°
Sud, le tout corrigé, la variation observée: 3° 30 nord
ouest. Dans la nuit, les vents ont été variables du Nord
Est à l'Est faibles. La voilure a varie selon ma position, les armées ont continué courir babord amures. Les
ennemis ont été toute la nuit à la vue, tenant le vent;
le temps étoit clair et beau. L'amiral ennemi a tiré
un coup de canon sur les neuf heures. Il l'a reppété
à quelque temps de la.

Jeudy sixième. Les vents toujours petit fraix à l'Est,
les deux armées en presence tenant le vent babord
amure au point du jour cinq vaisseaux ennemis étoient
occupés a changer des mâts d'hune. Il y en avoit un qui
m'a paru avoir le ton de son grand mât en domagé; à
huit heures et demie, la frégate l'Aigrette a été parler
au Languedoc. A neuf heures du matin, le vaisseau de
tête de l'armée ennemi a viré de bord et a couru la
bordée opposée pour se porter à la queue de sa ligne de
bataille pour ne pas trop approcher de notre armée;
cette manoeuvre a été continuée toute la journée; elle se
conservoit a environ deux lieues au vent; la terre paroissoit dans le Sud Ouest quart Sud à sept lieues environ.
A midy la latitude observée a été 36° 21 nord, la routte
estimée depuis hier au coucher du soleil a valu le Sus
Sud Est 3° Est; chemin dix huit lieues. La corrigée
Sud Sud Est 5°, chemin dix sept lieues, la longitude
arrivée Ouest soixante dis huit degrés quatorze. La
terre a été relevé au Sud Ouest quart Sud, distance sept

lieues. Les vents, dans le reste de la journee, ont été variables de l'Est Nord Est à l'Est petit vent. Les deux armées, courant toujours babord amures, les ennemis à trois lieues au vent restant au coucher du soleil dans la partie du Nord. Les terres les plus au Sud à l'Ouest Sud Ouest 2° Ouest, corrigé à sept lieues et demie. Dans la nuit, les vents ont varié, au Sud Est. A onze heures un quart, le général à fait le signal de virer vent devant tous à la fois; après que l'armée a en reviré aux amures sur tribord j'ay forcé de voile pour me mettre en avant tâcher de reconnoitre les ennemis; les vents étoient faibles, la mer clapoteuse, le temps nuageux; la reste de la nuit l'armée a tenu le vent toute voile dehors. (En marge: Le matin, à six heures et demie, le général a fait signal de prendre à la feuille numero un les signaux fait par un seul pavillon. A sept heures, ordre aux vaisseaux de tête de faire de la voile. A minuit trouvé vingt cinq brasses, sable gris fin.)

Vendredy septième. A cinq heures du matin, le peu d'air étoit au sud sud ouest presque calme; les ennemis étoient toujours dans le nord en calme ouest et mal en ordre. J'étois en avant de l'armée. A huit heures, la sonde a rapporté dix neuf brasses sable fin jaunâtre et coquillage brisé. Le calme a duré jusqu'a dix heures et demie du matin que les vents ont passé au Sud Est petit fraix et successivement au Sud Sud Ouest. A onze heures et demie, le général a fait signale à l'armée de former la ligne de bataille à l'ordre naturel; pour prendre mon poste il m'a fallu tenir le vent babord amure l'armée se formant aux amures sur tribord. A midy, latitude observée: 36° 6 nord, la routte depuis hier à midy a valu le Sud Est, chemin sept lieues et deux tiers, la longitude arrivée ouest soixante dix sept degrés cinquante six. A midy et demie j'ai viré et pris mon poste par les eaux du vaisseau l'Hector. A deux heures moins un quart, l'armée a eu ordre de virer lof pour lof touts à la fois. A deux heures, ralliement à l'ordre de bataille renversé, babord amure; à deux heures et demie ordre au vaisseau le Souverain de prendre la tête de l'armée à la place du vaisseau le Pluton qui, par les avaries qu'il a reçues dans ses mâts, ne pouvoit agir pour conduire la tête de l'armée. (En marge: le Pluton a eu sa mâture endommagée dans l'affaire du cinquieme, étant à la tête de la ligne.) A quatre heures, l'armée marchant sur la ligne du plus près babord amure à l'ordre renversé, le Souverain à la tête, le vaisseau l'Auguste commandant l'escadre bleue a fait signal aux vaisseaux de tête d'augmenter de voile. A quatre heure et quart le général a fait signal aux commandants des escadres qu'il les chargeoit de la police de la leur; immédiatement, il a signalé le mot d'ordre numero quarante sept. (En marge: A quatre heure et quart, l'Auguste a fait signal de serrer la ligne à son escadre). A cinq heures, la frégate l'Aigrette a prolongé la ligne et a dit à tous les vaisseaux de la part du général de faire attention que, le premier signal qu'il feroit pour tenir le vent, les vaisseaux fairoient porter à un quart largue et que lorsqu'il reppéteroit le même signal on tiendroit le plus près du vent. Les ennemis étoient alors occupés à former leur ligne de bataille à nos amures revirant par la contre marche et se formant sur le dernier vaisseau de leur armée. Ils étoient for sous le vent. A cinq heures et demie, le général a fait signal à l'armée de virer vent devant toute a la fois et aux vaisseaux de tête d'augmenter de voile et immediatement rallier l'armée à l'ordre d'échiquier sur la ligne du plus près babord,

[235]

amures, sur tribord au plus pres du vent. A six heures, l'armée a reviré aux amures sur tribord, après avoir reviré, elle a porté un quart largue. A sept heures, le général a fait le signal communiqué par l'Aigrette pour tenir le vent. A huit heures et demie, l'armée a tenir le vent sur tribord amure en ordre d'échiquier. Les vents étoient Sud Sud Ouest petit fraix. L'ennemi a reviré à nos amures avant la nuit. Le terre paroissoit, au coucher du soleil, au Sud Ouest quart Ouest, à sept lieues. La variation observée occase 4° Nord Ouest. Les vents ont été toute la nuit variables du Sud Ouest au Sud Sud Ouest petit fraix. J'ay tenir le vent au poste que j'avais dans l'armée sous differentes voilures. Le temps beau et clair.

Samedy huitième Septembre. A cinq heures du matin, les vents du Sud Ouest petit fraix, temps clair, le général a fait signal à l'armée de ralliement à l'ordre d'échiquier sur la ligne du plus près babord, sur tribord amure, la routte au plus près du vent, les ennemis restoient dans la partie du nord ouest. A trois lieues un tiers au même bord à sept heures du matin signal à l'armée de se rallier à l'ordre de bataille, renversé babord amures. L'armée a viré, vent devant, toute à la fois, d'après le signal fait; à sept heures et quart, ordre de serrer la ligne. L'ennemi a viré aussi par la contre marche à nos amures. A huit heures, le général a fait signal au vaisseau de tête de gouverner de manière à passer de l'avant du chef de file de l'ennemi. Le Souverain a fait porter plein sur les ordres qu'il avoit reçus pour approcher l'ennemi et luy passer au vent. A huit heures et quart, le général a fait signal de serrer la ligne; touts les vaisseaux, successivement, suivoient les mouvements du vaisseau de tête. A huit

heures trois quart, l'Auguste a fait signal qu'il découv-
roit des voiles sous le vent. C'était trois vaisseaux ou
frégates de l'armée ennemi qui rallioient. A neuf
heures et quart, l'Auguste a fait signal qu'il avoit attention aux signals du général, à neuf heures et demie, les
ennemis courant le même bord que nous, le général a
fait signal au vaisseau de tête de tenir le vent et successivement toute l'armée a tenu le vent babord amure toujours à l'ordre de bataille renversé; il y avoit à craindre
que les ennemis ne nous eussent gagné le vent si l'armée
avoit continué courir plein. (En marge: à dix heures
un quart, le Magnanime a signalé la terre au vent). Les
vents étoient toujours Sud Ouest petit frais. La partie
du Nord Ouest commençoit à devenir nuageuse. A
onze heures et quart, le général a fait signal de virer
vent devant touts à la fois; après que l'armée a eu reviré le général a fait signal de ralliement à l'ordre
d'échiquier sur la ligne du plus près babord sur tribord
amure, au plus près du vent. A midy, latitude observée
36° 2 nord; la routte, depuis hier, à midy, a valu le Sud
Sud Ouest 3° 30 sud, chemin une lieue un tiers; la longitude arrivée vaut 77° 58. Les vents toujours sud ouest
mais devenu faibles; l'ennemi a reviré à midy et quart.
A une heure apres midy, le général a reppété le signal
de l'ordre d'échéquier sur tribord amure. A trois heures,
les orages ont commencé de la partie du Nord Nord
Est, les vents fraix variant sans se fixer qu'à quatre
heures et quart au Nord Nord Est avec grosse pluye, le
temps devenu noir; le général a fait signal à l'armée de
virer lof pour lof touts à la fois babord amure; la pluye
et le tonnerre étoient en abondance; les vents faibles du
Nord Est au Nord Nord Est sur les cinq heures et par
raphales. L'armée après avoir reviré a tenu le vent en

ordre d'échiquier, babord amure; à huit heures du soir, le général a fait signal à l'armée de prendre tous les ris. Les vents commençoit à fraichir, le temps noir, la mer grosse. Après avoir pris les bas ris, j'ai forcé de voile pour rallier le vaisseau qui étoit de l'avant à moy et le général qui étoit en avant; à onze heures, me trouvant à portée de touts les vaisseaux j'ai diminué de voile et resté sous les huniers. Les vents étoient Nord Nord Est fraix et par raphales, le temps noir, des éclairs de partout, peu de pluye, ainsi que tout le reste de la nuit.

Dimanche neuvième. A cinq heures du matin, les vents ayant varié au Nord Est fraix, l'armée tenoit toujours le vent babord amure; les ennemis étoient dans la partie du nord à trois lieues et demie environ et à nos amures. Le général a fait signal à l'armée de se rallier à l'ordre naturel de bataille, babord amure. J'ay arrivé pour prendre mon poste à huit heures. Le signal a été fait pour tenir le vent et, à huit heures et demie, faire virer l'armée vent arrière tout à la fois. Le temps étoit obscur et un peu brumeux. Les ennemis paroissoient confusément et on ne pouvoit distinguer leurs manoeuvres; à neuf heures et quart, l'armée ayant reviré, le général a fait signal de retablir l'ordre de marche en échiquier sur la ligne du plus près babord sur tribord amures; à neuf heures et demie, les vents ont varié à l'Est Nord Est fraix, la mer grosse, le temps moins brumeux, tonjours nuageux. L'armée tenoit le plus près tous les huniers au bas viz et la mizaine. A midy, latitude observée 35° 41 nord; la routte estimée depuis hier à midy a valu le Sud Est quart Est; chemin dix lieues un tiers; la corrigé: le Sud Est quart Est 3° Sud, chemin douze lieues; la longitude arrivée ouest 77° 21. A trent quatre lieues du cap Henry au Nord Ouest quart

nord 4° 20 ouest. A une heure, les vents d'Est Nord
Est moins fort que la mer de Nord Nord Est qui exis-
toit grosse, le vaisseau, ayant de la peine à se porter sur
la lame, j'ai amuré ma grande voile. L'armée ennemie
a paru en ce moment courant la bordée du Sud Est
babord amure; elle restoit au Nord Ouest quart Ouest.
A une heure et demie, elle a reviré aux amures sur tribord par la contre marche et, après avoir reviré, elle a
serré le petit hunier pour ne pas trop courir dans le
Nord et conserver toujours l'avantage du vent. Elle
étoit à trois lieues et demie environ de notre armée. A
trois heures, le Caton a signalé avoir une voye d'eau.
Le général lui a repondu au feuillet numéro trois et,
ensuite, l'a renvoyé au Nord Ouest; finalement, il a
changé lof pour lof, mis en pane babord au vent, s'est
radoubé; à quatre heures, il a fait signal qu'il étoit
prest. Le général lui a repondu que l'armée réglera sa
voilure sur la sienne. Il a, cependant, forcé de voile
pour joindre et repris son poste. A neuf heures du soir,
les vents à l'Est fraix, beau temps, le général a fait
signal a l'armée qu'il étoit essentiel que chaque vaisseau
se tint à son poste et de serrer la ligne, l'ennemie étant
à notre vue. J'ai forcé de voile sans larguer les ris pour
me mettre en avant; à minuit j'étois de l'avant des généraux tenant le vent; j'ai diminué de voile en attendant;
les vents ont été Est Nord Est jusqu'au jour, beau temps
clair.

Lundy dizième. A six heures du matin, les vents toujours Est Nord Est petit fraix beau temps clair, l'armée
ennemie ne paroissant point le Souverain et le Citoyen
étoient en avant de l'armée; la vigie, du haut des mats,
a vu huit voiles dans l'Ouest Nord Ouest; on en voyoit
encore dans le Sud et lans le Sud Ouest. A six heures

et quart, le général a fait signal à l'armée de se rallier à l'ordre de bataille renversé sur tribord amure. A sept heures, faire passer l'Aigrette à poupe du général ainsi que le vaisseau le Pluton; mais, ce signal a été annulé par le Pluton. A sept heures et quart, ralliement à tous les vaisseaux et frégates qui chassoient sous le vent. A sept heures trois quart, faire forcer de voile à toute l'armée et reppéter tous les signaux. Le général a reppété le signal de l'ordre de bataille renversé sur tribord amure. J'étois par les eaux de l'Auguste; alors, suivant les mouvements qu'il faisoit manquant le Scipion pour se mettre en avant de moy et qui venoit prendre son poste quand le général à huit heures du matin a fait signal à l'armée de chasser sans ordre; dans le nord, l'armée l'ennemie ne paroissoit point; il paroissoit deux bâtiments de guerre dans le sud auest, à bord opposé à notre armée, à trois lieues environ de distance. A dix heures, le général a appelé les deux frégates qui étoient a chasser en avant. A midy, les vents étoient à l'Est faibles, le temps clair, latitude observée 36° 44 Nord; la routte, depuis hier, à midy: le nord quart Nord Ouest 3° 15; corrigé; chemin vingt deux lieues; la longitude arrivée, ouest, 77° 42. A seize lieues du cap Henry à l'Ouest Nord Ouest 4° 30 ouest. Le général, à, environ une heure après midy a indiqué la routte au Nord Nord Ouest. L'armée a singlé aussitôt dans la ditte partie; je chassois en avant de l'armée, hautes et basses bonnettes; à une heure precise, la vigie a découvert deux voiles dans le Sud Sud Ouest qui paroissoient courir la bordée au Nord Nord Est. Le général n'ayant pas répondu à mon signal et, à quatre heures, ayant fait celuy de diminuer de voile aux vaisseaux de tête, j'ai resté sous les huniers et arrivé au Sud Ouest pour me rallier indé-

pendemment des deux bâtiments signalés dans le Sud
Sud Ouest, il en paroissoit deux autres dans l'Ouest
courant à la bordée de l'armée, les vents étoient à l'Est
petit fraix. A huit heures du soir, la sonde a rapporté
vingt une brasses sable gris. A huit heures du soir, j'ai
mis en pane, le cap à la routte, pour ne pas trop faire
de chemin et attendre l'armée. J'ai ensuite porté au
Nord Ouest jusqu'à neuf heures et quart que j'ai fait
servir le grand hunier. Le vent étoit alors faible. A
deux heures j'ai trouvé douze brasses d'eau fond sable
jaune. Le reste de la nuit, les vents ont été très faibles
à l'Est, grosse mer du large, le temps clair. L'armée
a tenu le vent sur tribord amure à petite voile en attendant le jour. (En marge: Pendant la nuit, vu en différentes fois des fusées differentes des nôtres que les bâtiments de la pointe de l'ouest lançoient pour signaux de
reconnoissance.)

Mardy onzième. A six heures du matin, un vaisseau
de l'arrière de l'armée a signalé que les bâtiments que
l'on avoit chassée étoit françois ou allié. Effectivement,
c'étoit le Glorieux et la Diligente qui venoient joindre
l'armée. (En marge: les bâtiments qui restoient au
Sud Sud Ouest hier après midy.) A six heures et demie
du matin, le général a fait signal aux vaisseaux les plus
à portée des chasseurs de reppeter les signaux. A sept
heures et quart, signal au dixième vaisseau de l'escadre
blanche de passer à poupe de luy. (En marge: le Souverain.) A huit heures, signal de ralliement en toute
occasion. A huit heures et quart, vu la terre. L'armée
partoit au Nord Ouest quart Nord. Ensuite, elle a
singlé au Nord Ouest, toujours à petite voile. Les vents
étoient sud petit vent. Le cap Henry restoit au Ouest
quart Sud Ouest, corrigé distance: huit lieues. A neuf

heures environ, signal a l'armée de tenir le vent babord
amure. A neuf heures et quart, une frégate qui restoit
dans la partie du Nord Ouest courant la bordée aux
amures sur tribord a mis en pane après avoir reconnue
l'armée et fait des signaux de reconnoissance auxquels
le général a répondu aussitôt et, un instant après, le
général a mis son numéro. C'étoit la Concorde qui a
couru le bord au large pour luy passer à poupe. A dix
heures, le général a fait signal à l'armée de chasser son
ordre et de tenir le vent aux mêmes amures. Nous
étions à la vue de la baye de Chesapeak ou nous y
voyions l'escadre aux ordres de Mr. de Barras mouillié;
le Glorieux avoit mis son numéro; mais je n'étoit pas
encore rallié et, par conséquent, encore de l'arrière et
au vent de l'armée qui tenoit le plus près. Les vents
étoient Sud, petit fraix. Il empêchoit, par conséquent, ces
deux bâtimens étrangères à l'armée qui restoient dans la
partie de l'Ouest, hier, à prendre le large; toute l'armée,
qui chassoit pour approcher la côte, les empêchoit aussi
de courir Nord. A midy moins un quart, l'Auguste
qui étoit sous le vent au Citoyen a reviré de bord au
large. J'ay reviré aussi par les neuf brasses. (En
marge: le fond est sable jaune). A une lieue un tiers
de la côte, la latitude observée 36° 55 nord. La routte
depuis hier à midy: l'ouest nord ouest. Chemin treize
lieues un tiers. La corrigée: ouest un quart nord ouest
8° nord, treize lieues. La longitude arrivée: 78° 30
ouest, cap Henry Nord Ouest quart Ouest, restant à
trois lieues de distance. J'avois reviré sur tribord amure
toute voile dehors et passé au vent de tous les vaisseaux
qui étoient de l'arrière de moy. Le Glorieux, l'Aigrette
et la Diligente avoient signalé avoir espoir de joindre
ces bâtimens. Les vents qui étoient devenu assez frais

pour courir des bordées à trois heures et demie. J'ai
reviré à terre quand le vaisseau le Sceptre a fait signal
que les bâtiments chassés couroient vent arrière; effectivement, c'étoient deux frégates; elles avoient prolongé la cote ne pouvant courir au large et forçoient de
voile aussi proche de terre qu'elles pouvoient pour que
les vaisseaux ne pussent les approcher. Le Glorieux qui
les poursuivoit et qui couroit vent arrière comme elles
a canoné la dernière qui s'est aussitôt rendue; celle qui
étoit en avant a continué forcer de voiles; j'ai fait porter
plein sur la côte pour luy couper chemin et j'y serois
parvenu; mais, il y avoit tant des chasseurs à l'autour
de cette frégate qui ne pouvoit échaper le Glorieux sans
s'amurer au mariner le Richmond; celle qui venoit
d'être prise l'a laissée à la Bourgogne et a continué
chasser; à quatre heures et quart, le vaisseau la Bourgogne ayant fait le signal avec vaisseaux le plus à portée
de l'aider à amariner la prise, j'ai couru de ce cotté la,
pour cet effet; l'ayant joint, ainsi que le Pluton, sur les
cinq heures, j'ai mis mon canot à la mer pour l'envoyer
à bord de la Burgogne avec un officier prendre les ordres
de Monsieur de Charite; le canot a été mandé à bord
du Richmond; on luy a donné vingt huit prisonniers
et il est retourné à bord sur les cinq heures et demie;
cette frégate le Richmond, de trente deux canons, étoit
de compagnie avec celle qui étoit encore poursuivie qui
se nommoit l'Iris, re quarante canons, construite à Boston et prise par les Anglois; elles étoient bien armées en
équipages et en canons; elles venoient de Chesapeack;
par ordre du général qui commande l'armée anglaise,
elles avoient coupé les bouées de Nord Ouest ancres et
cherchoient leurs armées. Cette frégate, ditte l'Iris,
combattoient toujours et contre l'Aigrette et contres les

autres; mais, sur les cinq heures trois quarts, ayant été obligée d'arriver pour écarter la pointe Dingen qui va au large et qui est dans le Sud Est cap Henry, le vaisseau le plus à portée qui étoit le Palmier lui ayant coupé le grand mât d'hune, elle s'est rendue et a été conduite par l'armée dans la baye de Chesapeack qui y a été mouiller. A six heures et demie, le Pluton, nous ayant mis le pavillon de mouillage, il a fait servir, le cap Henry restoit, alors, au nord ouest; corrigé distance: quatre lieues. J'ai fait servir aussi et approcher le Pluton qui m'a dit qu'il mouilleroit le long de la côte en attendant le jour; pour aller mouiller dans la baye, j'ai singlé au nord nord ouest de l'arrière de luy et, à neuf heures, comme il a mouillé, je suis venu mouiller dans le nord de luy à environ un cable et demie de distance, les feux de l'armée restant au nord nord ouest; j'avois dix brasses, sable fin et jaune. La frégate a mouillé aussi entre nous, la Bourgogne a passé dans la baye. Les vents étoient sud sud est petit fraix variables au sud ouest, beau temps.—(En marge: Il nous est mort trois hommes.)

EXTRAIT DU LIVRE DE BORD DU VAISSEAU LE PLUTON[1]

3 septembre, 1781

Lundi trois. Nous avons sçu que dans les bâtiments pris hier au soir par l'Aigrete, l'un venoit de Charletown et de la Jamaique, avec beaucoup d'officiers allant à l'armée de Cornwalis. Le Souverain a appareillé pour rentrer plus en dedans.—Monsieur du Patail, commandant le génie dans l'armée du general Vasingthon est arrivé avec des lettre de ce général et de Monsieur de Rochambeau; il mandent à Monsieur de Grasse que sur la nouvelle de notre arrivée par la Concorde, ils étaient parti de leur camppes de Newyork avec toute l'armée françoise et un détachement considérable d'Américain pour gagner le bord de la baye de Chesapeak et qu'ils en avaient fait part à Monsieur de Barras afin qu'il vient les prendre à la rivière d'Elk ou ils sont actuellement, avec des bâtiment de transport pour les amener ici et qu'ils le prient de ne point attaquer Cornwalis sans eux, qui a quatre mille cinq cents hommes de troupes reglées. Le général a envoyé le Serpent porté la reponse qui est qu'il n'a point de bâtiment de transport et qu'il attendra Monsieur de Barras.

[1] Archives de la Marine, B⁴ 184, fol. 8ov°–9ov°.

APPENDIX I

FRANÇOIS JOSEPH PAUL DE GRASSE-ROUVILLE, Count de Grasse, Marquis de Tilly, was born in the commune of Bar-sur-Loup, Alpes-Maritimes, on the 13th September, 1722. When but 12 years old he entered the service of the Order of Malta as a Garde-Marine. In 1740 he joined the French navy; was made *capitaine de vaisseau* in 1762, served under D'Orvilliers in the Squadron of Evolutions in 1772, when he was highly commended as "a captain of the first distinction, made for a general officer and to conduct the squadrons and fleets of the King" (Lacour-Gayet, 390). He was in command of the "Robuste," 74 (again under D'Orvilliers), in the ineffective battle off Ushant, July, 1778, an action which brought the British commander-in-chief, Keppel, and one of his captains, Palliser, to a court-martial.

Raised to the rank of *chef d'escadre* (commodore) in this same year, he sailed in 1779 (still in the "Robuste"), with a squadron of four ships of the line, for the West Indies, where he served with credit under Guichen and D'Estaing. He returned with Guichen to France in January, 1781, and on March 22, the day he sailed from Brest in command of the fleet which was to be so effective an instrument in establishing American independence, was made lieutenant-general (the equivalent of rear-admiral in France at this period). His good fortune ended with his departure, November 4, 1781, from our waters. On April 12, 1782, he was defeated and made prisoner by Rodney (with 36 ships to the French 30, to which the latter had been reduced from 34 by collision and other accident), in the action usually known as Les Saintes, the small islands between Guadeloupe and Dominica. Though but six French ships were taken (one the flagship, the "Ville de Paris"), this battle warded off the contemplated attack on Jamaica and ended French naval influence in the West Indies. The loss of the battle was due (besides marked inferiority in guns and class of ships) to bad handling of the French fleet, which, in the beginning, scattered over a length of ten miles, never got into a real line of battle, and by standing south got into the light baffling airs of an almost calm day, under Dominica. Much has been written of Rodney's "breaking the line," but careful reading has convinced me that the breaking of the French line, as a special tactical move, is a myth. There was no real line to break. There were but disconnected and scattered units to attack. The beautiful regularity of printed plans is very misleading.

Of the six ships taken but two ever reached England. All were with Graves as part of the convoy of the great fleet of merchantmen which left the West Indies at the end of July, 1782. Two, the "Ville de Paris" and "Glorieux," foundered with all on board; the "Hector" sank later on her way to Halifax; the "Ardent" got into Halifax, where she was condemned; the "Caton," after repairs at Halifax, reached England. The "Jason" was the only one which weathered the gale without serious injury.

De Grasse sailed from Jamaica on May 25, 1782, in the "Sandwich," flag-ship of Admiral Peter Parker, for England. He reached Portsmouth on July 31; London on August 3. On August 9 he and all the French officers were presented to King George. He left London on August 12, reaching Paris on the 16th. On the 18th he was received by Louis XVI. He was granted a court. This, which inquired into the conduct of all the superior officers in the battle of Les Saintes, and many of lesser rank, was composed of fourteen officers and a judge-advocate. It did not render a decision until May 21, 1784. Many—in fact, most—of the charges brought by De Grasse were declared by the court "calumnious" and were ordered stricken from the record. He received a letter from the Minister of Marine (De Castries), saying: "His Majesty wishes to think you did all in your power to prevent the misfortunes of the day, but he cannot have the same indulgence in regard to the matters you impute unjustly to those officers of his navy who are found not guilty. His Majesty, dissatisfied with your conduct in this regard, forbids you to present yourself before him. It is with pain that I transmit his instructions and that I add the advice that, in the existing circumstances, you withdraw to your province." This De Grasse did. He saw no further service. Chevalier (Histoire de la Marine Française pendant la Guerre de L'Indépendance Américaine), who devotes several pages to the finding of the court (pp. 313–320), and several more to the result as it concerns De Grasse, says: "Beaten in the battle of Dominica, he honored himself by defending the ship in which flew his flag, with an energy difficult to surpass. His personal courage on this unhappy day was above all praise. In exchange for the services he had rendered, France owed him forgetfulness of the faults he committed on the 12th of April. As for himself, after the battle of Dominica he was under strict obligation to keep silence and live in seclusion. Instead of resigning himself to this rôle, the only one which became him, he gave himself up to sterile and unjust recriminations. He did not know—what, moreover, is the gift of but very few men—how to show dignity in misfortune." Americans, remembering their great debt to De Grasse, cannot but feel that he was harshly treated, and that this criticism was but the echo of a hundred-year-old dispute. Of De Grasse's courage there can be no doubt; of the value of his services there can be no question. He was a vital factor in the establishment of American independence. In the face of this fact, such errors as those quoted from his compatriot are as nothing.

De Grasse was married three times: first, in 1764, to Antoinette Rosalia Acaron, the daughter of a naval commissary. Of this marriage there were six children, Alexandre François Auguste, who died about 1849; Amélie Maxime Rosalie, who died unmarried; Adelaide, who died at Charleston, S. C., of yellow fever; Maxime, who died in 1773; Mélanie Véronique Maxime, who died also of yellow fever at Charleston, September 19, 1799; Silvie, who married Francis de Pau and died in New York, January 5, 1855, aged eighty-three. Mrs. de Pau left two sons and five daughters.[1] Of these, there are a number of descendants living in 1916.

The second wife of De Grasse was Catherine Pien, widow of a M. de Villeneuve; the third was Christine Marie Delphine Lazare de Cibon. Of these there were no children.

He died at Paris, January 11, 1788.[2]

APPENDIX II

GEORGE BRYDGES RODNEY (born 1719, died 1792) entered the navy in July, 1732, on board the "Sunderland," 60; in 1733 he was in the "Dreadnought"; in 1739, in the "Somerset," 80, where he was promoted lieutenant in October of the same year and sent to the "Dolphin," frigate. In 1741 he was in the "Essex" in the Channel, and in 1742 went to the Mediterranean with Admiral Mathews, by whom he was promoted captain of the "Plymouth," 60, when but

[1] De Grasse's four daughters came to Charleston during the French Revolution. On February 27, 1795, Washington, as President, approved an act of Congress granting them $1000 each. Amélie (Maxime Rosalie) died August 23, 1799, and Mélanie (Véronique Maxime) September 19 following. They were buried in the Catholic Cemetery at Charleston. The second daughter, Adelaide, was married to a Monsieur de Groschamps. The youngest, Silvie Alexandrine, was married to Francis de Pau of Charleston and later of New York. They had two sons and five daughters. The first child, a son, married a Miss Adams of Philadelphia; the second, Amelie, married Theodosius Fowler of New York; the third, Elizabeth, Samuel M. Fox of Philadelphia; the fourth, Silvie, Mortimer Livingston of New York; the fifth, Carolina, Henry W. Livingston of New York; the sixth, Stephania, Washington Coster of New York; the seventh, Louis, Angelina Thorne of New York.

[2] The data concerning De Grasse's family life are largely from the two journals of unknown officers in his fleet, printed by the Bradford Club, New York, 1864.

twenty-three years old. His promotion was confirmed by the Admiralty. In 1743 and 1744 he was in the "Sheerness" and "Ludlow Castle"; in 1745 was in command of the new 60-gun ship "Eagle"; was in the action in which the French under L'Étenduère were defeated in 1747. He was appointed to the "Rainbow," 40, in 1748, as Governor of Newfoundland; paid off in 1752. After several years' service in command of guard-ships at Portsmouth, he was, in February, 1757, given command of the "Dublin." He thus escaped being present at the execution of Byng (March 14, 1757), having the previous December escaped serving on the court-martial, on the plea of "a violent bilious colic." He was with Hawke in the expedition against the Basque Roads, and in 1758 was with Boscawen in North America, but took no part in the attack on Louisburg on account of sickness. He was made rear-admiral in 1759 and operated on the French coast that year and in 1760 (bombarding Havre July 4, 5 and 6 in the former year). In 1761 was in command in the West Indies; in 1762 was promoted vice-admiral; returned to England 1763; created baronet, 1764; governor of Greenwich Hospital, 1765, where he remained five years. He had a seat, as a nominee of the Government, in the House of Commons from 1751 to 1768, but in securing a seat in the latter year, through his own resources, is said to have spent £30,000. This crippled him financially for life. In 1771 he was nominated rear-admiral of Great Britain; was in the West Indies 1771–1774. On his return he was obliged to leave the country on account of debt, and thus lived in Paris over four years. In 1778 he was enabled to return to England through the kindness of the Maréchal de Biron, who advanced him 1000 louis. He was promoted admiral January 29, 1778, and at the end of 1779 was given a command in the West Indies. On his way, he was to relieve Gibraltar, having under his orders twenty-one ships of the line, some frigates, and some three hundred store-ships. On January 16, 1780, he came in contact with a Spanish squadron of eleven ships of the line off Cape St. Vincent. Only two of the latter escaped. After the relief of Gibraltar, he sailed with four ships of the line for the West Indies, where he had a notable career in which an unsuccessful action (through mistake of signals) against Guichen, the capture of St. Eustatius and its £3,000,000 of plunder (which carried Rodney off his head and led to financial ruin, partly through lawsuits, partly by reason of the capture by the French of the convoy conveying the booty to England), and the victory of the 12th of April, 1782, were the principal incidents.

For this victory over De Grasse he was made a peer with a pension of £2000, which in 1793 was settled on the title forever. He saw no further service. He was prematurely old through gout and dissipation and greatly harassed by lawsuits arising from his action at St. Eustatius. He died suddenly at his house in Hanover Square, London, on May 23, 1792. He was twice married, having two sons by his first wife, and two sons and three daughters by the second, who survived him thirty-seven years. His elder son, John, by his second wife, was a remarkable example of the favoritism of the times. Accompanying his father in the "Sandwich," he was made lieutenant, commander and captain at fifteen, being at this age in command of the "Boreas" frigate. These commissions were confirmed on his return to England in 1782. Accidentally, when just appointed in 1795 to the "Vengeance," he broke his leg, which had to be amputated, and he saw no further sea service. He died a captain on the retired list April 9, 1847.

Sir Samuel Hood, who had joined Rodney in December, 1780, as second in command, is very bitter in his criticisms of Rodney in his letters. In these, however, Hood's character does not show well. In his correspondence with Hood, Rodney was always appreciative and even affectionate, nor does Hood in his correspondence with Rodney ever show any but a very different sentiment from that of his private letters.

With all his faults, Rodney was a great commander.[1]

APPENDIX III

Admiral Samuel Hood was born December 12, 1724, the eldest son of the Reverend Samuel Hood. He entered the navy in 1741 as "captain's servant" and in 1743 was rated midshipman. He was such with Rodney in 1744 in the "Ludlow Castle." He was lieutenant in 1746 in the "Winchelsea" and was wounded when in her in an action with a French frigate which was captured. He served in the "Lyon" on the North American coast in 1748, returned to England the same year and was placed on half pay; he married in 1749. He was appointed to the "Invincible" guard-ship at Portsmouth in 1753; in 1754 had command of the "Jamaica" sloop of war, which he took to America. He returned thence in 1756 as captain of the "Grafton." In 1757 he had command of the "Antelope" of 50 guns, drove ashore on May 14 the French ship "Aquilon" of like force, and a week later captured two privateers. Was appointed to the "Bideford" frigate, July, 1757; to the "Vestal," February, 1758, and was with Hawke on his second and more successful attack on the Basque Roads. On February 12, 1759, he sailed in the "Vestal" for North America in a squadron under Commodore Holmes, but chasing a strange sail, which turned out to be the French frigate "Bellona," he captured her. His own ship after the action had only her badly

[1] Mainly from the British Dictionary of National Biography.—The Editor.

injured lower masts standing; his prize was wholly dismasted. He was thus obliged to return to refit. He then joined a squadron under command of Rodney, just promoted to flag rank, and took part in his attack on Havre, July, 1759. He was employed in the Mediterranean, 1760–1763; in 1765 carried a regiment of troops in the "Thunderer" to America; in 1767 was appointed commodore and commander-in-chief in North America, with his broad pennant in the "Romney." From 1771 to 1776 he commanded the guard-ship at Portsmouth. In 1778 he was appointed commissioner at Portsmouth, governor of the Naval Academy, and was made a baronet,—appointments which in the circumstances indicated retirement from active service. He was, however, promoted to rear-admiral of the Blue on September 26, 1780, and sent in December with a strong fleet to reinforce Rodney in the West Indies. The supposed explanation of these events was the difficulty in finding officers willing to serve in high commands under the Sandwich administration, which was politically so corrupt as to be in strong disfavor. Politics were never more disreputable than at this period. Hood, though he had made no particular reputation before, was to show marked ability in the West Indies and acquired a great reputation as a tactician. His conduct while North with Graves appears in the text, but his handling of his fleet at St. Kitts in the presence of De Grasse, where he occupied and held the anchorage against the latter, gave him a great reputation. He played a brilliant part as second in command on the 12th of April, 1782, which brought him a peerage (September 12, 1782).

He remained in the West Indies as second in command until the peace of 1783. Was returned in the general election of 1784 to Parliament (for Westminster). Was commander-in-chief at Portsmouth in 1787–88. Was promoted vice-admiral of the Blue, September 24, 1787, and in July, 1788, became a member of the Board of Admiralty, where he remained until the outbreak of war with France, February, 1793, when he was appointed commander-in-chief in the Mediterranean. His flag-ship was the "Victory." He arrived off Toulon on July 16, 1793. The extraordinary and dramatic events of Hood's command of a year and a half off Toulon must be read elsewhere for want of space here. He was promoted to admiral on April 12, 1794, and sailed for England on October 11, leaving Admiral Hotham in command. Hood was strongly criticized during this command, but Nelson's opinion is decisive. Said he:

"The fleet must regret the loss of Lord Hood, the best officer, take him altogether, that England has to boast of; great in all situations which an admiral can be placed in."

On June 1, 1796, he was created viscount; in March of the same year he had been appointed governor of Greenwich Hospital, which post he held in full possession of his faculties until his death on January 27, 1816, in his ninety-second year.

APPENDIX

APPENDIX IV

"Cape François, 27th Nov. 1781.

"The fleet in Lynnhaven-bay was waiting for news from General Washington, and the return of its boats, when, on the 5th of September, at eight in the morning, the lookout frigate made the signal of seeing twenty sail to the eastward, steering for the bay, the wind at N. E. It was soon discovered to be an enemy's fleet, and not that of the Compte de Barras, which was expected.

"The English fleet forcing sail was soon near enough to be perceived forming the line of battle a-head on the starboard tack, and placing its heaviest ships in the van.

"As soon as it was known to be the enemy's fleet, the Compte de Grasse gave orders to prepare for battle, to recall the boats from watering, and for the fleet to be ready to get under sail. At noon the tide permitted to get under sail; accordingly the signal was made, as also to form the line promiscuously as the ships could get under weigh.

"All the captains applied themselves so diligently to the manœuvre, that, notwithstanding the absence of ninety officers and eighteen hundred men, the fleet was under sail in less than three quarters of an hour, and the line formed in the following order: Pluton, Marseillois, Bourgogne, Reflechi, Auguste, L'Esprit, Caton, Cæsar, Ville de Paris, Victoire, Sceptre, Northumberland, Palmier, Solitaire, Citoyen, Scipion, Magnanime, Hercule, Languedoc, Zele, Hector, Souverain. The Languedoc, commanded by M. de Monteil, Commodore of the White and Blue squadron, happened to be the ship next a-head of the Ville de Paris; and the Compte de Grasse, observing that no general officer was in his rear, gave M. de Monteil a verbal order to go and take the command there.

"The enemy coming down took care in forming their line on the starboard tack, still to preserve the wind. At two o'clock they wore altogether, and formed their line upon the same tack as the French.

"In this position the two fleets were on the same tack, but by no means parallel, as the rear guard of Admiral Graves was infinitely to windward of his van.

"At three o'clock the headmost of the French ships, from the varying of the wind and current, finding themselves too far to windward for a well formed line, the Compte de Grasse made them bear up two points, that his ships might have the advantage of engaging together;

[1] From Beatson's Naval and Military Memoirs.

[253]

and they kept the wind as soon as they were sufficiently in line to lee-ward.

"The headmost ships of both fleets approached each other to within musquet-shot. At four the action commenced in the van, commanded by M. de Bougainville, by a very brisk fire, and the main body was successively engaged. At five the wind continuing to vary, even to four points, placed the vanguard still too much to windward. The Compte de Grasse ardently wished to make the action general, and to dispose the enemy to it, ordered again his vanguard to bear away; that of Admiral Graves was very ill treated, and he profited of the advantage the wind gave him to be master of his distance, and to avoid being attacked by the French rear, who were using their utmost endeavour to reach his rear and his centre.

"The setting of the sun at last terminated the battle. The English fleet kept their wind, and having preserved it, employed all the next day in repairing their damages.

"The 7th at noon, the wind changed in favour of the French, the Compte de Grasse approached the enemy, and manœuvred in the night so as to preserve the wind.

"At daybreak on the 8th, the wind favoured Admiral Graves, it enabled his ships to look up to windward of the French, who were then in bow and quarter line upon a wind on the starboard tack, but the Compte de Grasse perceiving it tacked his whole fleet together. They were by this movement in a well formed line approaching the enemy, who were upon the contrary tack in a line badly formed, and appeared inclined, notwithstanding their bad order, to dispute the wind. The Compte de Grasse made the signal for his van to pass close to windward of the enemy, who were now attempting to form the line of battle by tacking one ship after another, to come to the same tack with the fleet of France.

"Admiral Graves then perceived how dangerous such a movement would be, and that to continue it, would give opportunity to the French to attack him before his fleet was half formed; those of his ships had already tacked, when he made his fleet wear together, and form astern of his rear-guard, by which means he gave up the wea-ther-gage to the French, and made sail from them.

"In the nights of the 8th and 9th, another variation of wind gave them the weather-gage, but during the night of the 9th, the Compte de Grasse regained it by his manœuvres, for his ships having suffered less in the action, he had the advantage of carrying more sail than the enemy. In the nights of the 9th and 10th the English disappeared.

"The Compte de Grasse perceiving how difficult it was to bring Admiral Graves to action, and fearing that some variation in the wind might put it in his power to enter the bay before him, deter-mined to return to the Chesapeake, in order to continue his operations, and recover his absent people.

[254]

"The Glorieux and Diligente joined the fleet the 10th in the evening. On the 11th the two frigates, Richmond and Iris, which the evening before had come out of the bay, where they had cut away the buoys from the anchors of the French ships which had been obliged to cut their cables to get the sooner under sail, fell into the hands of the Compte de Grasse, who the same day anchored under Cape Henry, where the Compte de Barras had arrived the evening before; he had sailed from Newport the 30th of August. This arrival was of so much the more consequence, as he had on board the artillery for carrying on the siege.

"The fleet, in this affair, had twenty-four sail of the line and two frigates. Admiral Graves, reinforced by Admiral Hood, had twenty sail of the line, and nine frigates and sloops. He had sailed from New York the 31st of August, upon hearing of the movements Generals Washington and Rochambeau were making towards Philadelphia, and which then first discovered to the enemy, the projects intended to be executed.

"By the confession of the English, five of their ships were very much damaged, and particularly the Terrible, which they were obliged to burn. Only the fifteen headmost ships of the French could come into the action; and they had only an equal number of the enemy against them, for the five ships of the English rear-guard refused to come within cannon-shot.

"The French fleet has lost in this action, M. Boades, Capitaine de Vaisseau, commanding the Reflechi; Duke D'Orvault, Lieut. de Vaisseau, and Major of the Blue Squadron; Rhaub, Enseigne de Vaisseau, Suèdois on board the Caton; de la Villèon, auxiliary officer on board the Diadème; eighteen were wounded, and about 200 men were killed and wounded.

"The 18th, Generals Washington and Rochambeau came on board the Ville de Paris, to concert measures with M. de Grasse, for carrying on their future operations.

"The 19th, M. de Choisy passed York river, with the Legion of Lausun, and 2000 American troops, to go and invest Gloucester, where the enemy had 1500 men; he received almost as soon as he arrived, a reinforcement of 800 men from the ships of war.

"The fleet had quitted Lynnhaven bay, where the ships did not lie in safety, and moved above the middle ground and Horse-shoe, where they anchored in a line of battle within the entrance of those two banks, ready to oppose Admiral Graves, as he was reinforced by Admiral Digby, if he presented himself to succour Lord Cornwallis; besides, this position gave means to hasten the siege by a greater facility of transporting ammunition. Three ships were now to block up the entrance of James river.

"The 3rd of October, the enemy, distressed for want of forage, drowned 200 horses.

[255]

"On the night of the 6th and 7th, the trenches were opened both above and below York, within half cannon shot of the town.

"The 8th, a battery erected by the Touraine regiment obliged the Guadaloupe to cut her cables and run along shore under the protection of the batteries of the town. The same day they fired red-hot shot upon the Charon, and she was soon consumed.

"Everything was now ready for a general assault; when Lord Cornwallis, perceiving the great danger he was in, demanded on the 17th, a suspension of arms for twenty-four hours; only two were granted; and he signified that he was ready to capitulate.

"One day was employed to settle the articles of capitulation. Four years before this event (16th Oct. 1777), General Burgoyne signed the capitulation of Saratoga, where 6040 Brunswickers and Tories of the country surrendered themselves prisoners of war to General Gates.

"The enemy had 800 killed; our loss, with that of the Americans, was about 700 men. We have followed, for greater accuracy, the printed account, different journals, and particularly a copy of M. Rochambeau's, and others sent to us.

"The ships arrived last Tuesday are, the Provence, Victoire, Vaillant, and Triton, with the Ralieuse and Aigrette frigates. They quitted the Chesapeake, the 4th of this month, and M. de Grasse, four days after. The fleet of M. de Grasse is gone to Martinique, and the English are already sailed for the Windward Islands."

INDEX

INDEX

INDEX